DATE DUE			
Oct 6 '75			
Oct.20 '75			
Oct 27 79			
Nov30 79			
Nov 29 '82			

THE COSSACKS

The Cossacks

THE STORY OF A WARRIOR PEOPLE

by Maurice Hindus

947
H58c
90560
Nov. 1974

Preface

◆

THE YEAR 1944 marked the five hundredth anniversary of the appearance of the Cossack on the Russian scene.* Into these five centuries the Cossack has packed great history, now heroic, now perverse, always turbulent, rarely dull. Warrior and adventurer, rebel and killer, conqueror and crusader, martyr and persecutor, he has shaken thrones, convulsed nations. He has made rulers, Russian and foreign, tremble with panic and awe. He has added ignominy and ferocity, art and science to war, now and then to diplomacy.

Powerful and reckless, he has always been ready, especially in the early centuries of his career, to defy destiny and smite an enemy out of hate and revenge or out of folly and fun, out of love of liberty and hatred of tyranny, or out of mockery of liberty and in defense of tyranny. As warrior and individual he has etched himself with a gory and glamorous robustness on the pages of Russian history, on the fabric of Russian folkways.

Brimming over with physical vitality, he has survived every national calamity, every political upheaval, every social eruption, every natural catastrophe. Czars have come and gone. Pretenders to the throne have risen and fallen. Wars have swept the Russian land and spent themselves in ferocity and blood. Revolutions have shaken it and until the coming of the Soviets were smothered in fury and wrath. Plagues and famines have smitten now this, now the other part of the country. But the Cossack has remained. No other people in Russia have challenged fate so gaily, have courted death so riotously. Yet like the Russian steppe, the Russian forest, the Russian rivers, the Cossack seems an indestructible part of the Russian scene, of the very nature of the country.

*Bolshaya Entsiklopedia, St. Petersburg, 1903.

v

Under the Soviets he is living in a new social and political setting, at harsh and violent variance with anything he had known or dreamed in czarist days. Yet today as of yore he is still or again the man on horseback. In time of conflict with an outside enemy he is still the warrior supreme. Neither the tank nor the plane nor any other highly vaunted mechanized weapon has unseated him from his horse, has clanked the saber out of his hands. In World War II he has enacted some of the most sensational episodes. Not the conqueror that he once was, he still is the doughtiest of soldiers, with a technique, a tradition of his own, reinforced by inventions of the machine age. No other soldier in the Red Army has been more wily, more fierce, more unforgiving, more spectacular in battle. All Cossack armies have been elevated to the rank of Guard armies.

Immense has been the Cossack's contribution to Russian history, Russian geography, Russian military science. He has added vast territories to the Russian Empire. The Cossack Yermak Timofeyitch cut his way into Siberia, pushed deep into its vast primitiveness, conquered it and made it a part of the Russian domain, the Siberia without whose men and horses, bread and meat, planes and tanks, guns and shells Russia never would have won the war against Germany.

On January 8, 1654, in the town of Pereyaslavl, the Ukrainian Cossack Rada, Council, on the initiative of their leader Bogdan Khmelnitzky, from the Zaporog *setch*, voted unanimously to unite the Ukraine with Russia. Thereby they made Russia territorially the largest and economically the richest nation in Europe. In her march eastward into Asia and southwesternward into Europe, Russia in the course of the years might have achieved the annexation of Siberia and the union with the Ukraine anyway. But the historical fact is that these vast and extraordinarily rich countries became Russian—the one by conquest, the other by diplomacy—through Cossack initiative and Cossack adventure.

Nor is this all. Perennial frontiersman and border guard, the Cossack, more than any other soldier in the Russian armies, has held watch over Russian lands, the old and the newly acquired, in Europe and in Asia, against all enemies and all intruders. Without his passion for fighting, his lust for wandering, Russia might never have carved for herself one sixth of the land of the world.

Powerful has been the impress of the Cossack on Russia's political development. For centuries he was the unvanquished and invincible rebel and non-conformist. He was the audacious exponent of folk democracy. No one fought serfdom in Russia and in Poland as long and as implacably as the Cossack.

The Don Cossacks Stenka Razin and Yemelyan Pugatchev led two of the mightiest peasant revolutions in Russian history, one in the seventeenth, the other in the eighteenth century. In both instances Kalmyks, Tatars, Mordwins, Kirghiz, Bashkirs, and other alien peoples fought side by side with Russians, nor did either Razin or Pugatchev discriminate against them in the choice of their assistants. Whatever else this may mean, it demonstrates an absence of racial or national antipathy in the Russian folk mind.

Only when the Cossack's passion for revolt had in part spent itself in incessant fighting and was in part allayed by czarist rewards, of which a preferred social position and free land were the most enticing, did the Cossack become the unswerving supporter and the unrepentant defender of czarism. Yet in 1917 it was the Cossack who, by his refusal to fire on the crowds of rebellious civilians in the streets of Petrograd, the former capital of the czars, sealed the fate of the Romanov dynasty.

Invaluable has been the Cossack's contribution to the tradition and science of Russian arms. Other lands, Poland and Hungary in particular, have achieved renown for the high quality of their cavalry, the Cossack's military specialty. But no nation anywhere has cultivated a warrior and a human being like the Cossack. Lover of strong drink and rich food, of tender song and violent dance, of gay laughter and rowdy speech, of unruly living and reckless dying, he has ever been the playboy and the *bête noire*, the defamer and the defender of Russian civilization and its most undaunted warrior.

Napoleon spoke of him as "the disgrace of the human race," yet so captivated was he with the Cossack's soldierly qualities that he toyed with the idea of creating a similar type of soldier in the French Army. Nothing became of the idea, because, as one Russian writer expresses himself, "a Cossack is not made, he is born." Neither French history nor French geography had given birth to the type of frontiersman and adventurer out of which emerged the Cossack warrior.

While this is a book on Cossacks, in a larger sense it is a book on Russia in a new setting, with a social dispensation no different than that which obtains everywhere else, but with a past all its own, unique not only in Russia but in the world, rich in physical adventure, meager, except in the early centuries of his existence, in political self-scrutiny and cultural elevation.

Because his ancient heritage was more robust and his economic condition more opulent, the Cossack suffered greater shock and more violent uprooting at the hands of the Soviets than any other element in rural Russia. There were two stages to this uprooting, the civil war and collectivization. In both instances the Soviets were not without followers in Cossack villages. There were poor Cossacks with little land who responded to the promise of the Bolsheviks for a freer and more abundant life. Without the support of these Cossacks Semyon Budenny on the Don never could have mustered his Red cavalry which won decisive victories during the civil war, and Vanya Kochubey in the Kuban never could have gathered his formidable Red guerrillas.

But the rebellious Cossacks were in the minority. Overwhelmingly the Cossacks fought against the Lenin regime. Overwhelmingly they fought against Stalin's collectivization. Overwhelmingly they were defeated in both battles. They have known plenty of terror and woe. They have tasted deeply of humility and contrition. They have endured famine and exile. They have wept and cursed and hated. Yet defeat has not left them prostrate and helpless. Man has to live, and besides the Cossack never has been "soft." Centuries of Cossackhood have made him tough and energetic. Once the old way of life and landholding were banned, he resigned himself to the new order of things, and, speaking for the Kuban Cossack territory, which I know best, I must testify that nowhere else in Russia had collectivization in the prewar days risen to such heights of achievement. The rich earth of the Kuban, its magnificent climate, the Cossack's historic energies, his sturdiness of character, his naturally jovial disposition have, under the creative forces of the Revolution, given the Kuban, more vividly than any other part of rural Russia I have ever visited, the crystallized features of the civilization which the Soviets have been struggling to fashion—in part, I must emphasize, through theory and oratory, through hunger and heartache, but far more through sacrifice and toil, through faith and education. Nowhere else in Russia was the standard of living in prewar days rising so rapidly as in the Kuban, and it is my judgment that no other part of the Soviet Union will recover from the huge ravages of the war more rapidly.

There are eleven Cossack territories in Russia. I have limited myself in part to the Don but mostly to the Kuban Cossack country
because I know it best. The book is largely an outgrowth of three
journeys I made there: the first in 1926, when Russia was still groping its way to a conclusive plan of national action; the second in
1936, when collectivism in city and village was already entrenched;
the last in the summer of 1944, when, liberated from the rampant
German-Rumanian occupation, the Kuban was beginning to recover
its Cossack breath and its Cossack soul. I must warn the reader that
this is not a book of sensation. I have no state secrets to reveal. Russian leaders, as is well known, are not in the habit of drawing foreign
writers into their confidence. Nor have I any plots or counterplots to
expose, international conspiracies or scandals to unfold. Wherever I
have traveled—China, Japan, Germany, Poland, Russia, other lands—
I have never even sought interviews with the high and the mighty.
I have not allowed myself to be inspired or guided by official pronouncements, though I have not always ignored them. I have chosen
instead to mill about in my own leisurely manner among the common folk, for it is their life and their story, in Russia in particular,
that have always absorbed me.

Whatever the shortcomings of such a method of study and investigation, it has at least enabled me to observe, side by side with the
tragedies, also the triumphs of the Russian Revolution, triumphs
which for me have found their expression not so much in political
postulates and doctrinal proclamations, nor in the material lushness
of New York's Fifth Avenue or the material plenitude of Main Street
anywhere in America, as in new methods of plowing land, seeding
and harvesting grain, planting cabbage and cucumbers, Russia's
ancient and best-loved garden vegetables; acclimating new crops to
ancient lands; bringing water to sunbaked desert or draining moisture
out of what had for centuries been useless and hopeless marsh; new
appreciation of books and education; in short, a new approach to
nature and a new energy with which to whip increasing bounty out
of its immense storehouse of raw substance, and a new way of dis-
tributing this bounty. To me these little things have always been the
big things in Russia, and I have always linked them, not with any far-
flung conspiracy to suck the world into sanguinary uprisings and
Communist dictatorships, but with an effort to shake Russia out
of her centuries-old torpor and backwardness and drive her with

ruthless energy and will into the new world of science and the machine and what Cossacks speak of as "learning."

I realize, of course, that to the professional Sovietophobe and those who think as they do a book on Russia has little value or no validity unless it pictures the country as a land of atrocities and not much more. History does repeat itself. It was even so at the time of the French Revolution. Its havoc and horrors so frightened and incensed contemporaries that they refused to perceive anything positive or creative emerging out of the welter of agony and blood which it had invoked on France. They appraised the historic eruption in terms of their own peace and stability, their own comfort and pleasures, "the rights of man" from which they and their peoples had derived immense benefit but which had been flagrantly denied the common man in France. No more fierce indictment of the French Revolution was voiced by anyone, Frenchman or foreigner, than by Edmund Burke. In blistering rhetoric he denounced France as "not having sacrificed her virtue to her interest but having abandoned her interest that she might prostitute her virtue." Yet two years later, eminently honest as he was, Edmund Burke admitted that while the Revolution "has given me many anxious moments," those "who persist in opposing this mighty current in human affairs will appear rather to resist the decrees of Providence itself than the mere designs of men."

Only later, when British and other men of letters, however conservative-minded, viewed the Revolution in historical perspective, they spoke of it again and again as did Matthew Arnold when he wrote, "In spite of the crimes and follies in which it lost itself . . . it is—it will probably remain—the greatest and the most animated event in history." Speaking on the same subject, Sir Walter Scott makes Oldbuck, in *The Antiquary*, say, "It might be likened to a storm which, passing over a region, does great damage in its passage, yet sweeps away stagnant and unwholesome vapours and repays, in future health and fertility, its immediate ravage and desolation."

I shall not presume to foretell what the Matthew Arnolds and Walter Scotts of the future in England and elsewhere will say of the Soviet Revolution. Yet one need be neither scholar nor prophet to foresee that they will not be swayed by the emotions and hostilities of our own times. While taking cognizance of "crimes and follies" they will, as in the case of the French Revolution, accord more than modest tribute to the immense creativeness the Soviets have un-leashed. They will not fail to be impressed by the military strength the three Five-year Plans have given Russia or by the enormity of Russia's contribution to victory over Germany. The bankruptcy of Allied and German diplomatic and military intelligence in making even an approximate appraisal of Russia's fight-ing strength in the early months of the Russo-German war of 1941 is in this writer's judgment due chiefly to an unwillingness, or in-ability, or both, to identify, recognize, and appreciate the purely creative energies which the Soviet Revolution had whipped up and the resultant transformation of Russian industry, Russian agriculture, the character of the Russian people.

Whatever the faults of my writings on Russia in the past twenty years, I at least have the satisfaction of knowing, despite the sus-picions I have often invoked on myself on the part of the very diplo-mats and military observers who blithely prophesied in open inter-views, and even more in coded messages to their home offices, the collapse of Russia within three weeks, or three, or at most six, months, history has borne out my prognostications both as to the meaning of the Russo-German Pact of 1939 and the fighting powers of the Russian Army and the Russian people. On October 14, 1939, I spoke of the pact as a prelude not to peace but to war—"The more they co-operate now, the more cause they will have to clash later on"—and in September 1941, when the air was loud with prophecies of Rus-sia's imminent downfall, my publisher brought out my book *Hitler Cannot Conquer Russia*. I was not guessing, I was not making prophecies. I had seen too much of the transformation of the Russian land and the Russian people to be seriously impressed by the prophets and prophecies of collapse. Harsh and brutal as were the initial meth-ods of collectivization, resulting as they did in famine and in the butchery of livestock from which Russia had not fully recovered in the prewar years, it performed one of the greatest miracles in Russian history by making the peasant youth all over the country within the short space of five years both engine- and mechanical-minded. To me this alone was one of the greatest fighting assets Russia had acquired and without which, in this day of mechanized warfare, no nation can hope to win a war. I was also convinced that under collectivization there could be no breakdown in agriculture such as occurred under the Czar during World War I. I further realized that collectivization, however heavy and tragic the cost, was a newly created instrument which, barring a disastrous defeat in war, would in the future make impossible the recurrence of famines such as had periodically ravaged Russia, especially the peasantry, since the days of its recorded history.

Then, too, anyone with a rudimentary knowledge of agriculture and with an open mind could perceive that, once universally applied, the new method of tillage would put an end to parasitic farming—depleted soils would be rehabilitated and good soils would not be recklessly skimmed of fertility and abandoned to the mercy of winds, rains, and other disruptive natural forces.

One may loathe Russia and Sovietism as flamingly as one chooses, but a continued appraisal of Russia by diplomats, military observers, publicists of one type or another, purely or chiefly in terms of its negative features, will invite even graver errors of judgment than were committed in the prewar years, if only because, with the threat of future wars allayed, the creative energies of the Revolution will receive a fresh impetus, the most powerful they have yet been accorded. Nowhere else in Russia was this so manifest to me as during my journey in the Kuban Cossack country. In the years between my first visit there in 1926 and my last, in 1944, the Kuban had acquired more education, general and technical, had read more books, mastered more science, put on the land more up-to-date machinery, than in all the preceding years of its history, and in the light of all I saw and heard, barring another war or the real threat of one, past achievements are only a foundation for future efforts.

So while this is not a book of sensation, of power politics, of speculation on Russia's future international policies, it is the story, however inadequately told, of one of the most exciting peoples not only in Russia but in the world during one of the most decisive and dramatic turning points in its history.

I wish to express my thanks to Alfred Knopf, publisher, for permission to reprint certain passages from Sholokhov's novel, *Quiet Flows the Don.*

Particularly grateful am I to Babbette Deutsch for her excellent translation of the Stenka Razin ballad made specially for this book.

MAURICE HINDUS

Contents

Preface   v

PART ONE: THE MAN WITH THE SABER

I   The Ghost of Yesterday   3

II   The Voice of Today   8

PART TWO: THE COSSACK OF OLD

III   The Rebel Supreme   27

IV   The Cossack Republic   36

V   Yermak, the Conqueror of Siberia   42

VI   Stenka Razin   53

VII   Yemelyan Pugatchev   65

VIII   The End of the Dnieper Republic   78

IX   Warriors Supreme   83

X   Taras Bulba's "Grandson"   93

XI   The Great Reconciliation   102

PART THREE: THE COSSACK OF TODAY

XII   "You Are in America Now"   117

XIII   "The Gift of Catherine"   129

XIV The Man Who Was Dead   147

XV   The College President and His Sons   150

XVI The Two Russias   163

XVII The Open Road   174

XVIII "Our Outlet to the Sea"   182

XIX A Village Revisited   198

XX Cossack Girls   212

XXI The Boy with the Fiddle   219

XXII "We Were So Wild, So Wild"   231

XXIII Sex and Family among Cossacks   243

XXIV Religion among Cossacks   254

XXV Eating and Drinking among Cossacks   268

XXVI The Cossacks Discover America   281

PART FOUR: THE COSSACK OF TOMORROW

XXVII Work and Freedom   297

XXVIII The New Cossack   314

PART ONE

The Man with the Saber

CHAPTER I

The Ghost of Yesterday

———◆———

THE SUMMER OF 1942 was one of the most dismal in all Russian history. Frustrated during the preceding winter in their thrust against Moscow and Leningrad, the Germans were hurling their mightiest land and air armadas against central and southern Russia. With scarcely a battle, by sheer terror of their air assaults, they recaptured Rostov. In massed, powerful formations they were sweeping across the Don and the Kuban Cossack lands. They were roaring toward the Volga, the most Russian of rivers, toward the translucid, swift-rolling Terek, toward the oil fields of the North Caucasus—Grozny and Maikop—toward wind-blown Baku, heart of the nation's richest oil fields. On and on they were thundering toward the Caspian Sea, the Sea of Azov, the Black Sea, nearer and nearer toward the alluring and formidable Caucasus with its snow-capped mountains, its wine-growing valleys, its weather-tinted old fortresses. They were smashing their way toward the one part in European Russia that has the mildness and the balm of the semitropics, and the guile and the glory of a rich and yielding nature. Of this nature Russia's most gifted men of letters—Tolstoy, Lermontov, Pushkin—wrote with love and rapture. To this nature Russians everywhere—in Siberia, the arctic, Central Asia—dream of making a pilgrimage someday. All of it the Germans were now threatening to devour.

With subdued dismay the Russian press and radio reported the retreats and the defeats. Seeking to hearten the people with stories of transcendent heroism of individual men and women, with assurances of the nation's implacable will to fight and ample resources to win, neither the radio nor the press sought to conceal the mounting catastrophe at the front.

The Germans were obviously aiming to amputate Russia in the middle of her European center, to drain her indispensable life blood and wrest for themselves a fresh base from which to make the final leap on Moscow and Leningrad, on all European Russia.

Desperately Russia needed an incident, an adventure, a figure, a symbol, a *podvig* or feat, as Russians say, to demonstrate to themselves, to the outside world, and above all to Germans that a Russian fighting force, traditionally, historically, indigenously Russian, could even in the midst of his unchecked advances wreak ferocious vengeance on the armor-clad, seemingly all-powerful enemy. In the face of national calamity Russia had become sentimentally conscious of her Russianism, invoking past glories, past triumphs, past national leaders to sustain the spirit and strengthen the faith of today.

As if in answer to this quest, Nikolay Kirichenko, a Kuban Cossack general in command of a Cossack army, slipped through the German lines to the Cossack village of Kushtshevskaya. With his main force, under the immediate command of General Millerov, skillfully hidden and camouflaged in a valley, he sent out a small detachment to attract the attention of the Germans and then to feign a galloping retreat. When the Germans started in pursuit Kirichenko ordered the hidden army into action. Amidst thunderous shouts of "Hurrah, hurrah," the Cossacks galloped into the open. Flashing sabers, they pounced on the Germans and slashed away at them for three hours and forty minutes.

Caught unawares, the Germans were lost, without a plan of action or means of escape. Wherever they ran the Cossacks were upon them, wielding curved, narrow, gleaming sabers. The battle of cold steel, with only little fire power from the flanks, was fierce and unrelenting. Subsequently when I met Kirichenko and heard him describe this battle, he said, "It took the Germans eight days to bury their dead."

The battle over, the Cossacks picked their way back to the Russian rear with as little mishap and misadventure as they had made their advance. Despite all the mechanized equipment at their disposal, all the planes at their command to guard the Russian skies, to survey the Russian lands, the Germans were as powerless to thwart the withdrawal of the Cossacks as to halt their onslaught.

Here was something new in Russian tactics and in Russian fighting skill. In the prewar days Germans and other non-Russian military experts had doomed the Cossack to certain slaughter the moment he made his appearance on the battlefield. The tank, the plane, the motorized artillery, the high-powered infantry—so ran expert theory and prophecy—would find the man on horseback an easy, inviting target. In the profession of arms, to which he had for centuries lent luster and renown, the Cossack, it was confidently assumed, was hopelessly outclassed and outmoded. He was finished as a warrior every bit as much as the man with the bow or the tomahawk.

Hitler himself had as little faith in Cossack or any cavalry as his generals. The Reichswehr had not bothered to muster a sizable army of such troops. With his passion for the new, the thunderous, the spectacular, Hitler felt confident he could smash his way to victory in Russia, as he had done in Poland, France, and other western lands, on the wheels of the tank, on the wings of the plane. To him these were the decisive, all-powerful weapons of modern conquest. He considered even artillery of no primary importance, in contrast to Stalin, who hammered into the Russian Army and the Russian people the concept that "artillery is the god of war."

Yet here was Kushtshevskaya. Here was General Kirichenko. Here was the ancient saber. Here was the slaughter of a highly fortified German garrison deep within the German lines. A ghost of the past, the faraway primitive past, on whose power of action and resurrection the Germans had not counted, had risen out of the mist of history to taunt and terrorize the most scientifically minded armor-clad army of today.

Russian rapture was immense. The previous winter, in the battle of Moscow, General Lev Dovator, another Cossack leader who perished in the fighting, had distinguished himself with his attacks on the Germans. But Dovator's army was a link in a ring of armies—artillery, tanks, aviation, infantry. It acted according to a well-conceived plan by the Russian general staff. But Kirichenko was alone. He carried little armor, was escorted by no aviation. His was a dash into the unknown, and he had triumphed. The austere *Red Star*, which is chary of praising individual generals and which rarely dramatizes their personal accomplishments, dedicated all of its editorial space on February 22, 1942, to Kirichenko. It glorified him and his Cossacks as soldiers "setting an example of how to fight the Germans . . . that's how all forces in the Red Army should fight them." The Cossack was singled out as the model fighting man in the country, a eulogy *Red Star* has never to my knowledge given to any other fighting unit in the Red Army!

Not that Kirichenko was or is the ablest of Russian commanders. Master of Cossack warfare, matchless in the art of camouflage, of defying and eluding enemy scouts on land and in the air, of needling his way through enemy positions and springing surprise attacks on them, he has yet to demonstrate his skill in other branches of fighting, to attain the stature of Marshals Timoshenko, Rokossovski, Konev, Zhukov, Boltoukhin, Rotmistrov or such generals as the late Vatutin and the late and youthful Cherniakhovski.

Yet his achievements in Kushtshevskaya and subsequently in other places during the summer of 1942 proved among the most exhilarating episodes of the war. In Russia's overcast skies he was a bright and shining star, an envoy of hope, an augury of triumph. The soldierly qualities he displayed, the utter fearlessness and audacity which have ever been among the supreme virtues of the Cossacks, loomed for the moment as the most transcendent need of all armed forces. "If Kirichenko and his Cossacks could do it, so can we," was the slogan and the inspiration of military and political leaders everywhere in the Red Army.

In subsequent months Kirichenko and other Cossack generals, like Millerov, Taturinov, Belyayev, made spectacular history, as did all other forces in the Red Army. The Russian offensive swung out with new energy, past Stalingrad; Kursk, Voronezh, Kiev, and Dnieper regions were cleared of Germans. Leningrad was liberated from all threat of invasion and occupation. More and more of the Ukraine was reconquered. All of the North Caucasus was once more under Soviet rule and was beginning to hum with reconstruction. White Russia was wrested back. Baltic lands were again floating the Russian banner. Deeper and deeper was the Russian penetration into Poland, Rumania, Bulgaria, Jugoslavia, Finland, Slovakia, Hungary, Norway, East Prussia—nine foreign countries became highways for the onward sweep of Russian troops, and the end was not yet. All Poland was liberated. East Prussia was overrun. Silesia was in the grasp of the Russian pincers. Berlin and places beyond in the heart of Germany loomed up on the horizon as prize targets to be won.

Set against these campaigns and triumphs, in all of which the Cossack played a memorable part, Kirichenko's raid on Kushtshevskaya was like a fierce bolt of lightning compared to a shattering earthquake. He slaughtered the enemy but achieved no decision. He disrupted Nazi plans but did not paralyze their powers of advance. Kirichenko's own subsequent campaigns, particularly in Rostov and Taganrog, were militarily more fruitful of results. Yet because of what it had so spectacularly demonstrated in a grim hour of desperation and catastrophe, the Kushtshevskaya engagement remains an epochal event. It lifted the Cossack into the limelight, dramatized his daredevil audacity, glorified a purely Russian warrior and a purely Russian mode of warfare.

The Cossack refuses to be doomed or even pushed into the background of history. Quite the contrary. No longer the empire builder and empire maker that he once was, he can still give a powerful account of himself. Russian to the core, with the smell of sweat and horse about him, with the aura of steppe and forest, of marsh and mountain in his soul, with the zest of adventure and battle in his very breath, he is a living link between the Russia of today and the Russia of yesterday. Not exclusively the soldier that he once was, in time of war he is still the man of color and melodrama even as he was during the Seven Years' War when he rode triumphantly into the streets of Berlin and, during the Napoleonic Wars, into the streets of Paris, and again into Berlin in 1945!

CHAPTER II

The Voice of Today

GENERAL KIRICHENKO is forty-nine, of medium height, with upright shoulders, a massive back, a deep chest. Though he has been awarded a breastful of decorations, none adorns his smartly fitting khaki tunic, not even a ribbon. His handshake is powerful, his manner mild, informal. Neither his appearance nor his voice, least of all his vigorous but singularly chaste vocabulary, evoke the conventional image of a Cossack warrior.

His thick, dark hair is cut short and parted on the side in the style of an American businessman rather than a head-shaving or pompadour-loving Russian soldier or civilian. His dark brush-like brows are widely spaced. His broad ruddy face bears scarcely a trace of the strain he must have known during his many spectacular campaigns. It is a smooth, youthful, animated face. When he is contemplative the lids fall over his eyes; when he begins speaking they snap open and the eyes glow fresh and luminous. He walks with a sprightly tread, his lithe, tightly booted legs carrying his broad framed body with easy grace.

He was no longer at the front when I went to see him. As the nation's most successful exponent of Cossack warfare, he was brought to Moscow to assume charge of Russia's leading cavalry college, founded six years before Napoleon's invasion of Russia in 1812. Overwhelmingly the students of this college—the Budenny Cavalry Academy—came from the Don and Kuban Cossack countries.

The general's appearance was so disarming I could not help remarking that he in no way betrayed the supposed attributes of a man who had staged so many gory attacks on the enemy.

"When I am in the saddle," Kirichenko replied, "I am a general; when I am at my desk I am plain Nikolay Yakovlevitch."

He was that now, despite his uniform a civilian more than a general, a schoolmaster more than an army commander. His two adjutants, youthful Cossack officers, sat near by. They might have been casual visitors. There was no ostentatious clicking of heels, clanking of spurs, no profuse bowing, no effusive salutations, no dancing at attention on the "great man," for the "great man" was humble, friendly, and businesslike.

Though our conversation started with a discussion of the Cossack in modern war, it shifted to non-military, chiefly personal subjects. No people in the world, in these war times especially, are more difficult to approach than Russian leaders, military and civilian. Yet so inordinately inquisitive are the Russians that, once you are with them, they brim over with questions about foreign lands, America in particular, and they become chummy, personal, highly articulate. General Kirichenko was no exception. Freely he talked of himself. He came from the village of Staro-Kamenskaya, the Kuban, graduated in czarist days from a gymnasium (high school), fought in the civil war. On its conclusion he chose the Army as his profession and graduated from the academy he now heads.

"Have you a family, General?" I asked.

"Of course I have a family," he said. "I am a Russian, and a Russian always has a family."

He reached for his leather wallet, drew out a small photograph and passed it on to me. "My daughter," he said, "a splendid girl." The photograph showed a girl with large eyes, fluffy hair, a smiling face. On the back, written in a large, leisurely hand, was the inscription, "To my darling little father." "She is in college now here in Moscow," said the general. He also has two sons, both in the Army fighting—"not badly," he added.

We talked about novels, poetry, music, the theater in Russia and in America. The general was as eager to hear what I had to say about culture in America as I was to hear his opinions of culture in Russia. He loved literature; he said, "Without books a man withers away." He had read the Russian classics, Soviet authors, and Mark Twain. Rising from his desk, he walked over to a shelf, picked up an armful of books bound mostly in paper covers and laid them on his desk. One of the adjutants offered to carry the books, but the general thanked him and waved him aside.

I examined the books. They were autographed copies of the latest writings of Sholokhov, Ehrenburg, Sobelev, Simonov, and other outstanding Soviet authors. "Our writers are sending me books all the time," he said. "Often they ask me to write them what I think of their books, and I do it, too." Sending autographed copies of their books to generals is a vogue among Soviet writers.

Resuming the discussion of the Cossack as a warrior and the part he has played in the present war, Kirichenko said:

"The Germans laughed at us. They said they would blow the Cossack off the face of the earth with their planes, tanks, and high-powered artillery. They did their best to scare us with their mechanized monsters. These were terrible things to behold. Some of us fresh from the steppe were on first sight of them uneasy, all the more so because they made terrifying noises—screamed, wailed, shrieked until our ears nearly split. Germans are expert in attaching noise-making contraptions to their mechanized weapons. But we knew that our Cossack wisdom, our Cossack patience, our Cossack will would enable us to triumph over all their weapons, mechanical and psychological. Not

General Kirichenko

Cossacks on their way to battle

Kuban Cossack volunteers

in vain is red the color of our Kuban Cossacks. You've seen our uniforms, red-topped astrakhan hats, red bands on the trousers, red-lined hoods on our back, red breastpieces in our cloaks. Red is the symbol of our invincibility, of indifference to blood, of defiance of death. When blood courses down our breast the red frontpiece absorbs it, we don't see it and we keep on fighting."

I said: "It is five hundred years since the Cossack first appeared on the Russian scene. What is it that gives him the faculty of fitting himself into any age and any army, no matter how scientifically advanced?"

"The answer is simple. The Cossack does not permit himself to stagnate. He takes advantage of new experience, new invention, new modes of warfare. The Cossack of today has his own artillery, his own tanks, his own aviation, the best that our factories manufacture. He will have none other. He carries plenty of armor, yet never permits armor to weigh him down so as to endanger his chief soldierly asset, his mobility."

"Yet, basically," I said, "the Cossack of today, like the Cossack of hundreds of years ago, is a warrior of horseback."

"Quite true, basically he is that, and his greatest fighting virtues are those he has acquired in the centuries he has been a warrior on horseback. He has his own Cossack science and Cossack fighting traditions."

"What are they?"

Instead of answering, General Kirichenko arose, walked over to a large closet, and again waving aside an adjutant who offered to aid him, lifted a bulky album from a shelf and unfolded it before me. I turned the pages. From cover to cover they were pasted with photographs of Cossacks in war. The last pages of the album were devoted to photographs of Cossack families in Kirichenko's own army.

"Look at this photograph," he said, pointing with his fingers to one he uncovered. It showed a Cossack family in a trench eating dinner. "I know this family," Kirichenko went on. "The mother cooked the dinner, and it was excellent—I can vouch for that because I tasted it. Look at the grass in the trench and

the trees on the embankments, a perfect shelter as if fashioned
by nature. Only the Cossacks built it themselves. Look at the
faces of the people: no trace of worry or trouble, and one of
them, this young lad in the corner, is playing the accordion. Yet
at the time the photograph was taken German planes were roaring overhead, searching for just such shelters as this one." He
paused, looked lingeringly at the photograph as though reliving
the scene it portrayed.

"There is the Cossack for you, the entire family at the front."

"Who are they?"

"Countrymen of mine from the Kuban. When the war broke
out, the father came to the mobilization office with all his children. As is the custom among Cossacks, he enlisted himself
first—then one by one he called over his sons, the oldest first, the
youngest last, and had them registered. He did the same with his
daughters. When all the sons and daughters were enlisted, there
was nothing for the mother to do but follow suit, so she too enlisted. At the front the mother follows the family wherever
they go. She cooks meals for them, does their washing, looks
after their personal life. The daughters, of course, help her. The
remarkable thing about these Cossack mothers is that, no matter
where their families are, they always manage to find their way
to them with a load of thermos bottles containing hot home-
cooked food."

"Were there many such families in your army?" I asked.

"Not too many, but enough to demonstrate one outstanding
feature of Cossack life: its close family ties. Fighting is a family
tradition, has been for hundreds of years. The young Cossack
knows his father fought, his grandfather fought, all his male
ancestors fought. He knows his sons will fight, his grandsons
will fight, all his male descendants will fight if the country goes
to war. The heroes of the Cossack family are the men who attained glory in battle. The villains are the men who showed
cowardice under fire or were disloyal to the fatherland. Every
family knows the record of its ancestors. The fighting family
tradition of the Cossacks is one of his chief fighting assets. You've
been in our Kuban, you say?"

I nodded.

"You've noticed how broad our streets are, how immense the public squares. On these streets and squares boys acquire their skill in horsemanship and Cossack warfare. On Sundays and holidays the streets are often set out with rows of saplings, each sapling from eight to ten and fifteen meters from the other. Sometimes the saplings are topped with caps or earthen pots to represent human heads. While fathers and special teachers watch and instruct, the boys gallop past these saplings and slash away with their sabers."

"Cut off the tops?"

"Oh no, cut into them deep enough for them to settle down, but not to fall off."

"Don't heads roll on a Cossack battlefield?"

"Only when the Cossack is a poor fighter."

Laying the edge of his outspread hand to the side of his neck, Kirichenko continued, "A skilled Cossack cuts into here deep enough for the head to settle down. This is only one of the strokes we use in battle."

"What are the others?"

"There are many, each for a special occasion—depending on the situation at hand and on the personality of the enemy."

"You mean the personality of the enemy determines the stroke used in fighting him?"

"Precisely. When a Cossack picks out the man he is to strike he sizes him up in an instant and swiftly, as if by instinct, he decides which stroke will prove most effective. Therein lies the art and the science in Cossack fighting. If the enemy is a little fellow the Cossack will smite him on the head. If the enemy is a big fellow he will use some other stroke, the one I showed or straight over the neck or between the shoulder blades, or across the spine between shoulder and hip. There are many strokes, each, if executed with precision and energy, equally fatal. All these and others too the father or a special instructor teaches the Cossack youth, and d'you know how we can tell when a Cossack youth has achieved perfection in the use of the saber?"

I shook my head.

"When, leaping on horseback over a stream, he can swing down his body from the saddle and cleave the water with the saber without stirring any spray."

He paused as if waiting for the full meaning of his words to sink into my mind.

"I must repeat," he resumed, "the skilled Cossack father teaches the art of Cossack horsemanship and Cossack fighting to his son. The son takes pride in his father's achievements. This intensifies the family feeling in the Cossack household. And when war comes the father, grandfather, too, if he is in good health, ride off to war together, with sons and grandsons. Unless the higher command finds it necessary for purely military reasons to separate them, they stay together, fight together. Besides Cossacks usually fight in village *sotnyas*—hundreds—village regiments, district divisions. That's why many of our Kuban Cossack divisions and regiments are named after their villages. So all in all the Cossack has a multiple loyalty: he fights for the fatherland, for the family, for the village from which he comes. This multiple loyalty galvanizes his fighting spirit."

The general paused, nodded to the adjutant to pass around cigarettes, and after we started smoking he resumed talking.

"Our Cossack never knows the meaning of the word No. He knows only the meaning of the word Yes. From his earliest days he is trained to be master of any situation that might confront him. He is taught never to dodge but to overcome obstacles. A wall, a creek, a pond, a lake, a marsh, a storm, a flood, a fire, an explosion—any barrier, however hazardous, he must surmount. If he has to cross a windswept river or lake, he plunges into the water behind or beside his horse, often with one hand holding the horse's mane and swimming with the other. . . . He is a poor Cossack, a good-for-nothing Cossack, if he permits anything in nature or in man to hold him back or to scare him. . . . He grows up to fear nothing and nobody, neither nature nor man nor the devil himself. . . .

"Well, war comes. Consider the infantryman. He arises in

the morning, gets ready to advance. As he starts out he turns his eyes to the right and to the left, back or ahead of him. He is always on guard against this or that. Not the Cossack. He arises at the break of dawn or he starts out on a mission at the fall of night. He mounts his horse, pulls the cap over his ears, and sets off on his journey. He looks neither to the right nor to the left: he looks only ahead. If he wavers before an obstacle, the horse will pull him along. If the horse wavers, he stoops down, peppers the horse's feet with his lash or whip, and it ceases to waver. The Cossack rides on and on. Often he covers a distance of seventy miles a night. He cuts deep into the enemy's rear, plays havoc with communications, fuel supplies, food stores, munition dumps—above all with controlling staffs. I use the expression 'controlling' and not 'commanding' staffs because nowadays officers do not command, they control operations. By this work of destruction in the enemy's rear the Cossack cuts the nerves of the enemy's fighting organization, knocks out its brains, chokes the very breath of its mechanized monsters."

"But how do Cossacks fight tanks, General?" I asked.

"I'm coming to that. But first you must appreciate the relationship between the Cossack and his horse. The two must trust and love each other. They are not only companions but comrades in arms. The life of the one depends on the skill and devotion of the other. The horse must be sensitive to the will of the man on its back. It must not only fulfill but anticipate the right move, the right step, the right prance, the right maneuver. Quickly and faithfully it must respond to every sound, every gesture, every poke, every nudge of the man in the saddle. To rouse such response the Cossack must *never, never* neglect his horse. If there is only one piece of sugar, the horse gets it. If there is bread only for one, the horse comes first. If there is only one swallow of water, the Cossack himself goes thirsty and offers it to the horse. . . . The horse appreciates such attention and will fight for the Cossack to his last breath. Mistreat the horse, be negligent in your care of it, and it will throw you down or do just the opposite of what you want it to do in a critical moment, and then you and the horse are lost. . . . Do you know what we Cossacks call the horse?"

I shook my head.

"The Cossack speaks of the horse as *zhivoy motor*—the living engine. The horse moves like an engine—only it is a living engine, and is more amenable to the wishes of man than the mechanized engine. It is alive with rapture and fury, with courage and valor, with aim and achievement. The horse gives the Cossack his most precious asset—*dependable* mobility. Where the tank cannot pass, where the human foot cannot tread, the horse can make its way.

"Nor is this all. In darkness and in bad weather the tank and the plane have poor eyesight. The mechanized weapons cannot cope, or can cope only feebly, with fog and blizzard, precisely because of their poor eyesight. But the horse's eyesight is always keen. Therefore fog, storm, and blizzard are no enemies but friends of the Cossack. While the mechanized engine is stuck in mud, stalled in snow, while it waits for fog or darkness to lift or storms to subside, the Cossack's living engine moves on. That's what enables the Cossack to take the enemy by surprise—and surprise, as you know, often decides a battle before it has begun. There have been times when my Cossacks have played with tanks like a cat with a mouse."

"Do you mean you *advance* on tanks?" I asked.

"In the open steppe the horse, of course, is no match for armor. But we choose our own fighting terrain. We have to. Wooded rivers, deep gullies, broad ravines, overgrown hills, reedy or wooded marshlands with plenty of hinterland in which to hide and camouflage our presence—these are the terrains we must choose if we want to be successful in war. That's what we did in Kushtshevskaya. A small detachment of horsemen was sent into the clearing. When the Germans saw them they gave chase. The Cossacks feigned a swift retreat. The Germans thought themselves so certain of victory they intensified their pursuit. That's what we wanted them to do. Before the entire German garrison could be wakened and put into action, we were upon them, slashing away with our sabers. When the battle was over, hardly any Germans were left in that village."

"But such attacks," I said, "are enormously risky." I had read of similar Cossack attacks in the early months of the war which had resulted in gruesome catastrophes. The Germans had mowed down the horses and the men on their backs.

"Yes, such attacks are enormously risky. But in war, risk is a noble principle, and now that we've learned to choose the kind of terrain that gives us protection, we assume these risks quite readily. That's why Germans dread an encounter with Cossacks more than with any other force. They dread the saber far more than the bayonet. The bayonet they know. They are trained to use it, though not as well as our men. But the saber they don't know. Its very gleam and clank horrifies them. In revenge they seldom take Cossacks prisoners. Often they torture our men long before they kill them."

"I suppose Cossacks likewise don't bother with prisoners."

"Draw your own conclusions," he replied, and after a pause: "It depends on circumstances. But you want to know how Cossacks play cat and mouse with tanks. Well, once we learned of a concentration of two hundred German tanks. We wouldn't meet them in a frontal attack. So we plunged deep into their rear—under the cover of night, of course. We destroyed their controlling staffs. We cut off food, fuel, munitions. German planes dropped buckets of fuel in parachutes. We blew them up or set them afire. The tanks pulled one way or the other, but wherever they turned their communications were cut, their supplies were gone or beyond reach, and our anti-tank guns spattered them with bullets. They had no way of getting aid or advice. What could they do? Dig in, use up what ammunition they had—or try to escape. That's precisely what the German tank men tried to do. But they couldn't move far. They were stuck. We pounced on them with guns, sabers, pistols. We surrounded them, killed off the men, and the tanks were ours, most of them utterly undamaged. That's how we sometimes play cat and mouse with tanks."

"In the battle of Taganrog," I said, "you Cossacks are credited with taking a decisive part in the capture of the city. How did you do it?"

"That was one of our most magnificent campaigns. For nearly two years the Germans had been fortifying Taganrog. In the south they were protected by the Sea of Azov, in the east by Rostov. Everywhere else they had built chains of fortifications which bristled with fire power. A frontal attack was out of the question: we should've been slaughtered. So impregnable did the Germans deem themselves that in the pamphlets which they dropped on us they said if we rode within range of their big guns they'd tear us to pieces with their shells. But Cossacks aren't scared by German pamphlets or German fire power. After ou. infantry broke a lane through for us, we plunged ahead in the night into the German rear. We found their controlling staffs and annihilated them. We destroyed supplies and communications. The next night we plunged deeper still into the German rear and did the same thing all over. We got the German cards so badly mixed that they didn't know how to play them. The German armies back of us didn't know what was which and who was where. From our position we were pulling the entire German army of Taganrog backward, toward us. That's precisely what we were aiming at. The farther we pulled them toward us, the more confused they became. Then our infantry and other forces cut loose in a formidable attack. Cossacks coordinated action with theirs, and together we surrounded the German armies and destroyed most of them."

The general paused and reflected; then, with visible enthusiasm which showed itself in the deepening flush of his full smooth cheeks, he went on:

"Rostov was another magnificent Cossack campaign. Our armies were pushing the Germans hard, and they were fleeing across the Don River. They blew up the big bridge at Rostov. We didn't want to give the Germans a single spare hour in which to strengthen their fortifications inside and around the city. Every new pillbox they built, every new gun they installed, would cost us extra lives. So we Cossacks started as usual for their deep rear. We wanted to cut off the enemy forces in Rostov from all communication with controlling staffs and with supply stations. But on reaching the Don we found the river frozen solidly. Though it was dark, the ice gleamed like a mirror. We started to make our way across, but the ice was so slippery our horses slid and fell. We were in a desperate hurry. Every minute was precious. The more darkness we had to shelter us, the farther we could plunge into the enemy rear, and the more havoc we could wreak on him. What were we to do? Counsel came from an elderly Cossack. 'Brother Cossacks,' he said, 'let's roll the *burkas* [long black sleeveless cloaks] off our backs and spread them over the father Don.' The next instant hundreds of burkas flew off hundreds of Cossacks and were quickly spread over the ice from one bank to the other . . . Over this huge black carpet our Cossack divisions made their way across the river. We galloped for a distance of about twenty-two miles and got feverishly busy. We tore up rails. We blew up bridges. We laid waste to everything of use to the Germans but the earth. We captured eighteen carloads of munitions. We disorganized, confused, and terrorized the enemy. Tanks crews jumped out of their machines and fled. We jumped into the German tanks and fired at the fleeing men. Wherever they ran we were upon them with one weapon or another. Oh, how we slashed and fired away at them! We were fighting on land that was sacred to us—the land of our brothers, the Don Cossacks. We wanted to teach the Germans a lesson which their great-great-great-grandchildren would remember, which no Germans on this earth would ever forget. . . . We never fought any better. . . ."

The general sat back in his chair, drumming with his fingers on the table in imitation of galloping horses. Reflectively, almost dreamily, he said:

"Cossack campaigns can be most beautiful."

"Also terrible," I said.

"Most terrible. All war is terrible. I, a Cossack general, say so. It were better for mankind had there never been any war. Our Kuban Cossacks were peaceful citizens—no longer professional fighting men like their ancestors. They were tilling their lands, whitewashing their cottages, pruning their fruit trees, building new nurseries, new schools, new clubhouses, new cow stables, new jam factories. War was no longer their primary aim in life—no, sir, it was not. They were toiling to bring joy and happiness to their villages, their homes, themselves. The last thing they wanted was to drop their hoes and hammers for guns and sabers. But with fascism setting the world aflame with hate and murder, what else could they do?"

He paused, peered at me with the one gleam of fierceness I beheld in his eyes throughout the interview. Then, relaxing and leaning back in his chair, he resumed:

"Yet Cossack campaigns can be beautiful. One such campaign I remember with particular vividness. It was near the Miuse River by a small stream that flows into the Miuse. In anticipation of a German advance we burned the bridges over the stream, opened into it the sluices of a nearby kolhoz (collective farm) pond so as to swell its breadth and its depth. Securely hidden in a specially selected terrain, we waited for the Germans. They came in strong force, with much mechanized equipment. Our long-range artillery kept them from moving the equipment across the stream. Then in small boats they started sending their infantry across. They did it in a hurry. Soon masses of German infantry rolled on our side of the stream. We watched and waited. We didn't mind how much infantry they sent across. The more the better. We knew they would be no match for us. Promptly at eleven-thirty in the morning I ordered a sweeping advance. We started out in mass formation, on one side Kuban Cossacks, on the other Don Cossacks, the Kuban Cossacks in their red-topped caps, their flowing red hoods, the Don Cossacks with their blue epaulets, their blue caps, their flowing blue hoods, the blue bands on their trousers: waves and waves of red and blue billowing up and down the air, the horses trotting in rhythmic formation as if on parade. Such

magnificence, such pageantry I had never seen in all my life.
. . . Here was more than beauty, here were power, triumph,
joy, something so lovely, so enchanting that deep in my heart
I felt we'd win an overwhelming victory. Our artillery silenced
all or nearly all of the enemy's mechanized equipment, and we
plunged ahead only two kilometers and then galloped into the
attack. The battlefield was twelve kilometers [seven and a half
miles] deep. The Cossacks were in excellent condition. They
shouted and sabered, sabered and shouted—and we had plenty
of fire power, too, this time—until not one German infantryman
on our side of the stream was alive, not one. At two-thirty in
the afternoon I ordered the attack to cease. There were no more
enemies to fight, for the Germans on the other side of the stream
turned and fled. . . . Not a Cossack in this battle but had from
twelve to eighteen dead Germans to his credit. . . . It was one
of our most successful campaigns."

Dusk was falling over the long, thick-walled office. One of
the adjutants arose and turned on the lights. They burned feebly,
leaving pockets of darkness in the corners and imparting to the
room an eerie and ghostlike aspect, or so it seemed to me after
hearing the stories of Cossack battles, stories which belonged to
the faraway chivalric and primitive past rather than the harsh
engine-screaming present.

"The engineer is changing dynamos," explained the adjutant,
"so the current is feeble."

The ancient office remained in spectral semitwilight.

The general excused himself and walked out. An important
caller was waiting for him. Instantly the two adjutants stood up
and started talking.

"Isn't our general a wonderful man?" said one.

"He is always like that, simple and straightforward," said the
other.

"And how he loves children—you ought to see him play with
them in the orphan asylum."

"What orphan asylum?" I asked.

"The one we have adopted—right near our academy."

"They are war orphans, all of them."

"I visited them this afternoon, and they are all excited about the performance they are rehearsing for the New Year's party they are giving for the general. You must come to the party—the general will be glad to have you."

"Unfortunately," I said, "I shall not be in Moscow. I am leaving for home very soon."

"For America?"

"Yes."

Smiling, both youths looked at one another and at me with fresh inquisitiveness in the manner of adventurous boys who envy someone that is about to depart on a far and romantic journey. The very word America is magic for Russians, especially for youths who grow up on Jack London, Mark Twain, and Fenimore Cooper, and who associate our country with magic and miracles in scientific achievement.

"Too bad," said one of them, "you'd like the kids, and you'd enjoy their performance. We help them, of course. The general keeps telling us all the time we must love children, especially war orphans, and our students go there to teach them Cossack songs, Cossack dances, Cossack games. . . ."

"By the way," said the other adjutant, "when the general comes back ask him how many decorations he has been awarded. He's got a breastful of them, but won't tell how many."

Soon the general returned. When he sat down I said:

"How many decorations, General, have you been awarded?"

He motioned with his hand and made no answer. When I pressed him, he said:

"I'll tell you what. Let's finish the war first. Let's bring our infernal common enemy to his knees and keep him there. Then come to see me again and I'll tell you how many decorations I've been awarded and what they are. Anything else about the Cossack you especially wish to know?" he asked.

"Yes," I said. "What's his future? Won't new inventions, new weapons such as robot bombs, possibly robot lightning, robot flame throwers, make him obsolete?"

"Not at all," was the firm answer. "When all armies disappear, the Cossack will disappear. But as long as there are armies in the world, the Cossack will have his place in our Army. He has performed wonders in this war in spite of the plane, the tank, the motorized artillery. He will do so in the future, no matter what science brings forth. The Cossack won't stagnate. We shall not permit him to stagnate. We shall keep him attuned to new inventions, new techniques of warfare. We shall not allow him to remain content with his past achievements and past glories. The Cossack had his yesterday. He has his today. He has his tomorrow."

So the Cossack is here to stay! This is one of the most epochal and most striking phenomena in the evolution of the Soviet Revolution.

To appreciate the full meaning of this phenomenon we must know the origin of the Cossack and his past, its drama and melodrama, its romance and its reality.

PART TWO

The Cossack of Old

CHAPTER III

The Rebel Supreme

———◆———

FOR GENERATIONS West Europeans spoke of Russia as "the land of the Cossacks," meaning the land of barbarians. Nor did Russians themselves dissociate the Cossack from barbarism.

"Mothers," says U. Lukin, a Russian literary critic, "frightened unruly children by threatening to bring in a Cossack. On hearing the word, children shivered with fright . . . in countless songs the people remember with pain and wrath the Cossack lash. The very word Cossack evoked the image of a beast with a dangling forelock and a bloodstained whip in his hand."

A creature void of mercy and honor, fearing neither God nor devil—such was the popular conception of the Cossack. Nor was it unwarranted. Throughout the nineteenth century, which witnessed the flowering of Russian culture—literature and music, science and philosophy, a revolutionary consciousness and an immense humanitarianism—the Cossack became the symbol of Russian tyranny. At the bidding of the powers that ruled the country, he was always ready to shed blood. Student protests, workers' uprisings, peasant revolts—he trampled them all with zeal and ferocity. He was the champion suppressor of all liberties except his own. As long as he was the watchdog of the czars, the protector of the landed gentry, their power was secure, their destiny unshaken. Blindly he obeyed the orders of the *nachalstvo*, his superior officers. "Whatever father commander orders," runs a Cossack ditty, "we fulfill; we smite and stab and kill."

Yet it is not so in the beginning of Cossack history nor for centuries afterward. Quite the reverse. The Cossack had his being in revolt against the civilization in which he lived. He hated the rulers of his day and fought them. As rover horseman adventurer he could not help despising restraint or repression. For centuries the word *volnitsa*—liberty—was the Cossack's passion and battle cry, and he himself was the symbol of the common man's irrepressible urge toward freedom. He scoffed at the very concept of anyone's superiority to himself. Long before the world heard of the Russian Decembrists who rose in revolt against Czar Nicholas I or of any organized revolutionary party, such as the Populists, the Social Revolutionaries, the Social Democrats, the Mensheviks, or the Bolsheviks, the Cossack was the supreme rebel of Russia, heading in his day the mightiest revolutions in Russian history.

Without the aid of theorists or learned men of any kind, out of the perturbations and lessons of his everyday life, the Cossack created two of the most remarkable republics of his time. He was the champion crusader of folk democracy.

It is fiction to believe that the Cossack is an alien tribesman, "a savage Asiatic" whom czars had bribed or seduced into fighting for them. The Cossack borrowed much from alien tribes in dress, ways of living, methods of warfare, and much that may be understood as "wildness." But essentially he is Russian; he rises out of the soil of Russian history as the birch rises out of the Russian marsh.

Originally and in the main he was the humblest of the humble, the poorest of the poor. He was a religious nonconformist determined to worship God in his own way. He was a criminal fleeing from the law, an adventurer choosing to roam the wilds of nature rather than endure the monotony of a domestic existence. He was a sentry on a remote and turbulent frontier who tired of his post and ran away. He was a Tatar who fled from the repressions of the Tatar state. He was a straggling survivor of the massacres that rocked southern and southeast Russia when Tatar tribesmen swept over the boundless steppes, putting everything in their way to fire and sword. He was a Polish or Lithuanian peasant who broke away from the bonds which a haughty landed gentry foisted on him; he might be a Russian boyar or high official seeking respite from political obloquy, domestic scandal, or economic ruin. He might even be a Frenchman, a German, a Turk in search of a change of environment and of violent adventure.

Essentially the Cossack was a serf who made his way to freedom. Predominantly he was a peasant of the Orthodox faith. Predominantly he was a Slav, a Russian or Ukrainian. He was the voice of protest against the social inequalities and political barbarities of his age, the sword of vengeance against those responsible for both.

Were Russia a small country, surrounded by jealous and powerful neighbors, or if her southern and eastern borderland were governed by a strong state, there would be no place to which a rebel from the northern and the central part of the country might escape, safe from pursuit and capture. But the Ukraine, which is the Russian word for borderland, is immense and was sparsely settled. There was space in which to roam, there were fish and game on which to feed, rich land on which to grow grains and vegetables, excellent grass on which to breed horses and fatten cattle. The Don, the Dnieper, the Volga basins in these lands invited the newcomer. One could lose himself in their flat or rolling immensities. There no landlord's emissary would dare hunt fugitive serfs, no czarist agent would venture to clap chains over an outlaw or nonconformist.

The Ukraine was Russia's great Wild West, with no force other than a benevolent nature and a vengeful Mohammedan tribesman to threaten life and endanger liberty. Up north czars and boyars and a landed gentry were snuffing out the last vestiges of popular freedom. In such citadels of ancient democracy as Novgorod and Pskov, the *veche*—people's mass meeting—was suppressed. The Russian state was becoming more closely knit, more authoritarian, more autocratic, more contemptuous of the common man's rights. But Moscow had not yet laid a crushing hand on these faraway lands in the South. Here were no masters of the earth. Here no one had yet arrogated power and privilege unto his autocratic self. Here the common man—fugitive, serf, vagabond, nonconformist, bandit, whoever he might be, whatever his social and racial origin—might still assert his will and profess the dignity of his person. He still had the chance to initiate and cultivate his own democratic community.

This is exactly what the Cossack did. At first he was a peaceful tiller of the soil or a wanderer in search of food, freedom, and a new life. Fighting was a means to an end: physical survival. But alone he was no match for the galloping tribesman or the roving Mohammedan enemy. Besides he was unaccustomed to solitude. He came from a village and was irrepressibly gregarious. He craved society and companionship. For purposes of defense and camaraderie he banded together with others—strangers, wayfarers, adventurers like himself.

In time these voluntary bands expanded, their power became greater. They not only fought off attacks but launched onslaughts of their own on enemy hideouts or passing trade caravans. The more closely they drew together, the more they realized the need for common action and common usage, the readier they were to work out a body of unwritten laws and customs to govern their relations to one another and to the outside world. Out of these bands and communal associations there grew up, about the middle of the sixteenth century, two Cossack states, both republics, one on the Don, the other on the Dnieper —the one made up largely of Russians, the other of Ukrainians. The Don republic lost much of its independence, though not its rebelliousness, in 1614, but the one on the Dnieper held out until 1775.

The very name of the Dnieper republic—Zaporog *setch*—spells romance and adventure. Literally the words mean "a clearing beyond the rapids." An archipelago of islands juts out of the waters of the lower Dnieper; on one of these, the island Hortitse, the Cossacks cut down the dense growth of stunted wood and made a clearing for themselves. Hence the word *setch*—clearing.

Later they made similar clearings on other islands. Cut off by water from the mainland, protected from view by brush and timber, with log entrenchments and sod barriers blocking the approaches, the Cossack settlements were well sheltered against sudden raids and afforded excellent cover for sallies against enemies or neighbors.

Equality and liberty were the supreme law and custom of the Dnieper republic. Here were no private homes, only few and scanty private possessions. If the Cossack had a home with a landholding, it was outside the *setch*. Here he lived in the *kurenny*—barracks. These were built of brush and saplings with horsehides over the roofs. Each barracks elected its own hetman —leader—who administered its internal affairs. There was also the *Koshevoy* hetman—head of the republic, to whose authority the local hetmans had to submit. He too was elected and was responsible to the community. Only in wartime, as commander in chief of the fighting forces, did he exercise dictatorial powers. Even then, especially in a moment of reverses, might he turn to the mass meeting for guidance and counsel.

The governing body of the republic was the Rada—the circle —which was a kind of folk parliament. The Rada kept a close check on the *Koshevoy*. It had power of life and death over all members, including the hetmans. Every Cossack enjoyed the right to participate in the Rada, and once a year the main hetman rendered a report to this body. If he abused his powers, the Rada could sentence him to death. He was also subject to recall before his term of office expired.

The *setch* functioned only in summer. In winter the Cossacks went to their homes or wandered around the towns selling the loot they had acquired in the course of the summer's fighting and wandering.

Far and wide grew the fame of the Dnieper republic. The absence of class distinctions, of authoritarian rule, of the subjugation of one man by another, attracted an ever growing stream of adventurers and malcontents. For Russians in conflict with czarist law and the usages of the landed gentry, the Cossack republics on the Dnieper and on the Don had the same lure as newly discovered America held for the poor, the dissatisfied, and the persecuted in western Europe. They fled there for refuge and asylum. They needed less means than the migrant to America or no means at all, but infinitely more audacity, to reach the country of their choice. The departure was secret and full of danger. The infuriated landlords clamored for stiffer laws against runaway serfs, for harsher treatment of those captured. They reinforced the guards on their estates. More and more armed men prowled the open highways, haunted the remote lanes in search of deserters. But there was no stopping the clandestine exodus; the flood broke through all man-made barriers. Yet only the boldest and strongest risked their lives and fought their way to freedom. That is why, since the very beginning, the Cossack has been the pick of Russian manhood. Physically and mentally he was almost a race apart, fit for all trials and battles with men and nature.

Brief and simple were the tests to which the newcomer submitted on his arrival in the *setch*. According to Gogol the hetman said to him:

"Do you believe in Christ?"

"I do."

"Do you believe in the Holy Trinity?"

"I do."

"Show me how you cross yourself."

The applicant made the sign of the cross, and the examination was over. No inquiry was made into racial origin, personal character, political faith. These were of no consequence. The Cossacks were not predisposed to racial discrimination. They hated the Tatar, not because he was a Mongol but because he was a Mohammedan, therefore to them an infidel and also a foe. Yet the Cossack gladly sought the hand of the Tatar girl who struck his fancy or kidnaped her and made her his spouse. The Pole was a Roman Catholic, therefore to the Cossack an enemy of Orthodoxy, his personal enemy. Yet he did not disdain to ravish or marry the proverbially beautiful and cultivated Polish *panenka*—young lady.

Illuminating is an incident in the life of Yemelyan Pugatchev, the Don Cossack who shook Russia with his revolt against Catherine the Great. During the Seven Years' War, as during World War II, a Russian army swept into East Prussia and occupied Königsberg. Pugatchev was stationed in this old Prussian city. One evening he noticed a German laundrywoman and her daughter warming themselves by a Cossack bonfire. Captivated by the daughter, the impetuous Pugatchev proposed marriage. He had a wife at home, but that did not matter. The fact that he was fighting Germans, and moreover would continue to fight them, was no barrier. War was war, and a woman was a woman.

The Cossack's century-old ruthlessness toward the Pole, the Mohammedan, and the Jew had its roots essentially in his fanatical devotion to Orthodoxy at a time when religion was a universal source of conflict and war.

First of all a peasant in those days, the Cossack was overwhelmingly illiterate, with no business tradition, no knowledge, and no means of developing the agricultural and mineral riches of the country. Besides, the Cossack cherished no ambition to become a "gentleman," or a landlord with serfs of his own. He was no fortune hunter; professional traders he despised as much as officials or landlords. He was content to abide by his simple and elemental standard of living. To understand the retarded growth of private enterprise in old Russia one must remember, among other things, the Cossack's traditional contempt for it, the naturalness with which he, the freest of the free in Russia, clung to his primitive collectivism. In his backward environment, with his ignorance of the Western world and the individualist proclivities it was fostering, especially on the newly discovered American continent, there was not much to inspire him with an ambition to accumulate riches and to be lord and master of a personal domain or to give himself wholly, as did so many of the immigrants to America, to the pursuit of economic aggrandizement.

In later years, when individual landholding became a fixed practice, the Cossack became a landowner. He went through a

marked social differentiation. Some possessed much land and livestock, others little of both. Like the immigrant to America, the
Cossack was a pioneer and a colonizer, but unlike the immigrant
he was also a soldier. He never acquired the urge to wrest big
fortunes out of nature, to become a magnate of one kind or another. He was an empire builder not in an economic but in a
geographic sense. He might strive for the acquisition of more
land and tools, more cattle and horses, more silk and velvet, more
silver and gold, but he lived a divided life. Cossackhood was a
check on the economic man in him. Cossack lore and Cossack
lust of battle consumed much of his energy and his time. His
mind was too preoccupied with adventure. Like the sun, the
sky, the steppe, his Cossackhood was ever present within him,
so immutable a part of his being that rarely was he tempted to
pry his way into the business world, into trade, commerce, or
industry.

On the steppe the Cossack became a skilled horseman; he
mastered the lance, the dagger, the sword, and the gun. He
adapted himself superbly to the forces of nature around him. He
acquired a keen sense of direction and could go anywhere and
find his way about without map or compass. Sure of the right-
ness of his way of life, he frowned on laws and customs not his
own. Neither the property nor the person of others meant much
to him. He had no sense of the sanctity of human life. He raided
merchant vessels, ambushed trade caravans, indulged the passions
and habits of a warrior and a pirate. Fighting ceased to be a
means to an end and became an end in itself, a profession and a
pleasure, a game and a gamble.

The immediate neighbor of the Dnieper republic was Poland.
The long feud between the two is one of the bloodiest chapters
in the history of both. There were times when the two made
peace and fought together against a common foe, but the peace
did not last. It was too riddled with intrigue, too swollen with
contradiction; the Orthodoxy of the Cossack, the Roman Catholicism of the Pole, these alone barred a permanent and faithful
alliance. To the very end the Dnieper republic was a fighting

citadel of Orthodoxy. Yet from the Poles the Cossack borrowed much in manners, dress, swank, cooking, and talk.

The more numerous and the more powerful the Cossack became, the more completely he severed himself from his old ways of life. He enjoyed better food, better shelter, better clothes than he ever could in the serf-ridden town or village from which he fled. He now had freedom, pleasure, adventure. There was no master over him for whom to labor, on whom to fawn, before whom to prostrate himself. Not a shred remained of his old servility and self-pity. He had no more complaints against fate, no more quarrels with nature. He was a new man not only on the Russian but on the European scene, new in appearance, in dress, in manner, in character, in outlook on the world. He had no use for books and learning, but he wore new clothes rich in color and ornamentation and ample in size. He evolved his own "meteorology" and spoke of the "four winds" blowing from the four corners of the earth—from the direction of the Turk, the Teuton, the Pole, the Muscovite. He hated them all and intrigued with one against the other, yet always denying their right to intrude on his lands and disturb his independence.

Outdoor life, forays into Turkey, Poland, Muscovy, and other places toughened his body, sharpened his wit, tempered his soul. He grew increasingly restless, increasingly self-confident, increasingly audacious, increasingly warlike and in love with his Cossackhood. Nothing else held much lure for him or yielded as much satisfaction. Domestic ties were a burden, and he sloughed them off with no more compunction than he divested the passing trader of goods and valuables. Marriage was an incident or an accident and the family a by-product. Sex was a nuisance or a sin, at best no more than a flitting diversion. This may seem paradoxical, for nothing is more alien to the Cossack than asceticism. He revels in the joys of the flesh, in food, drink, play, rowdyism. But sex and family may drain a man's energies, impair his virtues as a warrior, weaken him for fighting—the supreme purpose and glory of Cossack life. Celibacy, therefore, became a cult, though not universally espoused, and the Dnieper republic was in some ways a semimonastic brotherhood. Women were barred, and married men had their families outside the *setch*.

This attitude is dramatized in the famous ballad which tells how the ataman Stenka Razin throws his bride into the Volga River to placate his Cossacks, who feel that the woman is robbing their chief of his prowess in war.

For over two centuries the Dnieper republic rocked with battle and adventure. No writer has described that life with greater vigor and authenticity than Nikolay Gogol. His novel *Taras Bulba* is one of the great epics in the Russian language and the most brilliant and full-bodied story of "the wood clearing beyond the rapids." The headstrong roistering Taras is the old Cossack at the height of his glory. Gogol shows him in all his boldness, all his vanity, all his triumph, and all his tragedy.

The story of Taras Bulba is our best source for knowing the robust heritage in the making of the Kuban Cossacks who are the principal subject of this book.

CHAPTER IV

The Cossack Republic

TARAS BULBA HAS TWO SONS, Ostap and Andrey. When they return home from their studies in the Kiev seminary wearing clerical garb, the father, on first seeing them, greets them with a burst of laughter and mockery. Embarrassed, then angered, Ostap warns his father to cease making fun of him and his brother. The warning infuriates Taras.

"Why shouldn't I laugh?" he roars.

"If you keep on," replies the son, "I'll beat you up."

The father is elated. The son is no "sissy." He has in him fighting Cossack blood. He asks Ostap whether they are to fight with fists.

"Any way you like," answers the son.

Taras rolls up his sleeves, and father and son pound mercilessly away with their fists at each other's ribs, back, and chest. After they soundly trounce each other, Taras embraces his son, kisses him and rhapsodizes aloud, "Wonderful boy! Be sure you pummel everyone as soundly as you've pummeled me." Turning to the other son, he scoffs at him and calls him a "lout" for standing with hands at his sides.

"Why don't you fight, you son of a bitch?" Taras says.

The mother appears and bursts into tears. The boys have just arrived. She has not said a word to them, has neither embraced nor kissed them, and here is the father having a fist fight with one and calling the other a son of a bitch for not fighting.

But the bellicose Taras is impervious to tears and lamentations. He glories in his sons. They are big, strong, bold, tough. The Kiev seminary has not robbed them of their Cossack fighting spirit. He proposes that they all go at once to the *setch*. He is impatient to show off his sons to his friends and to expose them to the strenuous life and the violent pastimes of the Cossack brotherhood on the Dnieper.

The mother protests and weeps. But what is a woman or a mother to the doughty Taras? "Enough," he scolds, "you've howled enough, old woman. A Cossack isn't born to run around with women."

True! To the Cossack of Taras Bulba's days and for centuries afterward, women are inferior creatures, a part of nature's, but not the Cossack's, scheme of things. They are never allowed in the *setch*. A mother who comes to see her son there risks losing her life; a Cossack appearing with a woman forfeits his. Women have their place in the world. They are homemakers outside the *setch*. They provide pleasure. They bear children. They rear the family. They till the land, tend the flocks, perpetuate the race, bring more Cossacks into the world. That is all they are good for.

But man has a special mission in life, holy and overpowering. In a toast to his son, Taras expounds this mission, which is "to beat the Mohammedan, the Turks, the Tatars" and the *Liakhs*— the Poles—too, if and when there is a clash with "our faith," which is Orthodoxy.

"Come," says Taras, "clink your glasses. . . . Is the brandy good? What's corn brandy in Latin? The Latins were stupid. They didn't know there was such a thing in the world as corn brandy. What was the name of the man who wrote Latin verses? . . . Wasn't it Horace?"

The mention of Horace startles the older son, and he exclaims:

"What a father! The old dog knows everything."

Taras doesn't resent being called a dog. He likes abusive language as much as violent action. He only hopes the classes in the Kiev academy haven't deadened his sons' appetite for brandy, "scorching corn brandy that foams and hisses like fury." To swill brandy and mead, old and potent mead, is as much a Cossack virtue and achievement as to gallop on a wild horse or to cleave with sword or saber the heads of Mussulmans, Tatars, Poles, and other enemies of the true faith or the Cossack's independence.

Taras is impatient with his wife's plea that he and the sons remain home awhile longer.

"Why should I wait here?" he remonstrates. "To become a buckwheat reaper and housekeeper? To tend the sheep, the swine, and loaf around with my wife? Damn such twaddle! I am a Cossack. I'll have none of it. What is there except war? . . . What's this hut to us?" To show his contempt for pots and pans and the ease and domesticity they symbolize, he smashes the crockery around him.

Such is the ancestor of the Kuban Cossack, restless, impetuous, hating work, hating outside rules whether Russian, Polish, Tatar, or Turkish, hating everything that doesn't stir his unbridled lust for excitement, for drink, for battle, for freedom.

Taras and his two sons arrive in the *setch*. Ostap and Andrey have their first glimpse and their first taste of the boisterous liberty which rules the place. Here are all the brandy and mead one wants to drink, and no one protests, no one moralizes, no one cares. Here are honey and *solomaha*—fermented rye dough— also meat and fish, fruit and cereal, above all thick rye flour soup, all one wants to eat. Here are freedom from care and worry, from fear and work. Here are no rich and no poor, no superiors and no inferiors, no caste and no outcast. Here are no sex and no love, not the sight or shadow of a woman. Here one may only dream of feminine beauty, feminine voluptuousness, feminine passion, feminine companionship.

Justice is simple and stern. Theft is a major crime. However trifling the object a Cossack steals from a fellow Cossack, he cannot count on forgiveness. His act is a disgrace, and all Cossacks participate in his punishment. He is tied to a post in the public square. Beside the post lies a stout club. The passer-by lifts the club and strikes the offender as hard as he likes. The clubbing continues until the thief is dead.

Refusal or inability to pay a debt is a serious misdemeanor. The guilty Cossack is chained to a cannon and remains chained until someone pays his debts.

Murder is brutally avenged. The cause, whether drunkenness, rage, revenge, jealousy, is of no consequence. A deep hole is dug in the ground, the murderer is thrown into the hole, the coffin with the corpse is lowered over him. The murderer is buried alive with his victim.

Ostap and Andrey revel in Cossack life. It is all so different from the routine and frustrations they knew in the Kiev seminary. Here they are free to give vent to their elemental nature, to the impulse for fun and excitement, to the lure of horse and steppe. But the interval of idleness and gaiety is brief; it always is in the *setch*, for it always alternates with intervals of battle and war. Fight the Cossack must if only to keep himself fit for war. Such is Taras Bulba's slogan. When no war is in sight to give his sons a chance to demonstrate their prowess, he urges the chief hetman to start a fight with the Turks. But the hetman reminds Taras that the treaty of peace between the Cossacks and the Turkish sultan forbids an attack. "But he is a Mohammedan," argues Taras; "God and Holy Writ command us to fight the Mohammedans." The hetman refuses to be stampeded into war. Incensed, Taras says:

"What do you mean? I have two sons, young fellows. Neither of them has known war, not once, and you say we have no right, and you say the Cossacks here must stay where they are?"

The hetman is firm, but Taras wants war; he must have it so his sons can prove their mettle as warriors. He starts a campaign against the *Koshevoy*, succeeds in having him recalled and a new man elected. Taras is overjoyed. But instead of Turkey, the Cossacks fight Poland. Taras and his sons fight with skill and ferocity. Then something happens which overwhelms Taras with shame and horror. Andrey receives word by secret messenger that the Polish princess with whom he fell in love during his student days in Kiev is in the town to which the Cossacks have laid siege. She is in dire circumstances, he is told, threatened with starvation and death and desperately in need of his help. Forgetting his father, Orthodoxy, and Cossackhood, he rushes to her rescue. On seeing her—young, beautiful, and helpless—he is so overwhelmed with love that he deserts the Cossacks, joins the Poles, fights with them against his own people and against everything the *setch* symbolizes.

Taras Bulba sees his son in battle leading a Polish regiment against Cossacks and fighting savagely. He seizes Andrey's horse by the reins and commands the son to climb down.

"I gave you birth," he said, "I shall end your life." With this, Taras shoots his son.

This is only the beginning of tragedy in Taras Bulba's family. Ostap is taken prisoner by the Poles. The father is heartbroken. With song and flattery, older Cossacks seek to divert him. But Taras won't be cheered. He cannot forget the handsome, dashing, jolly Ostap who had already been elevated to leadership among the Cossacks. Taras resolves that he will find his son wherever he may be, dead or alive. He makes his way secretly to Warsaw and joins the crowd watching the torture of his son. When Ostap falls bleeding and helpless to the ground, he mutters, "Father, where are you? Can you hear me?" High over the heads of the silent multitude rises Taras's booming voice, "I hear." The father's voice causes excitement and consternation. Instantly Polish horsemen start a search for the man whose voice they have heard. But Taras is nowhere to be found.

He returns to the Cossacks, makes his way at the head of his regiment deep into Polish territory and sacks, burns, slaughters all in revenge for the execution of Ostap. Finally he is taken prisoner and is sentenced to be publicly burned alive. Bound in chains, he is led to a tree, the limbs and top of which have been blasted by lightning. Hoisted to the top so all can see him, his hands are nailed to the trunk and a fire is started at its base.

But Taras disdains to look down to the rising flames. He is contemptuous of the enemy and of the death that is crawling toward him in bright flame. He searches the horizon, and when he sees Cossacks across the river he shouts, "Come on, boys! Quick, take that hillock yonder by the wood." With the hillock in their hands the Cossacks gain an immediate advantage over the enemy.

But the wind scatters his words, the Cossacks fail to hear his counsel. "Ah," moans Taras, "they'll perish, perish and in vain."

The flames rise higher and higher and begin to envelop Taras Bulba's body. But he is still indifferent to his own fate. Suddenly he sees a group of Cossacks leap out of a cluster of bushes. Taras is filled with rapture and once more shouts; "To shore, to shore, boys—there are boats beyond that hill—take them away so they cannot pursue you." This time the Cossacks hear Taras Bulba's words and follow his advice. Bullets whiz over their heads, but they keep on rowing. The flames leap higher and higher, but Taras's mind is clear and his head is unbowed. Triumphantly he shouts, "Good-by, boys . . . remember me— and next spring come here again and have a good time."

Here we have the Cossack of old in all his triumph and all

his tragedy. He lives boldly and boisterously and passes out of life tempestuously and prematurely.

It is out of such or a similar social and spiritual milieu that there rise in the course of the years Cossack leaders who become folk heroes and historical figures. The best-known of these come from the Don Cossack country, which espoused its own way of life in its own manner and in moments of crisis with no more regard for the law and order or even the wishes of Moscow than was evinced by the Zaporog Cossacks.

CHAPTER V

Yermak, the Conqueror of Siberia

"THE CONQUEROR OF SIBERIA," is the title which Russian historians and other writers, including Leo Tolstoy, have conferred on Yermak Timofeyitch, the Cossack rebel and outlaw who added to the Russian domain one of the vastest and richest areas in the world.

The monuments to Yermak in Tobolsk, Siberia, in Novocherkassk, the Don Cossack country, the many more that are certain to glorify his memory in the rising cities of the country he conquered, are an honor Yermak never dreamed of achieving. He was neither scientist nor explorer. He sought neither new routes to an old world nor old gold in a new world. He informed Czar Ivan the Terrible of his achievement, but there is no record anywhere that he regarded it as anything of stupendous consequence to posterity. Proud as he may have been of it, his conquest of Siberia was not the fulfillment of a long-cherished dream but the crowning incident or the monumental accident of his turbulent life, of pure Cossack adventure.

In subsequent centuries his deed so deeply stirred the folk mind of Russia that out of it, like the resplendent flowers that grew out of the fat Siberian earth, came a rich harvest of song and saga. Romance and sentiment fused his exploits into lyric and legend, at once tender and heroic, exultant and tragic. There are ballads that depict Yermak as the young son or the young nephew of Ilya Murometz, Russia's kindliest and mightiest folk hero. Others portray him as the young nephew of Prince Vladimir of Kiev, who antedates Yermak by six centuries. Like Ilya Murometz, Yermak is intrepid and invincible, slays the enemies of the people, is modest and jovial. He neither demands nor expects reward for his deeds. When, after a sensational triumph over the Tatar enemy, Prince Vladimir asks Yermak whether he will have his reward in land or gold, Yermak's reply is that all he wants is the privilege of free drinks in the prince's taverns.

Remote from historic fact, these ballads reveal something of the intrinsic nature of the man. Fame and riches held small lure for Yermak. He fought and conquered because he could not help himself; his Cossackhood had prepared him for nothing else, had inculcated in him no other ambition than to live a free, strenuous, adventurous life. His appetites were elemental and hearty, his wants were few, his tastes simple. He sought neither gaudy ornamentation nor gilded opulence. Love did not beguile him, sex did not ensnare him. When he was ruler of the town of Isker or Sibir, capital of the Tatar tribe that held sway over the country he conquered, a native prince called with his young daughter and offered her to Yermak for his pleasure. Yermak refused.

Little is known of Yermak's early life. His grandfather lived in Suzdal, a historic town in central Russia. Poor and beaten, he gathered his family and wandered forth in search of a better life elsewhere. Arrested and freed, the wanderer turned his footsteps southward. In his youth Yermak separated from his family and found work on boats and barges plying the waters of the Kama and the Volga. From the Volga he drifted to the Don and joined the Cossacks, known then as "the society of free people." Once a Cossack, he quickly mastered the art of Cossack warfare. With a good mind and a glib tongue, he attained the position of ataman.[1]

Within easy reach of the lower Don lies the lower Volga, a region then sparsely settled, feebly guarded by the czar's soldiers. A leading artery of commerce, with barges carrying goods and passengers to and from Persia, it lured Cossacks and other adventurers in quest of loot. The steep banks of the Volga, the rolling hills and dense forests in the hinterland, the immense caves, offered splendid protection against pursuers and intruders. Under the direction of atamans, Cossack bands of from two hundred to six hundred members roved the country, hunted, fished, and swooped down on passing barges and robbed them.

Yermak had the largest and most desperate band, numbering a thousand men. He was the most notorious outlaw on the Volga and staged the most spectacular raids. Merchants and soldiers dreaded an encounter with him, and for a long time he had his own way. Once a Persian ambassador, en route to visit the Moscow czar, found himself embroiled in a clash with Yermak. The ambassador's abusive language enraged the Cossack ataman, and the Cossack sword put the foreign emissary to death. Ivan the Terrible heard of it and dispatched a powerful force to avenge the murder of the Persian diplomat. Some of Yermak's men were seized, but the ataman himself and most of his band fled northward toward the Kama River and escaped.

About this time the enterprising Stroganov family had already carved for itself a gigantic empire along the banks of the Kama. Rich in forest and farm land, in fish and game, cattle and grasses, in salt and iron, in many natural resources, the rising Stroganov empire was subject to violent raids by Tatar bands. The Stroganovs needed a force to protect them. They sent an agent to Yermak's hideout with a message inviting him to come with his Cossacks and defend the new country from Tatar invasions.

Never averse to fresh adventure, Yermak and his Cossacks accepted the offer. They subdued the Tatars, and then the Cos-

[1] "Ataman" is the Russian, "hetman" is the Ukrainian for Cossack leader or chief.

sacks had no one to fight and nothing to do, so they started plundering the empire they had come to protect. Alarmed, the Stroganovs complained to Yermak. The ataman's answer was that as long as the Cossacks were idle they could not be stopped. He proposed that the Stroganovs provide work for the Cossacks, presumably of a kind to suit their roving and fighting nature.

The Stroganovs were impressed with Yermak's proposals. Pioneers and dreamers, their ambition was to expand their empire eastward, deep into the Urals and beyond. Expeditions had ventured into the unknown country but had neither explored nor conquered it. Novgorod merchants had voyaged to the Ob River. Twice Ivan III had sent forces to the Ob and subdued the Voguls and the Ostyaks. In the sixteenth century Russians knew the Siberian kingdom that lay along the Tura, Tobol, and Irtish rivers. In 1555 the kingdom acknowledged the rule of Moscow and agreed to pay an annual tax of 1,000 sables. But Moscow was far away. No Muscovites were around to enforce payment of the tax, and it lapsed. The kingdom again considered itself independent and beyond the reach of Moscow, then preoccupied with internal conflicts and problems. All that was known about the kingdom, all the Stroganovs had heard of it was that a Tatar khan named Kutchum was its czar. Once the capital of Kutchum was conquered and he and his subjects subdued, it would be open for exploration and exploitation and the Stroganovs would have a new world from which to gather wealth. They therefore proposed to Yermak that he go into the unknown land and conquer it.

The idea captivated Yermak. A new land meant fresh adventure and fresh loot. He called a mass meeting of the Cossacks, and before presenting the Stroganovs' proposal he upbraided them severely for their misbehavior. He told them they were disgracing themselves and need not think they could continue their rampage with impunity. He warned them that they need not think of returning to their old haunts on the Volga. They would be arrested and punished if they did. But if the road back was barred, the road ahead, he assured them, was wide open.

It was an untraveled road. No one knew where it led, what lay along its course, what enemies they might encounter, what battles they might have to fight. But the journey promised adventure and loot and the conquest of a new world. The mass meeting voted for the proposal.

The Stroganovs were overjoyed, and so was Yermak. Preparation for the arduous journey started at once. A hard bargainer, Yermak's demand for supplies—grain, flour, powder, firearms—and for guides and gunsmiths annoyed the Stroganovs. They made counterproposals, but Yermak was adamant. In the end the Stroganovs yielded. They did not want the Cossacks around any more, and they did covet new possessions in the East.

Rivers in those days were the chief highways of travel. On September 1, 1581, a flotilla of barges and boats carrying Yermak's 540 Cossacks and 300 of the Stroganovs' men, including German gunsmiths, started up the river Chusovaya. On reaching the Serebryannaya (Silver River), the expedition had to cross mountains. Since boats were useless, the Cossacks set about building carts and resumed their journey. For ten days the expedition plodded its way through dense forest and low mountains. It was traversing a country abounding in wood and land but empty of people. Not a single human being did the Cossacks see on the first part of their journey.

Again they came to a stream, the Zharovna River. Now carts were useless, so they abandoned these and built new boats. When the boats were ready, they floated away again. For five days they followed the course of the stream, passing through more country rich in land, in fresh-water lakes, in fish and game. The behavior of the wild animals surprised them. The animals showed no fear of man. This was a new experience to such seasoned hunters as Cossacks. They shot all the game they needed, caught all the fish they could use and rowed off again.

Soon they came to the river Tura. Here for the first time the Cossacks stumbled on a Tatar settlement. They gave battle to the hostile natives, and after inflicting small casualties on them they captured the settlement. They seized cattle, food, furs, pressed into service all of the more enlightened men of the community, and resumed their voyage. The deeper they penetrated the wilderness, the more impressed they were with its untouched riches, the more alluring was the scenery. The land was bursting with wealth. It was far away from czars, from the Stroganovs, from border sentries, and the Tatars were too impotent to challenge possession. Yet neither Yermak nor his men had any thought of settling to a life of comfort and riches. They were in quest not of aggrandizement but of adventure. The country fascinated them, and as they pressed onward they occupied more and more Tatar towns.

Finally they reached a settlement where they heard much of Czar Kutchum and of the town of Sibir which was his capital. An old man named Tauzik, an emissary of Kutchum, boasted that in the whole world there was no czar like Kutchum and no town like Sibir, that Kutchum's men and cattle were "as numerous as the stars." Yermak suspected the old man of guile, and by way of demonstrating his fearlessness of Kutchum and his powerful army he fired a gun at a tree that he specially selected for his purpose. The bullet split the tree in half. Other Cossacks fired their guns. Tauzik and the Tatars around were overawed. This was the first time they had seen firearms. The bow and the arrow, the iron or bone-pointed pick were the weapons they knew best. Tauzik fell on his knees, begged for mercy. Yermak did not take the old man prisoner, but ordered him to go to Kutchum and warn him that unless he was ready to surrender, he and his capital would be destroyed.

Tauzik departed, the Cossacks loaded up with fresh supplies and sailed on. They reached the Tobol, the largest river they had yet seen on their voyage. Soon they found themselves at the mouth of still another stream, the Bahasaan. On the banks sprawled a town. The natives came out and, like old Tauzik, started boasting of the powers of Kutchum and his son-in-law, whose name was Mametkul. Disregarding their boasts, the Cossacks made a landing, and to scare the natives they fired their guns. Terror-stricken, the natives held their tongues, saying no more of the invincible armies of Kutchum and his son-in-law.

The voyage was reaching a climax. The Cossacks were drawing closer and closer to the seat of Kutchum's power. They were ready for all eventualities. They cherished no doubts of victory, for they had weapons vastly superior and more deadly than anything the primitive tribesmen had known.

They streamed up the Irtish, broad, swift, cold, and alluring. They rowed all day and came to the largest town they had yet seen. Met by a hail of arrows, they fired their guns. Some of them fell dead, others were wounded. Never before had they suffered such casualties. But the battle was soon over. The Cossacks won. They entered the town and explored it. They found furs, rugs, cattle, homemade mead. They buried their dead, filled their boats with supplies and treasures, and proceeded farther up the Irtish. Another town loomed up before them, very large, surrounded by ditches and edged with palisades. Yermak knew what it meant. The Tatars had fortified the approaches. They planned to make a resolute stand. He knew the Cossacks were hopelessly outnumbered. He also knew guns alone, when there were so many of the enemy, were not likely to terrify them into flight and submission—not immediately. The battle promised to be protracted and savage. What was he to do?

He called a mass meeting. There was much heated discussion. The strain of the voyage proved too much for some of the men. They were weary and restless. They saw no limit to this land, no end to their voyage, and their troubles were mounting. If only they were within communicable distance of a base of supplies and reinforcements. But they were all alone. The Stroganovs were beyond reach. The Cossacks were completely cut off from the world from which they had come. Some were so unhappy and incensed that they wept. They demanded to know why they had come to this devilishly immense wilderness, where they were going and what save death was in store for them. There was clamor for a return home.

Yermak was facing the most acute crisis of his career as Cossack ataman. With his men demoralized and unhappy, further progress was unthinkable. He knew that Cossacks did not mind hardship if only there was hope ahead, triumph in the offing. But his men were sodden with defeat. Their language was violent and lugubrious. Their thoughts were not on the battle before them but on the misfortunes they were facing, on disaster and death. And there was not much time to lose. Kutchum had no firearms, but his forces were overwhelming and his men were boiling over with fury. They were fighting for their independence, and Yermak knew what that meant. But he too was fighting for a cause, a Cossack cause, the triumph over an enemy and sheer survival.

He listened to the tears and tirades. His own resolve was unshaken. However monumental the obstacles, they must be overpowered. His men must be refreshed and galvanized with faith in themselves, as Cossacks and warriors, as invincible crusaders against an ancient foe. He turned for counsel to Ivan Koltso, his closest associate and comrade. Koltso was not feeling happy over the crisis before them. But he would not surrender to defeat. The Cossacks, he said, must make a landing and fight Kutchum.

Heartened by Koltso's words, Yermak rose to speak. He harangued the Cossacks, scoffed at their tears, and shamed them for their cowardice. His speech bristled with censure and resentment. Yermak's scorching words filled the Cossacks with fresh energy and valor. Said one of them:

"You are wiser than we. Lead us wherever you choose. Twice it is impossible for us to die. Once we cannot escape death."

Other Cossacks echoed these sentiments. Their spirits revived, they clamored for action. They were Cossacks again, daredevil warriors, unafraid of Kutchum's numbers, ready for the sanguinary fray. Together they drew up a plan of battle. They were to advance with a center, a right wing, and a left wing. The center was to launch a frontal attack, the wings were to close in and wither the enemy with cross fire. To make their

numbers appear more formidable, they fashioned scarecrows
out of brush and scattered them, dressed as men, over the forest.

"If we win," said Yermak, "we become the czars here."

The battle started as the Cossacks planned. A deluge of arrows
descended on them. But the Tatars did not count on flank attacks. When bullets burst on them from right and left, they fled
in panic. The Cossacks triumphed. The supreme prize of their
journey, the town of Sibir, Kutchum's capital, was now in their
hands. The date was October 26, 1582, a little less than thirteen
months since they had started up the Chusovaya in the Urals.

Yermak and his men settled down in Sibir. Neighboring
princes came to pay homage and vow submission. The recalcitrant Tatars were easily overcome. There was peace and order
in the remote Siberian capital. Neither Yermak nor any of his
men harbored any ambitions to become the Stroganovs of the
vast new country which by right of exploration and conquest
was theirs. Free men, their tastes remained simple, their manner
of living unchanged, their democracy untainted. They elected
their atamans and all the other officials as in any other Cossack
community. They fished, hunted, brewed mead, regaled themselves with tales of Cossack heroism and Cossack achievement.
They sang and danced. They observed Orthodox fasts and festivals. They maintained Cossack discipline and ritual, honored
and obeyed the older folk, shared everything in common. There
were no rich and no poor among them. Offenders against public
order were put in chains for three or more days, depending on
the nature of the offense.

Life at first was easy and comfortable. In summer there were
hot sun and beautiful flowers, berries and wild fruit. There were
excellent hunting and fishing. Yet anxiety haunted the Cossacks.
Their numbers had dwindled, and there was no young generation
to fill the thinned ranks. The enemy was only outwardly submis-
sive. In his heart he rankled with hate and spite. Mametkul was
Yermak's prisoner, but Kutchum was at large in ominous hiding.
Yermak knew the Tatar czar was biding his time and would
strike when opportunity was ripe.

Immediately on the occupation of Sibir, Yermak sent a mission to the Stroganovs. "I have taken Kutchum's city," he wrote. "Mametkul is my prisoner. The people are under my rule. I have lost many Cossacks. I need men so we may regain our power here. This is a land of boundless wealth."

As a token of friendship and good will, Yermak loaded the emissaries with gifts for the Stroganovs, fox skins, sables, and other furs. To the Czar in Moscow he also sent emissaries and gifts. He informed the ruler of all Russia of his victory over the Tatars and his occupation of the Tatar capital. He also begged forgiveness for past sins.

The emissaries Yermak had sent to the Czar and to the Stroganovs returned, and Yermak learned the Czar had forgiven him his trespasses. In token of this forgiveness, the Czar sent him a cloak which he himself had worn and an armored coat. He also appointed Yermak commander of the small detachment of troops that came to the town of Sibir. In further appreciation of the ataman's achievement these troops, by order of the Czar, received the appellation of Cossacks, thus removing the stain of outlawry from the very word Cossack.

Yermak was happy, but not for long. He needed supplies and reinforcements, and none arrived. By the time spring came food was scarce and some of his men succumbed to scurvy. This was only a beginning of a mounting cycle of tragedy.

One day a Tatar chief came to Yermak with the complaint that a neighboring tribe was terrorizing his people. He asked for help to put down the threatening tribe and promised that his people would fight with the Cossacks. To refuse the request was to encourage the recalcitrant tribe in its depredations. So Yermak sent Koltso and forty men to fight it into submission. But the Tatars were treacherous; they slaughtered Koltso and his men.

The loss of his closest associate and forty men was a heavy blow to Yermak and his shrinking Cossack community. He had reason to fear further trouble. He knew the mind and ways of the natives. The successful perpetration of treachery was only the beginning of a determined crusade against himself and his men. He could not permit the assault to go unavenged. But his power was ebbing.

Shortly afterward Kutchum flaunted a fresh challenge. Traders from Bokhara in Central Asia, accompanied by a caravan of merchandise, were on their way to the annual fair in Sibir. Kutchum intercepted them and barred passage. When Yermak heard of this he resolved on prompt, decisive action. Summoning fifty men, he led them in person against the Tatar czar. One night while his men were asleep, Tatar sentinels betrayed them. Tatar soldiers pounced on them and killed them. Yermak was wakened and fought back. It was a hopeless fight. Wounded, he plunged into the Irtish and swam away. That was the last anyone ever saw him alive.

Thus ended the life of Yermak Timofeyitch, Cossack adventurer, conqueror of Siberia, folk hero and man of destiny.

Fresh expeditions followed in his footsteps. They were well armed and well led. Stubbornly Kutchum and his followers resisted the advent of the new armies. But the resistance was hopeless. By the end of 1598 the wilderness which Yermak had traversed in boats, on foot, in carts, with no compass, no map, no knowledge of astronomy or geography, with no benefit or guidance of science or scientific instruments, trusting solely to his Cossack intuition, his Cossack valor, and to the course of the swift-flowing Siberian rivers—that wilderness became Russian territory. It was the richest prize any Russian prince, peasant, czar, or serf had ever won for his people. The new country was named Siberia after the town of Sibir, the capital of Kutchum's Tatar empire.

In the old province of Samara, now known as Kuibyshev, whose hills, forests, and caves were the haunts of Yermak and his outlaw Cossack band, there are villages which bear the names of Yermakovka and Koltsovka, in memory of Yermak, the boldest Cossack ataman of his time, and of Ivan Koltso, his most trusted and intimate associate.

CHAPTER VI

Stenka Razin[1]

From the quiet island inlet
Out to where the stream flows deep,
Stenka Razin's painted galleys
Through the waters boldly sweep.

Stenka in the foremost galley
Has his princess at his side,
Drunk with wine and mirth together
As he clasps his new-won bride.

Sullen murmurs rise behind them:
"Chucked us for a wench! Why, true,
Just one night with her and Stenka
Has become a woman, too!"

Swelling now the angry mutter
Surges round the headman's ears,
And he holds his Persian beauty
All the closer at their jeers.

But his brows are scowling darkly.
Now a storm begins to rise.
There are swift and savage lightnings
In the headman's bloodshot eyes.

[1]Based on the folk song collected by Florence Hudson Botsford for her *Collection of Folk Songs.* Copyright, 1922, 1931, by G. Schirmer, Inc.

"Volga, Volga, Mother Volga,
Russian river, look upon
This my gift: you've not yet seen one
From a Cossack of the Don.

"In a fellowship of free men
Never shall a quarrel rise.
Volga, Volga, Mother Volga,
Take the beauty as your prize!"

High he lifts the lovely princess,
With his great arm's mighty sweep
Forth he hurls her, without looking,
Forth into the hungry deep.

"Why so glum, you devils? Stow it!
Filka, do a jig, you cur!
Thunder out a brave one, comrades,
All in memory of her!"

From the quiet island inlet
Cut to where the stream flows deep,
Stenka Razin's painted galleys
Through the waters boldly sweep.

IN HARBIN AND SHANGHAI, Mukden and Hong Kong, Novosibirsk and Leningrad, Moscow and Tiflis, London and Paris, Berlin and Hamburg, New York and San Francisco, everywhere during my years of travel I have heard, at one time or another, the tune of this ancient song about Stenka Razin. There is something in the appeal of the words and the melody that transcends the barriers of race, nationality, geography.

Much as the Nazis hated the Russians, vituperative as was their language against Russians, they placed no ban on this song when they came into power. Even in the fateful summer of 1939 I heard it played by a string orchestra in a Berlin café. In Russian cities and villages under the German occupation during World

War II, German soldiers and officers sang it, strummed it on guitars, played it on phonograph records, over and over. They offered chocolate bars, lumps of sugar, and other delicacies to Russian boys and girls who would sing it for them. I know of no Russian folk tune, not even the "Volga Boatman," whose appeal has been more universal than that of "Stenka Razin."

To non-Russians it is just a Russian song. But to those who are versed in Russian history it is a tribute to the most colorful and most dramatic figure in all Cossackdom. Pushkin speaks of Stenka Razin as "the only poetic figure in Russian history." So impressed was he with the poetic quality of the songs and ballads that Russian common folk in the hundreds of villages along the Volga and other places have woven about the life and deeds, real and imaginary, of the Cossack who led the first great people's rebellion in Russia, that he set out to collect them. When the collection was ready for publication, he submitted it to the censor. But publication was banned on the ground that the songs and ballads were "indecent" and about a man anathematized by the Church. Only in 1881 was the collection made available in print.

To the Russian people of his day and for centuries afterward Stenka Razin, as portrayed in old ballads, was the man who said, "I don't want to be czar; I only want to live with you like a brother." He was rebel and redeemer, warrior and folk hero, sorcerer and Little Father. There was nothing he was incapable of doing, and everything he did was for the good of man, the common man. He charmed snakes so they would not bite people. He was ready to charm mosquitoes so they would be harmless. When he fought for Astrakhan, which the folk tale describes as an Austrian city, he picked up the splinter of a lime tree, whittled off a shaving, flung it into the Volga, and out of the water rose a barge crowded with armed warriors ready to fight for him. He could swim over land, and did so all the way from Kazan to the market place of Saratov.

He buried packs and boatloads of treasures in the hills and caves along the Volga and other places. In a peasant hut a mysterious little goat crawled out from under the oven and a little boy started playing with it. Older people suspected the little goat was a carrier of one of Stenka's treasures and urged the boy to strike it. The boy did as told, and the little goat fell apart into clinking pieces of silver.

Stenka was still on earth fighting the battles of the poor and the lowly. He wandered around giving away his treasures to the needy and to the Church. He transformed himself into an immense black eagle and clove away at those who sinned against God. He disguised himself as an old beggar and roved everywhere, asking people how they lived and what complaints they had against those who ruled over them, and on the basis of the information he gathered he meted out retribution to evildoers.

Always he was a lover and protector of the poor and the lowly, their undying, ever watchful champion against the masters and rulers of the land. The folk literature about Stenka Razin in song and story is one of the richest in the Russian language. It testifies, as so many tales and ballads in Russian folklore, to the hard life of the muzhik in the days of serfdom and to his readiness to acclaim and glorify the men who fought for his emancipation.

Stenka Razin came from the Don country at the time when the ancestors of the Kuban Cossacks were still living in the Zaporog *setch* on the Dnieper, fighting their own battles against their own enemies and with much the same weapons which Razin used in all his campaigns. When Stenka came of age, "the society of free people," as the Don Cossack country was known, was no longer as free as it once was or as were the Cossacks in the Zaporog republic. It had already become a vassal of Moscow. Many of the Don Cossacks were no longer wanderers and warriors only; they were "homeowners," with homes and farms of their own. They no longer had to engage in brigandage for a living, or did so only periodically. They believed in a more or less orderly way of life.

But serfdom was becoming more and more deeply entrenched, runaway peasants and others came to the Don *cozakovat*—to live as free Cossacks. The "society of free people" no longer accepted them into its fold by merely subjecting them to a simple elementary test. First these newcomers had to work as hired hands for the "homeowners," then their application to membership had to be passed by the Cossack mass meeting. The result was that a new population was forming on the Don—the *golytba*—naked ones, men without land, without homes, without any possessions in the world. They followed in the footsteps of the original Cossacks, wandering, fighting, plundering. They constituted a powerful force of which one day Stenka was to make use.

Stenka himself came from a well-to-do family. His father had land and a home, and he grew up as a superb warrior. He made a pilgrimage to the Solovki monastery in the north, and in the course of the journey he saw much of Russia, heard the bitter words and loud wails of the muzhik. Serfdom was now an organized fact, a legalized institution. In 1592 Boris Godunov, under pressure of the landed nobility, issued a decree forbidding peasants dissatisfied with their place of work to move from one estate to another. Besides "czars and emperors," says Maxim Kovalevsky, one of Russia's most distinguished historians, "endowed members of the official classes with land often in disregard of their previous occupation by free communities, the members of which were forced to become the serfs of the persons who received the grant."

A freeborn Cossack, Stenka had only contempt for the scheme of things which prevailed in the non-Cossack lands of Russia. But he was not a part of it. He did not have to bow to the will or command of any master. He could pursue his own free life in his own adventurous way without fear of restraint, without thought of repression. Then something happened which set his soul aflame with rebellion.

In 1665 he and his two brothers participated in a campaign against Poland. His older brother was the ataman of the Cossack force in which he and his younger brother Frol fought. Prince Yurii Dolgorukii, who led the Russian army in the campaign, merged the Cossack force with his own army. By autumn

Stenka's brother informed Dolgorukii that his Cossacks wanted to go home to their farms on the Don. Being volunteer soldiers, like all Cossacks, neither the ataman nor any of his men felt under obligation to remain longer under the command of the Russian prince. But the prince forbade the Cossacks to leave. Thereupon the older Razin called a mass meeting of his men, informed them of the prince's order, and told them that since they were free men no one had the right to prevent them from going home. The Cossacks defied the prince and left. Dolgorukii sent a strong force to overtake them. Stenka's brother was seized and hanged. It was said that both Stenka and Frol witnessed the execution.

Stenka was outraged. His brother, a Cossack ataman, was strung up like a dog only for exercising the inalienable right of a free warrior, a free man, to do as he pleased. The rulers who oppressed the muzhik were now extending their dictatorial power over the Cossack. Stenka vowed vengeance and began to gather an army.

He was a tall, sturdy man of proud bearing and expansive manner, a leader of easy speech who understood the moods and the mind of the muzhiks and the poor Cossacks. He saw Russia seething with discontent. Desperate peasants fled from bondage, hid in forests, steppes, and caves and on riverbanks, set fire to landlords' mansions, murdered their owners. The peasants were ripe for rebellion. Loosely held together, the Russian state was unable to cope with the mutinous spirit brooding over the land. Stenka resolved to muster it for his own purposes.

Unlike Pugatchev, a century later, Stenka was not motivated by a desire to ascend the Russian throne. Nor did he aspire to possess himself of land and gold and to become a landlord or magnate. Like Yermak, he was too much of a Cossack to be lured by riches and material aggrandizement. Nor was he especially stirred to compassion by the dire lot of the muzhik. He was neither an idealist nor a social reformer. Compassion was an emotion alien to him as to all Cossacks. He had battled too often and too violently to be moved by the sight or thought of human suffering. But he had a grievance to settle with the Dolgorukiis of Russia. The thought of the wrong they had done his brother and all Cossackhood influenced his anger. Besides, he hated all rulers, their manners and ideas, their pomp and power.

Stenka's magnificent personality was an invaluable asset. He commanded admiration from friend and foe. A man of many and varied moods, now gay, now gloomy, now given to dissipation, now sunk in reverie, contemptuous of law and lawmakers, with no honor and no faith in his dealings with the enemy, he was yet truthful and generous with friends and followers. Commanding but not haughty, severe but not pompous, he was everyone's brother and everyone was his. Exceptionally democratic, he despised all caste, all sense and semblance of social superiority. His mother Matrena fought with him; so did another woman, Alena, who enticed seven thousand peasants into an uprising and into joining Stenka's army. In the days of his greatest triumph he lived in a sod hut like other Cossacks, ate the same food, wore the same clothes, though the booty he gathered made it possible for him to adorn himself in silk and velvet and all the finery of the gaudy and opulent Persian world.

He started his revolt in 1667. He was cautious in his first steps, as though groping his way toward the most effective method of action.

True to the spirit of the times, he embarked on his crusade of vengeance with an exploit of pure piracy. With a small band of Cossacks he captured on the Volga a fleet of barges hauling goods and prisoners in chains on their way to Astrakhan to serve their sentences. The captain and officers of the fleet and a monk in charge of a grain cargo, Stenka drowned in the river. The crews and prisoners he liberated, saying:

"I extend to you full freedom. I shall not compel any of you to stay with me. But whoever wants to join me shall become a free Cossack. I have come to wage war only on the boyars and the rich. I am prepared to share everything with the common people and the poor."

This was more than a call for support. It was a declaration of aims, the first Stenka Razin is known to have made public. As if carried by the wind, the declaration soared northward far and high, stirring commotion and hope in serf-ridden villages and towns. More and more men abandoned their homes and fled to enlist in Stenka's army. They saw Stenka, talked to him, called him affectionately "Little Father," trusted his wisdom, his good luck, his superhuman powers. With the passage of time Stenka's power grew, and his mastery of the spoken word, the manifestoes he issued, the "magnificent letters" he made public, stamped him as one of the shrewdest propagandists of all time. He organized a special corps of emissaries and sent them everywhere to make known his message to the common man. "We come," said these emissaries, "from our Little Father, Stepan Timofeyevitch, to destroy the *voyevodas* and to set you free." Usually the emissaries preceded Stenka's advance on a fortress or town. They propagandized the population, particularly the soldiers, and sought to win them over before the fighting began. Again and again they succeeded.

In the autumn of 1667 Stenka, with a fleet of thirty-five barges, sailed up the Caspian to the Yaik River in the Urals. There he and his army spent the winter. In spring they sailed out to sea again, raiding and sacking the lands along the coastline and taking the liberated serfs with them as Cossacks.

On reaching Persian shores Stenka sent a mission to the Shah with the request that he and his men be permitted to settle forever in Persia as they never wanted to return to the land of the hated Moscow boyars. In collusion with Moscow's representatives, the Persian shah issued orders for the seizure and the punishment of Stenka Razin's emissaries. When the Cossacks learned of it they swooped down on Persian towns and villages, looted them and laid them waste. The Shah was enraged and sent a flotilla of fifty ships to fight the Russian robber-warriors. The battle was desperate. Most of the Persian ships were sunk, but Stenka's losses were also heavy. He returned to the Volga, then to the Don, then again to the Volga all the way to Astrakhan, this time resolved to seize this rich and highly fortified city.

Inside Astrakhan, he had friends on whose support he could

count. He advanced on the city in barges, and before he was within attacking distance his propagandists were already inside, preaching the gospel of liberation. They assured soldiers and civilians that Stenka was their redeemer, that he had come to liberate them from the rule of the nobles and officials and that with their aid he could easily and swiftly capture the city. All its wealth then would be theirs to divide and enjoy.

The propaganda bore immediate fruit. Soldiers seized their officers, bound them, strangled them, flung them into the river. When Stenka drew near they shouted, "We greet you, Little Father, the subduer of all our tyrants." Stenka rose to the occasion with a memorable and inciting speech:

"I greet you, brothers! Revenge yourselves on your tormentors who have made you suffer more than the Turks and the Tatars. I have come to grant you liberties and privileges. You are my brothers, my children, and if you remain brave and faithful to me you shall be as rich as I am."

Loudly the soldiers cheered these words. Swiftly the message reached the people within the city—emissaries had carried it there—and it roused the common folk to action. Housemaids, cooks, janitors, street cleaners, coachmen, barge haulers, water carriers, men and women of the serf and servant class made common cause and launched a fierce onslaught on their masters. They swarmed round public buildings, jails, courthouses, military headquarters, smashed doors and windows, broke inside, seized papers and documents, threw them out of doors and windows and set them afire.

Delirious with joy and triumph, they danced round the leaping flames. By the time Stenka and his Cossacks had climbed over the high walls of the fortifications which the local military and state officials had built in anticipation of the battle, the city was already his. A crowd acclaimed him as their deliverer. Forthwith he announced to his followers that the city was theirs to do with as they chose.

Immediately they proceeded to take possession of the city. They moved into the homes of the rich, dressed in their clothes, ate their food, drank their wines, danced in their ballrooms, rode around in their carriages, married their daughters and wives. If the women resisted they were abused, punished, often put to death. Riotous was the anarchy roaring through the city. Triumph and revenge stalked the streets, haunted the waters of the Volga, carrying a burden of blood and death to the broad and silent Caspian.

There was little constructive statesmanship in anything Stenka did, little creative talent. There was only small effort to mobilize the torrents of unleashed energy and mold them into a positive social force, into a semblance of law and statehood. This was the fatal weakness of the rebellion. Yet it was gathering momentum. Stenka's propagandists were everywhere. They penetrated as far north as Vyatka and Vologda. With great eloquence they preached the same sermon—death to officials and rulers, to landlords and princes, liberty and land to the serf and the common man. Kamish, Saratov, Samara, all Volga towns, heaved with revolt. Tsaritsyn, now Stalingrad, fell; Tambov, Pensa, Nizhny Novgorod, and Kazan responded to the call for action. Even Moscow province buzzed with disaffection. Town after town capitulated to Stenka Razin. Armies sent against him were again and again persuaded to turn against their officers and join the rebels. In Moscow, citadel of officialdom and landlordism, there were voices which advised opening the gates of the city to the Cossack chieftain and welcoming him with bread and salt.

The defeatist counsel only intensified the resolution of the government to crush the rebellion. It launched a barrage of counterpropaganda against Stenka. Knowing that the peasant was czar-minded and loyal to the Church, the official propaganda branded Razin as a foe of both, a traitor and a heathen. Priests proclaimed him the anti-Christ, Satan incarnate, seeking to lure Christians to sin and damnation.

Losing no time, Stenka struck back with vigor. He too knew that the muzhik was czar-minded and Church-minded and would allow the enemy no chance to galvanize these loyalties into a rallying slogan against himself and the rebellion. He therefore announced that he was fighting neither czar nor Church but only those who were in league with the nobles and the landlords. The ruling czar and the ruling priests, he charged, were in the pay of nobles and landlords and were enemies of the people. He promised to put a new czar on the throne, the son of the reigning czar. The royal heir had actually died, but Stenka proclaimed him alive and announced that he had fled from the tyranny of his father and was now in his keeping. The czarevitch, he assured his followers, was a friend of the common man and welcomed the extermination of the nobles and officials. As for the Church, Stenka said that he would place at its head the deposed patriarch Nikon, a man of God and lover of the people.

Nor did Stenka content himself with mere oratory. He chose two impostors to take the place of the dead czarevitch and of the deposed patriarch. One was a Cherkess prince whom his Cossacks had captured, the other was an obscure monk. The prince traveled in one barge, lined with red plush, the monk in another lined with black cloth.

Stenka moved deeper and deeper northward. The rebellion which had started with an act of piracy became a national crusade which lasted from 1667 to 1671. Yet it was doomed to failure. Militarily its chief defect was the absence of a closely knit central organization, experienced officers, and, save for the Cossacks, trained soldiers. In the end the Moscow government strangled the movement. Stenka and his brother Frol were betrayed and captured.

Put in chains and hitched to a lumber cart, the two brothers were led on foot over public highways all the way to the capital so that the populace could see them in their defeat and disgrace. Frol complained of his tortures and wept. But not Stenka. He uttered no word of complaint. Both were ordered to confess their guilt. Both refused. They were tortured brutally. Stenka's bones were broken one by one. His hands and feet were twisted, turned, and wrenched; water, alternately hot, cold, and salted, was poured over his bleeding flesh. But Stenka refused to confess any guilt. To the end he was conscious of the righteousness of his cause and of his moral superiority to his tormentors. When his brother weakened and was ready to confess, Stenka shouted to him:

"Hold your tongue, you dog!"

To the very last he remained unrepentant. On June 6, 1671, he was quartered alive.

The Stenka Razin revolt tells us much about the Cossacks and about Russia. The Cossack and the bonded peasant fought savagely against tyranny, but their conception of freedom was as vague as it was elementary. It had scarcely any political or institutional meaning. Anything else would have been impossible in those days when Russia's backwardness was immense compared to western Europe, when the dark heritage of the Tatar invasion which lasted for over two centuries was still crippling the social awakening and the intellectual unfolding of the country.

When Stenka Razin rose in rebellion, England had already had her Christopher Marlowe, Francis Bacon, and William Shakespeare. Italy had already given the world Dante's *Divine Comedy*, Petrarch's sonnets, and Galileo's momentous discoveries in astronomy and physics. Corneille and Racine had passed in France; Cervantes was long dead and long remembered in Spain; and the Pilgrim Fathers and English cavaliers had already settled the Atlantic seaboard of the New World. No such advances in knowledge and culture had been made in Russia, which was some three centuries behind the development of western Europe.

One of Stenka Razin's great contemporaries was John Milton, who created not only *Paradise Lost*, but as spokesman for the Puritan Revolution and a member of Cromwell's government, wrote the world's most eloquent defense of free speech in the *Areopagitica*. It is impossible to make any comparison between Cromwell and Stenka Razin at any point; for while both led popular revolutions in the seventeenth century, and only a few years apart from one another, Russia was still wallowing in the Middle Ages, with neither people nor rebel leaders manifesting any consciousness of law and government and the organized social discipline which Cromwell brought to England.

It was not until the twentieth century that Russia, with a

speed that has no precedent, leaped over the centuries and, amidst iron and blood, with the aid of the spoken word and the written document, sought to catch up with the modern world at its most advanced point.

But the historic facts and the romantic legends about Stenka Razin will always remain a tempestuous expression of a people's will and struggle for liberty.

CHAPTER VII

Yemelyan Pugatchev

THIS IS THE PICTURE Pushkin, Russia's greatest poet, gives of Yemelyan Putgatchev: "His appearance was striking. He was about forty, of medium height, lean and with broad shoulders. Gray was beginning to show in his black beard, his large lively eyes never were still. His face had a pleasant but crafty expression. His head was cropped like that of a peasant, and he wore a ragged jacket and Turkish trousers."

There was nothing prepossessing about the man, his appearance, or his manner. He never attended school, could neither read nor write, and signed his name with a coarse scrawl. He was sly and dissolute; orgies of drinking and sex in the days of his greatest triumph evoked harsh comments from his more religious followers. He loved gaudiness, he loved swank. Yet he led a mighty revolution against Catherine the Great. Unlike Stenka Razin, he was consumed not only with a passion for revenge but with the ambition to ascend the Russian throne. Though unlettered, he had a sense of history as well as destiny. Being a Cossack, a freeborn man, he frowned on all superiors, including the greatest czarina Russia ever had. Until the coming of the

Soviets his was the most stupendous and most sanguinary revolution in Russian history.

This revolution was all the more remarkable because it occurred in the "glamorous age" of Catherine the Great, one of the most fabulous women of her time. During the thirty-four years of her reign she filled the Russia of the court and of St. Petersburg society with a lavish flow of Western culture, chiefly French. Though of German origin, French was the language she liked best; she spoke it fluently, and, busy as she was with state affairs, she found time to translate French novels into Russian. French architecture, French art won her hearty admiration, and she imported both to Russia. She enriched Russia's art galleries with one of the finest Rembrandt collections, today a priceless possession of the Hermitage in Leningrad, Russia's most famous art museum.

Among Catherine's friends were some of the greatest French writers and thinkers of her day. She carried on a spirited and voluminous correspondence with Voltaire, the French writer and philosopher. Twice she invited D'Alambert, philosopher and mathematician, to Russia. He refused both invitations. Yet when the Czarina learned that he was facing hard times, she granted him a pension for life.

So impressed was Voltaire with Catherine's charm, wit, intellectual acumen, that he spoke of her as "my Cato." Stanchly he defended her against the attacks of her critics and enemies for the severity of her rule. When Voltaire died, the Empress hastened to buy from his nephew his personal library of seven thousand volumes and twenty volumes of manuscripts and letters. The books in this library are in French, English, Italian, and Spanish, and the pages are interspersed with comments and criticisms in Voltaire's own handwriting. Catherine paid thirty thousand rubles for the collection. Today the Leningrad state library considers it one of the greatest literary treasures in the world, worth millions of American dollars.

Denis Diderot, Encyclopedist and critic, was another celebrated French writer with whom Catherine corresponded. When

Yemelyan Pugatchev

Yermak, the conqueror of Siberia

she learned of his financial distress she came to his rescue in original fashion. She bought his private library for fifty thousand livres, allowed him to keep it, appointed him its custodian at an annual salary of a thousand livres, and paid it to him for fifty years in advance.

The fact that she was German, the princess of Anhalt-Zerbst, did not prevent her from heartily disliking German culture and German politics. She cleansed the Russian court of the pro-German camarilla that infested it during the brief reign of Peter III, her murdered husband. On his mother's side this haughty and frivolous Czar was a grandson of Peter the Great, but his father was the Prussian Duke Charles Frederick. He was so passionately German, so hero-worshiping an admirer of Frederick the Great, with whom Russia was at war, that on his ascension to the throne, and in violation of Russia's alliance with Austria and France, he concluded peace with the Prussian King, returned to him all Russian conquests, which included nearly all of East Prussia, and promised him an army for the war against Denmark. After his death Catherine reversed Russian policy toward Frederick the Great. Among her favorites and advisers were no German or pro-German conspirators. She maintained her position so firmly that Frederick stopped plotting against Russia.

Catherine cultivated the friendship not only of French literary men but of British statesmen. She knew and practiced the art of political flattery. Because he defended her eloquently in Parliament, she had a bust made of Charles James Fox and commissioned the Russian ambassador in London to inform the British Liberal that she had placed it between the busts of Cicero and Demosthenes. Until the German invasion of Tsarskoye Selo, former residence of the czars and a national museum under the Soviets, Fox's bust was on exhibition in the Cameron Library. Out of vengeance against her anglophile policy as much as out of sheer vandalism, the German occupants broke the bust.

William Pitt was another British statesman whom Catherine greatly admired.

The brilliance of Catherine's court astounded European statesmen, even as the brilliance of her diplomacy confounded them. A fluent writer, a spirited conversationalist, gifted with an extraordinary amount of guile, wit, and audacity, no foreign diplomat outguessed, outsmarted, outbargained her. In all her diplomacy Russia came first. Eugene Tarle, Soviet Russia's greatest living historian, speaks of her as "a genius in foreign diplomacy." Under her rule Russia became large, more respected, more appreciated as a world power than under any former rule.

Her private life was shadowed and illumined by sensation and melodrama. Her pulchritude, her intrigues with and against her lovers, her illegitimate son, her miscarriages, her will to power, her love of ostentation, make her a topic of spicy gossip in the chancellories and salons of Europe. But because of her rich contribution to Russia as a state, a nation, a world power, and because of the many foreign and enlightened streams of culture with which she refreshed and fertilized Russia's social and intellectual life, she is today being accorded ever rising acclaim by Russian writers and historians.

But to the common man in Russia she was no heroine. Though she liked to think of herself as "the Great Mother of Great Russia," she offered little comfort to the enslaved muzhik. Under her Russia flowered at the top but rotted at the bottom. Despite all her glib flirtation with French liberalism, she did not rise perceptibly above the political milieu of her Russian surroundings, particularly the landed gentry. Serfdom attained new heights. She pushed it into the Ukraine. To her lovers and favorites she made gifts of immense estates to which were attached one and a half million serfs. She toyed with the idea of abolishing serfdom but did nothing about it. When Grigory Orloff, for a long time one of her most intimate favorites, urged her to act on the question, her reply was: "The landlords would hang me before the peasants could rescue me." So indifferent was she to serfdom that an advertisement in a St. Petersburg newspaper read as follows: "Two young girls for sale, attractive, deep-breasted, can sew and launder, price 100 rubles; also for sale a colt, a bull, 50 hunting dogs, prices moderate." Serfs were not only sold but were offered as stakes in card games. They were bought and bartered like chattels.

Catherine abolished compulsory military service for the gentry. Because he was made to believe that serf labor compensated the gentry for military service, the peasant now expected his liberation as a serf. But there was no liberation. There was only an intensification of peasant bondage. Consequently the grumbling of the muzhik grew increasingly loud. There were fresh repressions, widespread and cruel. There were also vast areas of the country that were striken by famine and epidemics. Therefore to the millions of muzhiks neither the splendor of Catherine's personality, the brilliance of her court, nor the triumph of her diplomacy had any meaning or yielded any satisfaction.

Nor did they to the crafty, illiterate, black-bearded Cossack who proclaimed himself the Czarina's dead husband in whose death she had connived and challenged by force of arms her right to the throne. From that moment Pugatchev and the rebellious, freedom-loving Cossacks haunted Catherine's mind, though not her conscience, and drove her into action against them and into the dissolution of the Cossack republic on the Dnieper and the subordination of all Cossacks all over the country to St. Petersburg rule.

We know more about Yemelyan Pugatchev than about Stenka Razin. He never stirred the folk imagination like Stenka and never became as exalted a folk hero. But Russian writers have gathered an extraordinary amount of authentic information about his life and times and his explosive career as a revolutionary leader. A century had made a difference in Russia's internal development. Stenka Razin became legendary, but Pugatchev remained an historical figure.

Born in the village of Zimoveyskaya, Pugatchev came from a poor Cossack family with not enough land to provide a competent living. In his boyhood Yemelyan, or Yemelko as he was nicknamed, was given to rough banter and rough brawls. He thrived on boyish mischief. Crafty and dishonest, he stole melons and fruit in neighbors' gardens and orchards. Handsome and well built, cunning and strong, fond of song and dance, he became the leader among his playmates. He heard much of the Cossack republic on the Dnieper and tried to emulate its adventurous way of living. With a party of Cossack boys he formed his own "setch." He "communized" property, and the boys threw into a common store all their possessions—eggs, fruitcakes, wooden containers of homemade mead. They armed themselves with bows and arrows, with wooden lances, wooden sabers. For fun they tied the leg of a rooster to a little cart. They invited a girl named Sonka, who happened to be visiting the village with her aunt, to join them in the "setch." In the Dnieper republic women had no place. But the presence of a girl livened up the adventure of the boys and lent it a touch of originality. Yemelyan prided himself on his gift for originality.

Naturally he became leader of the "setch." He had Sonka clip his head with sheep shears, leaving the traditional wild forelock dangling over the top of the head. To add to the fierce authenticity of his appearance, he pasted a mustache of horsehair to his upper lip.

At night the alarm was sounded. Sonka wildly beat a club against the cooking kettle. The "Cossacks" sprang to their feet. "Onto your horses!" Yemelko ordered. "Straight for Czargrad!" —the ancient capital of Orthodoxy.

For Czargrad the boys chose a neighbor's melon patch and apiary. They captured the "enemy," who happened to be the beekeeper and at the moment quite drunk, tied him up and ordered him to pick the ripest melons. Playing and singing, they ate the melons. As a demonstration of the discipline of their "republic" they whipped one of the "Cossacks" for pulling Sonka's tresses.

In the morning the village was astir with commotion. Yemelko received a violent thrashing from his father. He was the object of loud tirades and curses. A melon patch was a source of food to the Cossack family, and stealing in one's own village, from one's own neighbors, was one of the grossest sins a Cossack could commit.

Yemelko became more cautious in his escapades, but not too cautious. He never lacked audacity or ingenuity to perpetrate his own pranks in his own way. He was always an ebullient mischief-maker.

At seventeen he married Sonka and soon went to war. He fought in the Seven Years' War, a daring soldier. While in East Prussia he suffered one of the most painful humiliations in his life. He was orderly to a Colonel Denisov. For going off to battle instead of looking after Denisov's horse, the colonel ordered Pugatchev to lower his trousers and to submit to a whipping. Yemelyan was puzzled. He thought the colonel was joking. But the colonel was bursting with rage; he commanded other Cossacks to seize Pugatchev and whip him. They threw Pugatchev to the ground and beat him mercilessly. His eyes shut, his teeth dug into the earth, Pugatchev endured the punishment in silence. But he never forgot the ignominy perpetrated on him. Someday he would wreak brutal vengeance on men like, Colonel Denisov and those whose rule and power he symbolized.

Pugatchev fought on in East Prussia. Then he went to Poland and Turkey. On his return to the village of Zimoveyskaya he felt disgusted with his lowly poverty, his utter inability to provide a comfortable living for his family. He ran away to the Terek Cossack country. Sagacious and scheming, he tried to become ataman. He almost succeeded, but was arrested instead and returned to his native village. He escaped again, was once more arrested and this time was chained to a block of wood with a guard over him. But he did not remain a prisoner long. His persuasive talk came to his rescue, and he ran away together with the guard. Now he was seeking not only refuge but fortune. He wandered and traded and tried his hand at several tasks, but never succeeded in any of them. One day he made the acquaintance of a fugitive like himself whose name was Semyonov. They became friends, discussed the problems and trials they were facing, and once Semyonov said to Pugatchev: "You resemble

Peter." He meant Peter III, the murdered husband of the reigning Czarina. Pugatchev was impressed. The suggestion fitted into
many things he had been secretly and earnestly contemplating.

Meanwhile everywhere he went, to inns and taverns on road-
sides, he heard much talk about the dead Czar who was not dead
but alive. Rumor had it that it was not he but someone else who
had been murdered by the court conspirators. These rumors
and Semyonov's suggestion preyed on Pugatchev's mind. He conjured up visions of glory and power and made his way to the
Cossack territory on the Yaik River in the Urals. Here, in protest against being made a part of the regular czarist army, the
Cossacks teemed with revolt. Like the serfs they were ripe for
an uprising and for vengeance against the powers determined
to strip them of their traditional Cossack independence. Because
of the tension and turbulence in the Yaik, Pugatchev had no
difficulty in making himself accepted as the living Czar whose
throne Catherine had usurped. He promised the Yaik Cossacks
restitution of all their rights and all their liberties.

Rapidly the news spread not only in the Yaik country but
in other places that the real Czar was alive, that he was "the
muzhik Czar" and would overthrow not only the Czarina but
the landed gentry and would liberate the serfs, give them land,
and make them free Cossacks.

The response to Pugatchev's declaration was swift and momentous. Not only Cossacks and muzhiks but, as in the days of
Stenka Razin's rebellion, non-Russian peoples like the Bashkirs,
the Kalmyks, the Mordwins, others, chafing under repression
and aflame with Pugatchev's promises, enlisted under his banner
and fought in his rapidly growing armies. It is not without significance that both Stenka Razin and Yemelyan Pugatchev
catered to the non-Slavic peoples in Russia, which only em-
phasizes the absence of what we speak of today as racism in
the leaders of the Cossack and peasant revolutions of the past.

The faith of the peasantry in Pugatchev was strikingly revealed
in the conversation between Lieutenant Colonel Michelson, a
Russian officer of Scotch descent, and the muzhiks in the village

of Kudravinskaya, about twenty-five miles from the town of Zlatoust in the Urals. Michelson, whom Pugatchev had borne on a stretcher in East Prussia after he was wounded, was now in command of an army hunting for the Cossack impostor. On reaching Kudravinskaya, Michelson was met by the elder of the village and others, including women and children.

"Have you heard anything about the scoundrel Pugatchev?" Michelson asked.

"There was a rumor—a rumor," the elder replied hesitantly. "The rumor was that Pugatchev's army had been beaten."

"Why are your houses closed? Where are the people?"

"Who knows where they are? They got together and started off, and it's two weeks since they've gone."

"Where?"

"Naturally to *him*—to no other place. . . . His soldiers came, read a manifesto—a brief one—and said: 'Submit to Czar Pyotr Fedoritch or your homes'll be set afire'—and, sir, you know we are a dark people, afraid, and so many submitted to him."

"What does this scoundrel Pugatchev offer you to tempt fools into submission?"

"Who knows? You'd better come into the house, sir. Our houses are quite filthy with cockroaches and other vile things, we live so badly, sir, a plagued muzhik's life."

Michelson knew the elder was deliberately stalling and lying, and he became angry.

"Well," he shouted, "did the scoundrel and state criminal Pugatchev promise you all the land, abolition of taxes, exemption from military service?"

Now all the peasants broke into talk.

"Yes," they said, "he's promised all this, all this."

"And to string up the nobility and the officials?"

"Yes, but we are a dark people, maybe he is a deceiver and scoundrel. How do we know? And maybe he is the Czar."

The peasants knew they were talking to an enemy of Pugatchev and were cautious in their replies. But in their hearts they were with Pugatchev. They believed he was "the muzhik Czar" and that he would fulfill his promises. No one else had made such promises. No one else offered respite from poverty and oppression. So not only in the Urals but all over the land, especially on the Don and Volga, the muzhik was ready for battle. Whole villages abandoned their homes and enlisted in Pugatchev's army. Among his soldiers were not only serfs on the land, but serfs in the factories of the Urals. They forged weapons for the rebels, including artillery, and gave Pugatchev a military strength of which Stenka Razin had never dreamed.

Russia thundered with revolt and civil war. Catherine became increasingly anxious and sent army after army against the pretender. But the black-bearded Cossack leader struck back with ferocity. He hanged Catherine's officers, judges, officials, nobles. He sacked estates, burned castles, laid waste the land of the gentry. He acted the part of a muzhik czar. Only Cossacks and muzhiks and other common folk, he proclaimed, had the right to rule and own the Russian earth.

On July 12, 1774, Pugatchev took Kazan, all but the kremlin inside the city. The victory stirred fresh enthusiasm for him and his cause. More and more peasants flocked to offer themselves as soldiers. They were as cruelly vindictive with their landlord-masters as Pugatchev himself. They killed and sacked and burned estates, divided loot, and swelled Pugatchev's fighting legions.

After nearly three years of rebellion Pugatchev found himself staggering farther and farther south. He was no match for Catherine's armies. On the conclusion of the war with Turkey, the Empress sent fresh forces against the rebels, better organized, better led, and better equipped than the mass of unwieldy manpower at Pugatchev's command. On the twenty-sixth of August, Pugatchev and Catherine's armies fought a decisive battle in the town of Sarepta. Hunger sped the disintegration of Pugatchev's forces and on the twenty-sixth of September 1774 two Cossack elders, Tvorogov and Chumakov, betrayed him to his enemies.

He was bound in chains and taken to Moscow. He was questioned and tortured day after day, week after week, and for a long time he refused to confess his guilt. But the tortures grew more and more unendurable. A weaker man than Stenka Razin, he finally broke down, made a full confession of his plot to overthrow the Czarina and make himself Czar of Russia.

"Do you sincerely repent your wrongs?" asked A. Vyazemsky, the imperial prosecutor.

"I repent before God," replied the swollen and battered Pugatchev, "and before the most merciless Empress and before the entire Christian world."

His confession is perhaps one reason why he never became the exalted folk hero that Stenka Razin is.

On January 10, 1775, he was taken in a high sled to the same square and the same place in Moscow where Stenka Razin was executed. Here, as if in pity for "the muzhik Czar," the muzhik executioner first severed Pugatchev's head, then quartered his body.

Voltaire was disturbed by the news of the brutal execution and wrote to Catherine, making inquiry as to its cause and the nature of the Pugatchev rebellion. In her reply the Empress blithely dismissed it as an "insignificant incident" perpetrated by a "pathetic vagabond," to whom she referred ironically as "Marquis Pugatchev."

Thirty-seven years later, when Napoleon was in Moscow, he thought of Pugatchev and of the peasant revolution he had led. Three times Napoleon had addressed himself to Alexander I, the Russian Emperor, with an offer of a "magnanimous peace." Alexander ignored the offers, never replied to Napoleon. Napoleon then wondered what he could do to salvage the victory which threatened to ruin him. The muzhiks were still serfs. They might be ripe for another uprising against the Czar and the gentry. Seriously Napoleon considered staging such an uprising. He ordered a detailed study of Pugatchev, his method, his weapons, his achievements. But in the end Napoleon changed his mind. A peasant revolution might slip out of hand, and then there would be none with whom to conclude the favorable peace he sought.

The year that Pugatchev was executed, the embattled farmers

of New England fought the Battle of Concord and Lexington. The following year came the Declaration of Independence; and within four years the great French Revolution. It is startling to think of the illiterate Pugatchev, with his false claims to the Russian throne, as a contemporary of Mirabeau, Jefferson, and Burke; of Voltaire, Goethe, Kant, and the Declaration of the Rights of Man. But here, as in the case of Stenka Razin, the cultural lag that separated Russia from the Western world was enormous and momentous.

Americans in the days of Jefferson considered the idea of abolishing slavery; conditions made it impossible until the days of Lincoln. So, too, Catherine the Great thought of the abolition of serfdom, but it was not until the days of Lincoln's contemporary, Alexander II, that the serfs were liberated. The Russian people were illiterate, economically and politically backward, and a leader like Pugatchev expressed both their resentment against oppression and their limitations in achieving freedom.

The England of the Glorious Revolution which placed William and Mary on the throne shortly after Stenka Razin's death was a first-rate mercantile power; the America of John Adams and Alexander Hamilton was also a great mercantile power; and the France of Danton, Napoleon, and Talleyrand was a country of businessmen and bankers, as well as farmers and workers. In America, France, and England there was a powerful, highly advanced intellectual class. But not in Russia. An intelligentsia was only beginning to rise. Russia was hopelessly behind the political and cultural procession of the West. The court of Catherine the Great and the estates of the nobles rested on a country of illiterate serfs with only a small, ineffective middle class of merchants and businessmen. The immense commercial revolution which had been transforming the West since the Crusades—with its discoveries in the Americas, Africa, and the Far East, its revival of classical learning, its advance of modern science and the democratic idea—had created a culture which Catherine could admire, but which history made it impossible for her to transplant to the whole of Russia. It could only remain the private luxury of a few intellectual aristocrats. The country was agrarian, and its revolutions, like its economy, were bound to be agrarian and anarchic.

And so, even in the eighteenth century of Pugatchev, as in the seventeenth of Stenka Razin, the Cossack could be the leader only of elemental, popular rebellions against oppression, without envisioning a new state society or new relations between man and man. Razin and Pugatchev were not statesmen standing at the peak of a culture developed over eight centuries, with Greece and Rome as a recovered heritage, but primitive chieftains whose vision of the world was molded by the Cossack community, Cossack emotion, Cossack adventure. Their slogans were simple: free land, free Cossacks, free living—and in the case of Pugatchev, freedom from taxation and from military service, an advance over the ideas of Stenka Razin. These were the dreams of the Cossack, the serf, the muzhik; and the atamans gave them leadership and fighting force. But they did not know how to transform these ideas into a political force; they were no ideologues or statesmen or even politicians. They knew the elementary communal system of the Cossack village and no more. There was Cossack hatred of tyranny, primitive fury at oppression, trained love of battle, a strong sense of separatism and individualism, but there was no one in Russia then to tell them how to transform these into a national movement for liberation, and if anyone did tell them they would not understand, and if they understood they could do no more about it than Catherine herself. Their time had not come; it was not to come for a century and a half; but in their time the lovers of liberty who followed Stenka Razin and Yemelyan Pugatchev planted seeds of freedom which the Russian people would remember for a thousand years and longer.

CHAPTER VIII

The End of the Dnieper Republic

THE DNIEPER REPUBLIC spread over an immense area, embracing the former province of Yekaterinoslav, a large part of the province of Kherson, a broad slice of the Don country.

The capital was no longer on the island of Hortitse but in Kosh, on the river Podolnaya, Dnieper tributary.

In 1768 the Cossacks assembled for an election of their *Koshevoy* hetman. The leading candidate was a Cossack named Kolnyshewski, a name suggesting Polish influence. In the years when the Cossacks had been Poland's neighbors, they had quarreled with the Poles, fought with them and against them, traded with them, looted them, compromised with them. They had regaled themselves with Polish food, drinks, and women; they had learned to flaunt Polish swank and now were often putting a Polish ending to their names. Russian or Ukrainian by origin, the Cossack had acquired a perceptible, often garish, veneer of Polish culture.

Kolnyshewski was elected, and old Cossacks with white, bushy mustachios and long forelocks, themselves former hetmen, proceeded to anoint the newly chosen leader. Gathering moist earth in their hands, earth which the Cossack boot had trodden, they spread it thick over the hetman's bared head. The mud rolled down his face and mustache, dribbled into his eyes and mouth, but not a sound of displeasure issued from his lips. He knew what it meant, for despite fanatical devotion to Orthodoxy, all was dust and rot to the Cossack—all but his liberties and the glory of his unvanquished arms.

"Rule over us," solemnly intoned the assembly, "and may the Lord bless you with the age of the swan and the clacking voice of the crane."

To this day the crane is a revered bird, symbol of beauty, friendship, and independence, a harbinger of good luck. Therefore no one molests its ample nests on the treetop or barrack roofs.

The anointment over, the mass meeting adjourned to church for a special Mass. After the reading of the Scripture, as if in response to a military command, all half unsheathed their sabers and vowed to defend to their last drop of blood the things they held sacred: Orthodoxy, freedom, and the *setch.*

Outwardly their life had undergone slight change in the two hundred years they had been maintaining the *setch.* But their meteorology was forecasting portentous weather: wind from the north—that is, from Moscow, the Moscow which hated freedom and tyrannized over the muzhik, that was seeking to encroach on Cossack independence, that was already making a vassal of the Don Cossack, and that was sending judges, prosecuting attorneys, other officials to the *setch.*

Yet apprehension over the storm from the north did not bar the Cossacks from unleashing one of their own in the west. Within easy reach of the *setch* lay the Polish town of Uman. A strong force of Cossacks descended on it and staged one of the most horrible massacres of their career. Invasion of Cossack territory by Poles and of Polish territory by Cossacks seemed almost a law of nature. Neither scrupled to cross into the other's land and steal herds of cattle and droves of horses. But this was no adventure in plunder. This was the "Uman Butchery." The Cossacks burned the town and killed soldiers, civilians, priests, Jews, women, old people.

News of the massacre reached Catherine the Great. She was no friend of Poland. She was to connive in its partition. But the unruly Cossacks disturbed her. She had had trouble with them in many parts of Russia. They were rebelling against being drawn into the national scheme of things. She knew how dangerous, revengeful, and unreliable they were. On a previous occasion in a crucial moment of Russian history, they had betrayed the Russian Czar. During the battle of Poltava between Peter the Great and Charles XII of Sweden, the hetman Mazeppa had fought against Peter. In retaliation the Czar executed the Cossack rebels. On May 14, 1709, his armies occupied the *setch* and broke up its entrenchments. By special decree Peter abolished the *setch* and forbade the Cossacks to cross into Russian territory.

But Peter's successors needed the Cossacks to hold down the marauding Tatar and Turkish tribes. They made peace with them, allowed them to re-establish the *setch*, to rebuild their earth and timber fortifications, and to resume their own way of living. To dim their own memory of Mazeppa's treachery, the Cossacks created a triumphant legend. Peter, runs the legend, became so firmly convinced of the friendship and loyalty of the Cossacks that on a stone which he buried he had inscribed the words, "Cursed, cursed be he who shall destroy the *setch*, which is loyal to me, or who shall requisition the Zaporog lands."

Of his own lands, the Cossack was fiercely jealous. Though now and again Poland and Turkey lay claim to them, he never acknowledged their right to the claim. But now times were changing. New political currents and new social moods were sweeping over the Russian scene. Particularly marked were these changes in 1775, the year of Pugatchev's execution. More than ever Catherine was shaken with distrust and anxiety. Twice within a century the Cossack had lifted the sword against the Russian throne. He had built up a tradition of revolt which was taking root in the mind of the serf. Warlike and far from the capital, the Cossack, left to himself, to his old rights, his old independence, and his old wildness, would continue to be a threat and an evil. Catherine had already allotted some Cossack lands to Serbian settlers. But that was not enough. She was determined to make the Cossack a part of the Russian state, the Russian fighting forces. He must obey the law and fear the throne. Never again must there be a Stenka Razin, a Yemelyan

Pugatchev. Never again must St. Petersburg be harassed by peasant uprisings and Cossack rebellions.

On their part the Cossacks were aroused by the settlement of Serbian colonizers on lands they deemed immutably and indisputably theirs. They sent emissaries to the Czarina to voice their protest and to beg her to reverse the new policy of the disposition of their lands. But St. Petersburg was frigid to any petition coming from such hell-raisers as Cossacks.

Said Pyotr Panin, one of Catherine's closest advisers and who as much as anyone was instrumental in bringing the Pugatchev rebellion to a violent end: "They [the Cossacks] are murderers, useless creatures; they have outlived their day."

Said A. Vyazemsky, the man who prosecuted Pugatchev and wrung a confession of guilt from "the muzhik Czar": "They are thieves; they deny the family, property, the state; nor do they feel any shame for their wicked deeds."

The Cossacks found only one friend in court circles. He was Grigory Potemkin (Potyomkin), high in the graces and favors of the Empress, one of her most brilliant diplomats and empire builders, founder of the cities of Yekaterinoslav, Nikolayev, and Kherson, and builder of Russia's first fleet in the Black Sea. He always admired the Cossack as an individual and as a warrior and valued the immense service he had rendered Russia with his wars against the Poles, the Tatars, the Turks, and other Mohammedan tribesmen in the west and south. Potemkin received the emissaries from the *setch,* listened to their complaints, entertained them. He expressed sympathy for them, but he too remembered Pugatchev, he too was conscious of the tradition of revolt which the very word Cossack implied. "Now that you have weakened the Turks and the Poles," he said, "you want to clasp your spurs around Moscow." The Cossacks disavowed such an intention. They swore nothing was further from their minds. But what was an oath to the Cossack? Besides, even while the emissaries were in St. Petersburg, their men in the *setch* raided Serbian settlements and set them afire.

Catherine sent an army against the *setch,* a powerful army, fifty regiments of lancers and hussars, ten thousand infantrymen. They came up unexpectedly and paused a short distance outside the *setch*. They demanded instant and peaceful submission. Startled and incensed, the Cossacks called a mass meeting.

"Are we to give up our mother *setch?*" a Cossack shouted.

"Never, not as long as the sun shines."

"Whoever believes in God, draw your saber and sound the alarm."

"We shall crush the Muscovites like flies."

There was acrimony and much heated defiance. But it was all useless. The Czarina's infantry seized the powder cellars, the treasury, the offices, the cannon. On June 5, 1775, the *setch* was occupied without a battle, and the conquerors lost no time in stripping the Cossacks of weapons and in imposing on them a new discipline. They gave them passports, which Cossacks never had known and could not but despise because to them such documents were symbols of the tyranny they had always fought. They grumbled and fumed. They threatened reprisals and revenge. Some there were who wept at the ignominy that had come to the Cossack, the freest of all men in the steppe, but all in vain. Neither tears nor fury could bring back the old days and the old independence. The fate of the Cossack was sealed. The *setch* was at an end. The Dnieper republic, like all free Cossack societies, was dead.

To legalize and dramatize the demise of the *setch*, Catherine the Great issued a manifesto on August 5, 1775, which in part read:

"There is no more a *setch* in its political ugliness. There shall be instead a place and an abode for permanent settlers equal to all others and useful to the fatherland."

In disgust some Cossacks took to their boats, fled to Turkey, and founded there a new *setch*. Most of them migrated to the Black Sea and from there subsequently to the Kuban, a land rich in steppe, in mountain, in forest, in stream, in grass, in honey, in fruit, and pathetically uninhabited. They had to subdue the roving native tribesmen before they could call the land their own. But battling the "Mohammedan infidels" was no new experience to them. They were amply prepared for the task, and it offered them an outlet for their fighting energies.

CHAPTER IX

Warriors Supreme

On my arrival in Baku early in June 1942, the first thing that struck my attention as I looked out of the window of my hotel was the double line of school children, boys and girls, not over fifteen years of age, who were having military drill in a small playground by the Caspian Sea.

On my previous journeys to Russia I had seen school children marching in military formation, performing military drill, playing war games. But this time the exercises had special meaning. Baku was still far away from the fighting lines, but the Germans were set for a thrust southward toward the rich oil city on the Caspian. The school children of the city were drilling for possible action against the enemy.

They were learning to march, to handle guns, to throw hand grenades, and to crawl *po plastunski*. That crawl proved the most assiduous part of the drill and the most fascinating to watch. One at a time the boys and girls crawled on their bellies, their heads down, almost boring into the earth, and with a snake-like twist of their bodies. Often they co-ordinated the crawl with the hurl of the block of wood that represented the hand grenade. There was no laughter. There was no sense of play. Earnestly these boys and girls were training for possible house-to-house fighting or for guerrilla warfare.

I had been away from Russia for six years, the stormiest the country had known since the civil war. During this interval much had happened to change not only the mood but the vocabulary of the people. Now it was rich with military phrases. On reading back numbers of Baku and Moscow newspapers, the new phrase that captivated my attention was the one that designated the special crawl—*po plastunski*—the school children were learning to master. I had never before heard it. I inquired around as to its meaning and import and received varied technical explanations.

It was not until I came to the Kuban in 1944 that I learned the historic origin and the dramatic significance of the expression. It dates back to the beginning of the nineteenth century, only a few years after the Cossacks came to the Kuban. It is the Kuban Cossacks who invented and perfected the crawl and gave it its name. It is derived from the word *plast*—layer of earth. To crawl *po plastunski* is to crawl like a layer of earth, and a *plastun* is a Cossack infantryman who masters this crawl. When he is proficient in it he can crawl or lie for hours in mud, marsh, amidst reeds, shrubbery, tall grass, sometimes up to his neck in water or slush and in no way betray his presence or invoke the suspicion of the loitering or galloping enemy. Such a soldier makes a superb scout, and originally the *plastun* was essentially engaged in reconnaissance.

In time the Cossack developed further talents. With the swiftness and secrecy of a snake he made his way to an enemy guard or an enemy gunner and struck a fatal blow. It was as though an unseen spirit had struck it. So inaudible and invisible was the *plastun* that the fallen man was scarcely aware of the action.

The grenade was the *plastun's* favorite weapon. He was skilled in throwing it. But it was not his sole weapon. Wearing the Cossack *cherkesska*—flowing black cloak—the famed Caucasian hood, the Cossack sheepskin cap, pigskin boots, he carried, in addition to a tea kettle and biscuits which were tied to his belt, the carbine to which was screwed a short sword and a goathorn of powder. Sniper, crawler, observer, listener, the *plastun* could stab, shoot, or kill his man with the grenade, or get him with his *arkan*—a lasso made of horsehair. Lying like a *plast*, he threw it cowboy fashion at a charging cavalryman, a prowling scout, a watchful or unwatchful guard. He might strangle his victim or make him prisoner and use him as a "tongue"—informer.

The *plastun* cultivated not only special physical but specific mental faculties. He became a keen observer of nature. The rise of a swarm of mosquitoes or the disorderly flight of a bat told him of the presence of man; so did the cries of crows and other birds, the rustle of trees, the swaying of shrubbery. He attuned his eyes and his ears to all sights and all sounds of nature. He learned to identify the tracks of men and animals in mud, sand, marsh, in the woods, steppe, anywhere. He moved about in such a way as to cover up or falsify his own footsteps. He learned to walk forward by walking backward, turning his head no more than necessary to make certain of his bearings. However short or long the distance he negotiated in such fashion, it was with no more effort than his *plastunski* crawl.

He evolved new methods of communication with his fellow Cossacks who might be out on the same or some other mission. He learned to croak like a frog, caw like a crow, howl like a wolf, grunt like a boar. He imitated the sounds of other birds and animals. Every sound uttered carried its own message.

Above all, the *plastun* was a man of extraordinary strength, endurance, and patience. He knew loneliness and privation. Constantly he faced mishap and hazard. He was ever awake to unforeseen encounters and to methods of grappling with them. He was ever ready to avail himself of anything about him—climate, lay of the land, movement or sounds of living things—to attack the enemy, spy on him, ambush him, pick him off swiftly and noiselessly wherever possible. He terrorized the enemy, made him afraid of marshes, ponds, rivers, tall grass, trees, any topographical or botanical situation which permitted the new Cossack infantryman to operate.

The *plastun* therefore is no invention from above, no result of experiments or orders from the Russian general staff. The mode of warfare he symbolizes is an outgrowth of the Cossack's fighting experience in the Kuban.

His greatest enemies were the native tribesmen, cunning and daring warriors and magnificent horsemen. Ignorant, primitive, as wild as the mountains in which they lived, they resented the coming of the Russians to their far-flung, sparsely settled lands. They were as vindictive as the American Indians when the white man started encroaching on their domain, and battled as fiercely. Now and then, like the Indians, they made peace with the Russians, but the peace did not long endure.

In 1778 General Alexander Suvorov came to the Kuban, which, together with the Crimea, was ceded by Turkey to Russia four years earlier. The natives refused to recognize Russian rule and ownership. They regarded themselves as subjects of Turkey. Fanatical, fighting Mohammedans, they did not want Christians or aliens on the land, which had not been Russian since the twelfth century, when the Black Sea was known as the Russian Sea.

Suvorov was a soldier and a diplomat. While building defenses in the Kuban he kept wooing the natives. He wanted to make friends with them, draw them into his confidence. Once he gave them a banquet for which he ordered one hundred oxen, eight hundred sheep, five hundred buckets of vodka. The banquet was a hilarious success. It ended in gay dances and exciting horse races. Suvorov was pleased. The natives appeared reconciled. But they were not. Soon after he left there were fresh raids and fresh skirmishes. The Kuban continued to be a scene of sanguinary feuds.

To subdue the natives, the Cossack had to outmatch him in every form of fighting. So he experimented with new weapons, new tactics, new modes of warfare. He improvised. He studied the enemy, imitated him, borrowed from him. He did things he never was called upon to do in the *setch*. He became an expert mountain climber; he mastered the art of fording rivers, ponds, and lakes; and he evolved the *plastun* infantryman. He learned

Cossack gunners in action

General I. A. Pliyev

A Cossack charge

Kuban Cossacks

to sail the sea, for the Sea of Azov and the Black Sea washed the lands of the Kuban.

So impressed was the Russian general staff with the fighting of the Kuban Cossacks, particularly with the *plastun*, that in 1840 it ordered the formation of two *plastun* battalions, one in the village of Yelizavetskaya, the other in Maryanskaya.

From generation to generation, not only in the Kuban but everywhere in the army, the *plastun* was emulated. Finally he became a tradition under the Soviets even more than under the Czar. Every soldier in the Red Army learns to crawl *po plastunski*. One reason Russian guerrillas during World War II were successful in outwitting, outmatching, outfighting German troops was because of the lessons and traditions of Cossack warfare and all that it implies in tactics and strategy, in individual cunning and individual initiative.

One of the largest and liveliest villages in the Kuban is named Plastunovkskaya.

In the 170 years that the Cossack has been in the Kuban he has participated in every war Russia has since fought. He has won the battle against the natives, has brought peace to the Kuban and adjacent lands. With his triumph villages sprang up. Towns arose. Population increased. No one needed to fear sudden raids or sudden death.

In 1760 fathers of the Kuban Cossacks marched with General Chernyshev into Berlin and occupied it. In 1790, soon after they came to the Kuban, they helped Suvorov storm Izamail, the mighty Turkish fortress on the Danube. "The Cossacks perform miracles," said Suvorov. A year earlier they fought with Kutuzov, entered the town now known as Odessa, other towns in the Odessa-Dniester territory.

During the Napoleonic invasion in the village of Ponemuni, the Kuban Cossacks and the Cossacks from the Bug, were the first to fire on General de Veux's infantry as it crossed the Niemen River. Throughout the Russian retreat to Borodino they were in the thick of the rear-guard fighting. At Mozhaisk they held up the French army for four hours. They were on the right flank of the Russian armies in the battle of Borodino. They proved audacious scouts and guerrillas. Together with the Don Cossacks they formed "the flying corps," and when the French army was in retreat they ambushed it, pounced on it, slashed it to pieces, unit by unit. Neither the Don nor the Kuban Cossacks took prisoners. That was no Cossack practice, still rarely is. On and on they pursued the fleeing enemy. With General Platov, of whom Tolstoy writes in *War and Peace*, they marched into Paris.

During the Crimean War (1854–56) they were triumphantly again in the forefront of the fighting. Their *plastuns* attained fresh distinction and were awarded the banner of St. George.

In the Turkish and in all other subsequent wars, they fought with their usual zeal and ferocity. With thunderous shouts of "Hurrah," their red-lined hoods waving like flames of fire, they galloped into enemy formations and slashed away with their narrow gleaming sabers. In the Far Eastern war of 1904, the Japanese spoke of them as "devils in skirts"; the "skirts" were their flowing black cloaks. Their slogans always were: "The Cossacks know no defeat, they know only victory" and "The Cossacks neither take nor become prisoners." In the first World War, according to information given me in Krasnodar, only 118 Kuban Cossacks fell into German hands alive. . . .

Warriors supreme, loving war as much as ever, the Kuban Cossacks also became settlers and colonizers. They tamed the Kuban, and the Kuban tamed them. The idea of celibacy, so widespread in the *setch*, had lost its spell. The denial of the family no longer prevailed; indifference to it invited ridicule and condemnation.

The Cossack usually married young. He assumed the responsibilities of a husband, the duties of a father. He was no puritan; he did not disdain relationships with other women. A passionate creature, his appetite for sex was violent. Yet there was no divorce. The Cossack's Orthodoxy forbade it, public opinion condemned it. Once married always married, "until death do us part." And the more children the better, especially if they were sons. A son meant a new allotment of land, a new Cossack warrior, fresh honor and glory for the family. Beat his wife the Cossack might, not always with impunity, for a Cossack woman might have the courage and the strength to strike back with fist, with club, with lash.

On holidays and festivals the Cossack had his fun. He drank inordinately. Taras Bulba's "science of drinking" was still in vogue, still a source of wanton pleasure. When inebriated, the Cossack became explosively impulsive, his nature welled up, his fists flailed away at the willing or unwilling antagonist or onlooker. Fist fighting was a pleasure, an adventure, a custom, an achievement. A Sunday and holiday without a fist fight was as rare as one without a sumptuous dinner. Often there was a murder—a Cossack in rage or in a burst of jealousy stabbing an antagonist with the ever ready dagger.

The Cossack no longer wore the uniform of the *setch*, with its Polish and Tatar decorations. Taras Bulba's red morocco boots with silver heels gave way to knee-high snug-fitting black boots; the baggy trousers with "countless folds and pleats" were discarded. The tighter-fitting garment was more easy to wear, to hold up, to sit within the saddle. The scarlet jacket was exchanged for the *cherkesska*—the flowing cloak of the native mountaineer. The sheepskin cap remained, now christened the Kubanka. Black with a scarlet crown crossed with gold lacings, the Cossack wore it summer and winter. His weapons were always with him—the dagger, the sword, the lance.

More than ever the Cossack continued to regard himself superior to others. In his own mind there was no one like him. The intellectual, the town burgher, the merchant, the ordinary official, the foreigner, all were inferior. None had his valor, his sense of robust adventure, his feeling of triumph over everyone, including nature. In his eyes the muzhik was a low and contemptible creature, with neither the will nor the audacity to battle his way to freedom, to shake off, as did his own Cossack ancestors, the evil plague of serfdom or landlordism.

His Orthodoxy the Cossack cherished as devoutly as his ancestors had done in the *setch*. He was still its supreme defender and protector. The Orthodox priest forgave his sins, heard his confessions, prayed for good crops and for victory, christened the newly born, married the young, buried the dead, yet contained within him something that was wholly evil. The Cossack did not mind swearing at the priest, telling ribald tales about him or his wife, and if the priest crossed the street, he never would follow, would always turn back lest ill luck strike him.

Books did not tempt the Cossack. If he was literate he might read them. But learning held no lure. Cossack wisdom was to him the florescence of the human intellect. He wanted no improvement on it, did not believe any existed anywhere. Sometimes a son or daughter displayed unexpected love of books. The son the father might encourage in this love. The daughter he mocked. What did a woman want with learning? Not for her was the university; land she could till without it, children she could bear, the household she could manage, all her other duties she could perform, as her mother, grandmother, great-grandmother had done, without ever looking into a book. There were exceptions, of course, but not too frequent.

One of the Cossack's great loves was the horse. Not the work horse, which was a drudge and a slave, like the muzhik in the days of serfdom. The work horse he did not mind lashing. But the saddle horse was a personality. He fondled it, flattered it, whistled to it, sang to it, bestowed on it his deepest solicitude, his tenderest words. It was his comrade in arms, it carried him to faraway lands and battlefields. It shared with him sorrow and joy, want and triumph. It anticipated and fulfilled his will, especially in battle. All he was in life, all he had been in history—freeman, brigand, adventurer, conqueror, colonizer—the horse had made possible. When the horse was wounded he sighed with sorrow, or ranted with rage when the horse was killed. He buried it with honor if conditions allowed.

In the Kuban the Cossack carried to new heights of achievement his warrior traditions and fighting prowess. As ever he was born "not with a silver spoon but with a saber," but he no longer scoffed at the state or defied it. He fought not for his *volnitsa—* liberty—as did Taras Bulba, but for the Czar. Catherine the Great closed one chapter in his history and opened another. She supplanted or transmuted his denial of the state into subordination to the throne.

In the accomplishment of this far-reaching goal Catherine used compulsion, but after the suppression of the Pugatchev revolution she cautiously avoided violence and resorted to it when other methods failed. In the disbandment of the *setch* there was little bloodshed. Those who did not flee to Turkey were subsequently "exiled" to the Black Sea, and then migrated to the Kuban. "Nobody would mind being exiled to the Kuban," said an intellectual in Krasnodar with whom I discussed the past of the Cossacks. "Nobody could possibly object to living in so bright, sunny, beautiful, rich a country when it was so sparsely settled, particularly if one got free land as the Cossack did."

Whenever a boy was born to the Kuban Cossack he was allotted, automatically with his registration, a holding from eighteen to forty acres. In pre-Soviet days Cossack holdings in the Kuban attained an area of nearly seventeen million acres. The boy started his Cossack career as soon as he was old enough to care for a colt. He grew up with the còlt, as the colt grew up to be a Cossack war horse. As soon as the boy was old enough to balance himself on the back of a horse or mount a saddle, he started riding. By the time he was eighteen, when he entered regular service, he was a magnificent horseman. He remained in the service officially twenty years, unofficially all his life, for there was nothing he loved so much as Cossackhood—fighting, roving, adventuring, conquering.

Out of this Cossack society in the Kuban came few intellectuals, few priests, few merchants, few businessmen, hardly any industrialists. Sons followed in the footsteps of fathers, grandfathers, remained professional warriors.

The czars cultivated the Cossack, catered to his love of war and adventure, pampered his vanity. They elevated him into a caste, the vaunted Cossack caste, which further fortified his exclusiveness, his sense of superiority to others. Himself largely a descendant of muzhiks, he deemed himself a personage of transcendent importance, for a special career, special privileges, special compensations, and special dispensations.

In return for the Czar's benevolence, the Cossack was ever ready for war and for the fulfillment of the Czar's commands. He kept himself, his horse, his saddle, his weapons, his uniform, all of which he obtained with his own funds, ready for duty. He journeyed to St. Petersburg and enrolled in the Emperor's personal bodyguard. Not for him to know what the Czar wanted to do or what happened to others whom he scarcely knew and whom he was again and again summoned to suppress or hack to pieces. Gone was the tradition of Pugatchev, of Razin, of the other stalwart champions of the lowly muzhik and others who felt aggrieved and abused. Dead was Taras Bulba's hatred of rulers and landlords, his love for the all-embracing Cossack *volnitsa*. True, during the Revolution of 1905 the Urubsky regiment in the Kuban rebelled against the Czar. But that was only one regiment. The Cossack not only in the Kuban but on the Don, the Terek, in all the eleven territories where he lived and prospered, forgot his once lowly muzhik origin, his once buoyant, stalwart defense of the underdog. No one now despised the muzhik more than he. No one was more ready to exploit him, insult him, strike him down. Once the great rebel against absolutism in Russia, the Cossack now became its mightiest defender. The Czar's personal guard in peacetime included 2,575 Cossack officers and 60,532 men! The chief mission of the Cossack was not to build a new culture or a new society, but to uphold the power of the Czar and fight for him inside and outside of the country. So universal grew his reputation for reaction and brutality that Webster's dictionary gives as one of the definitions of "Cossack": "One of an armed contingent employed by reactionaries to suppress liberals or other opponents, especially by force."

Only in 1917 did an awakening come. Czarism had lost the

war and had so discredited itself with corruption and incompetence, court intrigues and pro-German machinations, that when the people in Petrograd rose in revolt, the Cossack gave them his blessing and joined them in the battle against the Romanov dynasty.

CHAPTER X

Taras Bulba's "Grandson"

WITH THE COLLAPSE of the Czar the Kuban and other Cossacks faced one of the sternest crises they had ever known in their century-old career as warriors. With violent emotion and inflammatory appeal such as "land, bread, peace," reminiscent in their simplicity and explosiveness of the slogans and battle cries of Stenka Razin and Yemelyan Pugatchev, the Soviets were splitting the country into warring camps.

Though far away from Petrograd and Moscow, citadels of the new revolution that was threatening to engulf the entire country, the Cossack territories remained neither unimpressed nor unshaken. When the civil war erupted they too took sides, and out of those who joined the Soviets none had attained the distinction as a warrior and as a leader of warriors that was won by Budenny, a mere cavalry sergeant in the Czar's army, and Vanya Kochubey, the Kuban Cossack who was not even a sergeant. Budenny is now a marshal and well known all over the world, but Kochubey was not destined to enjoy Budenny's triumph. Yet in the Kuban his name spells epic and legend. He was a true son of the Zaporog Cossacks, from whom he was descended, a roistering, boisterous Taras Bulba of the twentieth century.

There is hardly a Cossack home in the Kuban that has not on its book shelf a copy of the biographical novel *Kochubey*, by Arkady Peventsev, himself a Kuban Cossack, of which over a million copies have already been sold.

Ivan Kochubey—Vanya or Vanka for short—was a dashing, hot-tempered Kuban Cossack from the village of Alexandro-Nevskaya. He was married to a mild-mannered, motherly woman named Nastya, who was so enamored of him, his physical strength, his air of mastery, and his immense popularity, that she always addressed him by the polite *vy*—you—and dared not speak to him aloud or seriously to disagree with him even when she knew he was wrong and he knew it too.

Vanya never went to school. He was illiterate. When he had to sign a document, he made a cross with a pen or with a finger dipped in ink. He loved songs, stories, adventure, and fighting. He was indifferent to religion but had his share of Cossack superstitions. He would not pass a woman with an empty pail and refused to go down a street which a priest had crossed. Doing otherwise meant misfortune. A hen that crowed like a cock was to him a harbinger of calamity.

Kochubey was short and tough, with a war scar on his forehead. His eyes were gray and bright; when he was angry they glowed with fire. His lips were narrow, his chin strong, his neck a copper band of muscle, his expression sullen. His speech was as tough as his appearance and as picturesque. In all the Kuban there was no more daring horseman, no more skilled wielder of the saber. On tiptoe, from a knee-bending position, he could leap into the saddle without the use of his hands. With a circular stroke of the saber he could sever a man's head. He knew neither danger nor fear. He did not care for pomp or formality. He was simple and direct. There was nothing he loved more than the old-fashioned Cossack *volnitsa* (liberty), which recognized no repression from above, no subjection from below. He resented the social and economic cleavages in the Cossack village, the unquestioned power of the Cossack ataman. Poor and uneducated himself, he was steeped with Cossack pride and Cossack self-reliance. Wholeheartedly he subscribed to the Cossack motto: "Don't unsheath the sword unless you have to; don't sheath it without glory."

In the first World War, Kochubey fought on the Turkish front under the Cossack colonel Andrey Grigoryevitch Shkuro. On returning home he responded with eagerness to the revolutionary call of 1917. Though Cossacks possessed ten times as much land as the muzhiks, there was among them a sharp differentiation in well-being. Some were nearly as well off as landlords, others had sunk to the destitution of lowly muzhiks. Revolutionary slogans denouncing existing inequalities stirred Kochubey's blood. He wandered off to Tikhoretskaya and with a squad of his own men, all in uniform, joined the Revolution. He carried about him two Mausers, a Belgian revolver, a Browning, a dagger, and a sword. He fought to save the cities of Bataisk, Vyselki, and Krasnodar. His fame as a Cossack rebel spread, and men flocked to him on their own horses, in their own uniforms, with their own weapons, and said: *"Primi, batko* [Take us into your ranks, Father]." His army grew and his fighting zeal mounted, but he understood the Revolution in his own way. He was for Lenin and the Bolsheviks, but not for the Communists. Lenin was a Russian name, Bolshevism a Russian word; Kochubey understood and appreciated both. But Communism was an alien word; as yet he did not associate it with Lenin and Bolshevism.

Above all, Kochubey was against his former chief, Colonel Shkuro, now a general fighting in the Kuban against the Revolution. He wanted to fight it out with Shkuro single-handed with any weapon or with no weapon, with bare fists. Shkuro resented and ignored the challenge, yet recognized in his former Cossack a valiant and dangerous antagonist.

Kochubey's fame reached the Bolsheviks. They appreciated his fighting qualities and his popularity in the Kuban. They wanted to make him a part of their fighting forces and to subordinate him to their political program. They knew history well enough to realize that rebel Cossack leaders, if successful in battle, might run away with their triumphs. Unless they were drawn into the framework of a political cause, they might turn into brigands and hoist high the banner of anarchy. Such dangerous men had already appeared in the Kuban.

The Bolsheviks sent a commissar named Lyakhov to accompany Kochubey. He lasted only three days. During a battle he showed fright and Kochubey denounced him as a coward. The Bolsheviks sent another commissar named Kondybin. Kochubey stared and sneered at him with contempt. The word "commissar" conveyed to him the concept of cowardice. Kondybin knew it and racked his brain for a key to Kochubey's respect and good will. He could not depend on the help of Communists in Kochubey's ranks, because there were none—not one. But Commissar Kondybin was himself a Cossack, daring in the saddle, skilled with the saber. Kochubey did not know it. He tolerated Kondybin but did not disguise his contempt for him. The two men spent the night in the same room in a Cossack cottage, Kondybin wrapped in an overcoat. In the morning Kochubey waked him with a kick.

"You think you've come here to sleep?" he snarled.

Kondybin did not protest. He was biding his time to prove his mettle. The time came soon. Kochubey received orders to drive Shkuro's forces out of the village of Vorovskolskaya. If he failed to take the village he was to burn it. He must act at once, for Shkuro was seeking to outflank him.

The key to the village was a hill. The hill must be taken, and Kochubey ordered Kondybin to take it.

"If you fail," he warned him, "I'll cut your head off."

His contempt for the commissar was so pronounced that he presented him with a horse that had been wounded and which the Cossacks had nicknamed "the three-legged fool." With saber unsheathed, Kondybin led his men into the charge. Through his binoculars Kochubey watched the fight. Kondybin won. So overjoyed was Kochubey that when his Cossacks lined up in the church square, he publicly embraced the commissar and kissed him.

"From now on," he said, "you must call me Vanka." In further appreciation he presented the commissar with a thorough-bred saddle horse.

Kochubey was in high spirits. On learning that the priest of the village had fled, he said a church without a priest was of no use and ordered it burned. Cossacks started fetching straw into the church, but Kondybin protested. He branded the act as "counterrevolutionary," and asked Kochubey to rescind the order. The Cossack leader was dismayed and angered. He was not accustomed to being overruled, and refused to rescind the order for the burning of the church. Thereupon Kondybin said he would do so on his own authority. Incensed, Kochubey seized the commissar by the breast and shook him violently. But the commissar, too, was angry. Now he would have a showdown with the hot-tempered Cossack leader. Instantly he drew his dagger and pointed it at Kochubey. Kochubey drew his gun, leveled it at the commissar. Both men were ready for a duel. But there was no duel. Kochubey was thrilled with the commissar's fighting courage.

"That's a commissar!" he exclaimed. "Now we shall be comrades." They remained comrades to the end.

Kochubey's popularity in the Kuban and his success as a leader in the Revolution made him an increasingly dangerous antagonist of the Whites, of Shkuro and of Denikin, under whom Shkuro fought. The Whites offered a bounty of "two sackfuls of coins" —as Kochubey laughingly expressed himself—for his head or his person. But Kochubey remained at the head of his fighting Cossacks.

Denikin's army received aid from the Allies. His men in the Kuban had more and better weapons. They pressed harder and harder against the revolutionary Cossacks. Kochubey was driven from one position to another. His men wore out their clothes; they looked unkempt. Often they went without food; many were sick, many died from disease. Whenever possible they were buried with a semblance of ceremony and in new shirts. Kochubey insisted on that.

Yet Kochubey was unbroken. His men were loyal. They

fought and fought. When a battle was over, and whether won or lost, they broke into song to the accompaniment of an accordion:

> *"Don't weep, don't weep,*
> *Marusya darling,*
> *Don't weep, don't censure,*
> *And for your beloved little Cossack*
> *Offer a prayer to the Good Lord."*

"They sing beautifully," Kochubey rhapsodized. "Wonderful Cossacks!"

Hungry and rumpled, journeying in dust and rain, in wind and frost, "scathed again and again like hemp in a bouncer," they were light of heart, buoyant of spirit. Kochubey was immensely proud of his men.

Yet misfortune continued to trail after him. Once on the road he ran into a little cart in which he recognized the Red Cross nurse Natalya, who had been tending his wounded men. He stopped the cart, dismounted from his horse, lifted the felt cloth, and under it saw his wife Nastya. She lay crouched and feverish; her eyes were red and watery. She was ill with typhus. But there was little he could do for her. He, too, contracted the disease. For two days he had been burning up with fever. To add to his troubles, Pelipnek, one of his favorite Cossacks, had been killed on a mission. Seventeen other Cossacks with him also lost their lives. Their bodies were brought back slung over saddles. There was no time for a burial service; they were laid at rest in haste in the village of Kurshava.

The village was in danger of falling into Shkuro's hands. Retreat was unavoidable. The roads were cluttered with carts and people seeking refuge. Wives, mothers, and children of Kochubey's men were among these wanderers. There was no way of insuring their safe retreat. So they were ordered to remain behind and trust themselves to the mercy of the enemy. The Cossacks protested. What would Shkuro do to their families? But there was no time for debate. Ill with typhus, thin and feeble, Kochubey gnashed his teeth as always when in anger and shouted: "All families are to be left behind in Kurshava!" The Cossacks bade their families good-by. They kissed wives, children, mothers, sisters. They might never see one another again. But there was no loud grief.

The retreat started. A trainload of supplies and wounded men followed east. Kochubey and his men protected it from Shkuro's bands. Finally Kochubey became so ill he could not remain in the saddle. There was no place for him in the train, and he was carried inside the snow-swept tender. He was so cold that Akhmet, his aide, warmed him with his body. All along the road of retreat there was misery and death.

Then Kochubey regained his health. He needed rest and treatment. Yet there was no time for anything but the revolutionary war for a new Russia. The time was February 1919. The train reached Kisliar, the terminal point of the railroad. Thence they must make their way on horseback to Astrakhan. Otherwise they were in danger of being captured and annihilated. The direction was straight north and the distance from Kisliar to Astrakhan was not great—less than two hundred miles. But the Kalmyk desert which they must cross was swept by a blizzard. Besides, the country was barren, desolate, sparsely settled, and Kochubey had only fourteen men left. There was no place to stop and rest. Yet there was no turning back. The mass of Cossacks were with Shkuro, who was in control of the lands they had left behind and was determined to capture Kochubey.

A band of Shkuro's Cossacks appeared in the steppes, and Kochubey was again smitten with typhus. One of his adjutants took command and ordered the men to lie down with their horses and fight it out with the enemy. But superior numbers and superior weapons overpowered the rebel Cossacks. Ignat, Kochubey's brother, was killed. The others were hacked to death with sabers. Kochubey himself was spared. There was a heavy reward for his capture. Besides, he might be a priceless asset to the Whites and their cause. So Colonel Poznakov tied him in ropes and took him to the village of *Sviatokrestovskaya* (Holy

Cross). Though Kochubey was ill and unconscious, Poznakov ordered two hundred of his men to escort the bound Cossack to the village.

The Whites treated Kochubey with unexpected mercy and solicitude. They sent a physician, two nurses, and a woman caretaker to look after him. Kochubey had a weakness for feather pillows and feather beds. Nothing rested him so well or gave him such a deep sense of comfort. So he was laid in a feather bed with feather pillows at his head.

He responded to treatment. An Armenian barber came to cut his hair and shave him. Barber fashion, he talked to Kochubey and answered questions as to what was happening in the outside world. What particularly impressed Kochubey was the news that the Whites were hanging captured rebels everywhere.

The Whites sent a spokesman and offered Kochubey the opportunity of escaping such a fate. A hero in the Kuban, his allegiance to the cause of the Whites would bring it much-needed prestige and support and would be a blow to the revolutionary crusade among the Cossacks. His fame would rally fresh masses of them to the banner of the counterrevolution.

General Denikin, commander in chief of the White armies, approved the proposal to persuade and bribe Kochubey into joining their forces. An officer came to make Kochubey a flattering offer. The rank of colonel and all the rewards and glories that went with it were his if he allied himself with the Whites.

But Kochubey was not the old type of Cossack warrior who loved war for its own sake and no more. Through Commissar Kondybin he had learned to read and write a little, and while he had read no books, his thoughts, sentiments, ambitions, and hopes were inextricably linked with the ideas of the Revolution as he understood them. "Land, peace, freedom" to every Cossack as poor as himself who dug and grubbed in land for a living was a stirring message, transcending in appeal anything else he had heard or known. He had in him the resoluteness of Stenka Razin or Taras Bulba, could neither be flattered nor bribed into betraying the things he believed in and for which he had fought so zealously. Gnashing his teeth, he rejected the bribe of money and honor that the White officer had offered him.

The Whites did not lose hope. They put Kochubey on trial. The doctor protested. Kochubey, he said, had not yet sufficiently recovered to endure the strain of a trial. The doctor was over-ruled. The matter would brook no delay. Bluntly Kochubey was told that his choice was between "ignominious death" or "glorious achievement." He was still a very sick man, thin and pale, a shadow of his former self. But only outwardly. Inwardly he was as much the Cossack rebel as when he commanded victorious troops on the steppes and in the mountains of the Kuban. For him there could be no choice. Gruffly he said that if he ever recovered his health he would like to meet General Denikin in person and cut his throat.

His fate was sealed. The sentence was death.

In the public square a gallows was erected. The Whites turned out as if on parade—columns and columns of mounted Cossacks. Thin, haggard, frail Kochubey was led to the gallows. The noose was flung over his neck and his body sprang into the air, with a plywood board on his breast marked "Red Bandit Kochubey!"

In the Soviet Kuban, Vanya Kochubey, from the village of Alexandro-Nevskaya, is today a legend and a hero. He is the reincarnation of the Taras Bulba from whom he was descended, the Taras who with his own hands shot his older son for betraying the Cossacks and who in the end burned to death shouting defiance at the enemy.

CHAPTER XI

The Great Reconciliation

IN THE SUMMER OF 1926, only a few years after the end of the
civil war, I went to the Kuban for the first time in my life. As
I wandered around the *stanitsas*—villages—the largest and most
populous villages in Russia, I observed nowhere, save in the
appearance of the cottages, streets, and public squares, any signs
or symbols of Cossackdom. No uniforms, no banners, no galloping horsemen, no *dzhigitovkas*—Cossack war games on horseback.
Something had erased every visible mark of the once picturesque,
valiant, ruthless military caste. Nearly five centuries of history
and battle, conquest and triumph, had, to all outward appear-
ances, gone up in smoke. Only the ancient names of villages
remained. Some, like *Plastunovskaya, Vasurinskaya*, were taken
from the names of regimental barracks at the long-defunct *setch;*
others, like *Otvazhanaya* (the Daring), *Pregradnaya* (the Barring), *Upornaya* (the Stubborn), *Storozhevaya* (the Guarding),
Besstrashanaya (the Fearless), *Grosnaya* (the Stern), expressed
the soldierly qualities or duties of the Cossacks.

The civil war seemed to have dealt Cossackdom a mortal blow.
At that time I wrote an account of my trip under the title, "The
End of the Cossack." Repeating what I had heard from Soviet
officials, and from Cossacks themselves, I said that history was
through with this "magnificent barbarian." He had played his
part in expanding the Russian Empire and making Russia an
immense fighting nation in Europe and Asia, but he had miscalculated the powers of the Soviet Revolution. For once he had

encountered an antagonist immeasurably stronger than himself, one from whose stern reckoning there was no escape.

Of course there were pro-Soviet Cossacks. There was Vanya Kochubey, as gallant and sturdy a warrior as had ever arisen out of the Kuban or other Cossack ranks. And there was the Don Cossack Budenny, today a marshal in the Red Army, but only a sergeant at the beginning of the civil war. Budenny's First Cavalry army, more numerous, better equipped than Kochubey's guerrillas, stormed and won many White strongholds. The Cossacks who were with the Revolution were mostly the *golytba*—the naked ones; that is to say, the poor ones. They came from the same ranks as those that had once supported Stenka Razin, Pugatchev, and other Cossack rebels. They constituted an intrepid fighting force and won many decisive battles for the Soviets. But the overwhelming mass of Cossacks defied the new order and vowed to drown it in blood. The territories of the Don, the Kuban, and the Terek became for a time strongholds of the counterrevolution. The very slogans under which White Cossack armies were fighting were symbolic of their irreconcilable antagonism.

"We don't want to be the equals of muzhiks; as formerly, we shall be masters and the muzhiks shall submit to us," read one slogan. Others read:

"The possessions of each Cossack must remain undivided, inviolate!"

"Never recognize the Soviet state."

"For the rights of Cossacks and against the muzhik interloper."

Politics, property, prestige, social superiority, Orthodoxy were the main motives that nurtured the hostility of the Cossack White armies. Let it be remembered that in the Kuban the landholdings of the Cossacks embraced an area of about seventeen million acres.

There were Cossack leaders in these armies who, because of the growing power of the Soviets in the central and northern territories, proclaimed the Cossacks a separate nation with a way of life and a body of rights all their own. They sought to lure the Cossack masses into a movement for the formation of a federalist Cossack state. They banked on universal Cossack solidarity. They played on every conceivable Cossack trait—vanity, love of war, contempt for the muzhik—to keep aflame his hate of the Revolution and his will to make an end of it.

But the Kochubeys and Budennys had their followers. Cossack communities were as torn by family feuds and tragedies as the rest of Russia. Unforgettable is Babel's short story, "The Letter," in which a young Cossack describes to his mother how his father, a White soldier, executed one of his brothers and how later another brother, a Red soldier, captured the father and executed him.

But the White Cossack was fighting a losing battle. In the spring of 1919 Kuban Cossacks made up forty per cent of Denikin's forces. When summer arrived, they constituted only fifteen per cent of Denikin's armies, and by the beginning of 1920 only ten per cent. More and more of the middle Cossacks, no landed proprietors but with a large enough holding to live comfortably, deserted the White generals. In January 1920 the Kuban Cossack garrison in Eisk refused to fight Soviet groups. In the end all Cossack opposition collapsed.

This was not the first time that the Cossack was overpowered in war. But on previous occasions there was always a remote territory to which he could withdraw, nurture his wounds, gather fresh strength, and perpetuate uncurbed his military way of life. In dissolving the *setch* in 1775, Catherine the Great put an end to the sole surviving Cossack republic, but she kept alive and fostered, as did all subsequent czars, the social and military aspects of Cossackdom. This time, excepting those who migrated to foreign lands, where their Cossackhood was doomed anyway, there was no free territory in which to settle. The Red flag triumphed everywhere.

During my journey through the Kuban in 1926 I spent a Sunday in the village of Pashkovskaya, on the outskirts of Krasnodar. This was one of the most czarist-minded communities in the Kuban. The Czar had visited it during the first World War. Grand Duke Nikolay Nikolayevitch was its sponsor, and the Cossacks derived much glory and some profit from this guardianship. Now the Czar was dead, the Grand Duke was in exile, and the Cossack caste, like all other castes, was scrapped. Nothing was left of its former power, glitter, or tradition. Cossacks had been leveled to the status of the lowly muzhik.

It was a bright and sunny morning in midsummer. Church bells were ringing, and people were flocking to Mass—nearly all women. The men were gathering in the ungainly, weed-grown public square. They were tall, sturdy, with broad shoulders and faces and swarthy complexions. Many of them clung to the long, bushy mustachios, and older men cherished their ample beards —the special pride and glory of the Cossack *starik* (old man). They stood around or sat on the empty market tables and benches munching sunflower seeds and talking. No one was in uniform, though most wore the Kubanka, the black sheepskin cap with its shirred scarlet top. The Cossack uniform was outlawed; the dagger and the sword were forbidden. The older men looked sullen and subdued, though the younger men, as is always the way of youth, talked and laughed aloud and went in for horseplay.

The Cossacks were full of talk. There were no more Cossacks in Russia, they wailed, the Russia once known as the land of the Cossack. Only the name remained, now an insult, now an execration.

One man invited me to his house. From a trunk in the unlit storage room he hunted out the old *cherkesska*—the Cossack's traditional cloak—and an old hood and brought them to the living room. Holding both in his hands and waving them around as if enjoying once more the sight of the bands of red and black and the fusion of colors, he railed against the evil times that had come upon the Cossack when he was no longer permitted to don his uniform even on Sundays and holidays. Gone was everything the Cossack cherished. No more Cossack war games, no more

Cossack crusades, no more Cossack celebrations, no more Cossack *volnitsa*, no more Cossack saddle and horse, no more Cossack anything! A muzhik—lowly, unclean, poor and grubby—that was all the Cossack had become. He had neither fatherland nor government any more. He was the stepson of his own country, reviled, despised, an outcast of outcasts. He was not even permitted to serve in the Army. Only Cossacks who had fought for the Revolution were taken into the Red Army, but even they were no longer Cossacks, and they were not always allowed to serve as cavalrymen.

Yet toward evening that day the Cossack world suddenly came to life again, not with uniforms and horses, but with song and dance. An accordion player appeared in the public square, and soon the place teemed with young people—Cossack boys in boots, Cossack girls in white kerchiefs. Older men and women formed a circle several rows deep, and inside the circle the young Cossacks sang and danced with as much vigor and exuberance as their fathers and mothers, their grandfathers and grandmothers when they were young, though with a good deal more sobriety. Late into the evening the accordion played, and the young people sang and danced the Ukrainian *hopack* and other favorite dances.

The civil war was over and done, but the Revolution had another battle to wage with the Cossacks—the battle of collectivization. And now again the Cossacks were divided. Those with small landholdings were usually willing enough to give the new system a trial, but those with substantial land allotments would not hear of collectivization. In the *stanitsa* Troitskaya near the banks of the Kuban River, the priest appeared one Sunday morning in the pulpit and said to his people:

"There will be no service this morning. There is a task for you to perform. Go and perform it."

The task was a demonstration against collectivization. The congregation marched out, in disorderly, tumultuous fashion, an embittered crowd of men and women. They made their way to the village Soviet. Loud and angry were their shouts of protest and indignation. Some men dressed up as women and joined the mob, shouting wildly, shaking fists, threatening rebellion. Their disguise insured them against possible violence. They knew women might be arrested, but in a scuffle they would not be beaten. Some of these disguised men had little clubs and other missiles hidden in the folds of their skirts or in their bosoms.

The Soviet officials were helpless. There were only a few of them. They talked, argued, and pleaded, all in vain. The angry crowd would not allow them to talk, would only compel them to listen. From a neighboring village a young Cossack, a Soviet official, arrived on the train. As soon as he stepped out, he was knocked down and beaten mercilessly. He himself told me of the incident. He bled profusely, he said, and did not know whether or not he would be beaten to death, as some Soviet officials had been. Soon afterward the priest disappeared.

So widespread and acrimonious were the protests against collectivization that in 1930 Vyacheslav Molotov, then Premier of the Soviet Union, made a journey to the Kuban. He tried in person to win the Cossack population to the new system of landholding and land tillage. So enraged were the Cossacks that at first they refused to hear him. From five in the afternoon until two in the morning he argued and pleaded, but his words fell on deaf ears. Some Cossacks were so embittered they threatened to beat up Molotov.

Not only the Kuban but the Don and the Terek heaved and flamed with violence, disorder, and family feuds. There was fighting with fists, clubs, and machine guns; there was blood and death. Nowhere else in Russia was the antagonism to collectivization, and the liquidation of kulaks, so intense and tumultuous. Several of the more rebellious *stanitsas* were forcibly evacuated. Some Cossacks were exiled to the nearby province of Stavropol, others to faraway places in Central Asia. Whole villages were removed—men, women, and children, the rich and the poor.

As during the civil war, the Soviets, now supported by the loyal and powerful Red Army, were determined to battle Cossack opposition to the finish. Nowhere else in Russia was the fight so prolonged and tragic in its consequences. There was wholesale sabotage of tillage. There was mass slaughter of live-stock. There were mass arrests and mass exile. There was famine. But the Soviets won.

Twice, then, within a decade and a half the Cossack was fought into submission. Yet when the fight was over and the Cossack bowed in defeat, the Soviets hastened to woo him not only with verbal promises but with material gifts. They sent to the Kuban tractors and combines, purchased mostly in America; grain drills, disk harrows, other mechanized implements; train-loads of flour for bread and trainloads of grain for seed; select seed, the choicest available in the country; and a body of new leaders, the most firm but also the most seasoned, the most tactful, the most able in the land.

Brilliantly and movingly, the great Cossack writer, Mikhail Sholokhov, has told the story of collectivization among the Cos-sacks in his novel *Broken Earth*.

In the summer of 1936 I was again on my way to the Kuban. I stopped in the city of Rostov, capital of the Don Cossacks. As I was strolling along the main avenue I noticed a young man in Cossack uniform. The last time I had seen that uniform was in the secrecy of a Cossack home in the village of Pashkovskaya; since then I had not seen it anywhere else in all the Soviet Union, except on the stage—black sheepskin cap with the scarlet top, flowing black *cherkesska* with scarlet shirt front, purple-lined hood gleaming in the sun and at the belt a sword and a dagger—the uniform of a Kuban Cossack! The old uniform was legal again. It was once more a part of the Russian scene. It was an attribute no longer of reaction and barbarity but of manliness and valor—above all, of patriotism. . . . The Cossack had re-gained his fatherland and with it some of the picturesqueness that was his in the days of his glory.

History was being reshuffled. The old and the new were no longer in mortal clash. The older generation might still long for the past; the new generation saw chiefly the present. And past and present, like two estranged friends, were coming together again. Chastened by the great conflict, carefully avoiding mention of old memories and grievances, the Cossack and the new rulers were seeking an alliance on a basis of a fresh understanding and a fresh respect for each other.

Russia was once more wooing the Cossack, beckoning to him, flattering him, giving him a place in the sun. The void he had left made it inevitable that he should fill again. Collectivization had come to stay. The battle against it was as futile as the battle of the artisan in the early years of the industrial age against the coming of the machine and the factory. No power anywhere could dislodge the tractor and the combine from the immense wheatlands of the Kuban. In his own arsenal there was no weapon with which the Cossack could combat the machine age which the Soviets had spread even more energetically over the plains and valleys of the Cossack regions than over the rest of Russia. The old generation might grumble and long for the day when they could do as they pleased—swear, smoke, drink, revel, loaf, fight, make faces at the whole world, and deem themselves and their ways of life superior to those of anyone else, anywhere, and everywhere else. But they were powerless. They had to reconcile themselves to the new dispensation and to reaping the rewards of their toil within the framework of the new communal order and the highly mechanized implements out of which it was being forged.

Significantly, the Russians have incorporated in their language the American words "tractor" and "combine," words symbolizing the most powerful weapons with which the Soviets won the battle of collectivization. Without these two American inventions there would have been no collectivization of the land.

Mikhail Sholokhov's brilliant portrayals of the Cossack during the years of turmoil and readjustment have helped cleanse the Cossacks, especially the Cossack youth, of their old political antagonisms and emotional hostility. In Sholokhov's moving pages, millions of Soviet-minded Russians have seen the Cossack in a new light, a human being caught in a gigantic historic tempest and swept on to a new fate. No other Soviet novelist has been read so widely or moved his readers so profoundly. Sholokhov made the Russian people and the Cossack himself see through his great and truthful art that the Cossack had sinned but that he had also suffered and was no longer in a position to indulge in his ancient sins; he was fit for a new day and a new society.

Meanwhile fascism was sweeping Europe. It was high-lighted by Hitler's rise to power and the triumph of Franco in Spain. War clouds were gathering; Russia was in danger. In the defensive measures of Russia's military leaders the Cossack was again a man of consequence. German and other engine-minded military experts might deride the use of cavalry in modern battle; they might pitch their hopes so high on the airplane and the tank that they saw little or no contribution cavalry could make today. But the Russians, more historical-minded than ever, were impressed with the Cossack's contribution to military science and to Russia's military might in past wars. They refused to dismiss cavalry as outmoded. . . . Besides, they planned to mechanize the Cossack warrior. They would arm him with machine guns, with light and heavy artillery. They would replace his old rifle with new guns. They would strengthen his ranks with tanks and planes. They would fit him, more than any czar had ever done, for infantry as well as for cavalry. Russia was a land of plains, marshes, and forests, in which the mechanized weapon might at times be stalled and only the horse could traverse with ease and safety. For scouting purposes, for rear-guard action in advance or retreat, for ambushing the enemy in woods and marshes, for terrorizing him when caught unawares in a village or a series of villages, for charging on him with sharp sabers and wild shouts of "Hurrah! hurrah!" and for encircling the enemy, the Cossack had his ample uses. He had outlived only his primitive mode of warfare, but not combat.

Above all, the Cossack's warrior spirit counted. His very presence in the Army would lend it color and toughness. His songs and stories would stir the martial spirit of others and remind them of the former victories of Russian arms.

On April 20, 1936, the Central Executive Committee of the U.S.S.R. issued a decree containing this passage:

"Considering the devotion of the Cossacks to the Soviet Government and also the desire of Cossacks actively to be drawn into the cause of national defense, the Central Executive Committee of the Soviet Union hereby provides: to remove from Cossacks all previously existing limitations on military service in the ranks of the Peasants' and Workers' Red Army."

Three days later Klementi Voroshilov, Commissar of National Defense, issued an order for renaming various existing cavalry divisions, making them Cossack troops and inducting into their ranks boys from the Cossack territories of the Kuban, the Don, and Stavropol—all excepting the mountaineers.

These military provisions were followed by an unwritten social classification of far-reaching consequence. The people living in the *stanitsas* were now all considered Cossacks whether or not they were so recorded in pre-revolutionary years.

In one village I came upon a Gypsy family whose men wore Cossack uniforms.

"What does it mean?" I asked.

"I am a Cossack now," said a tall, swarthy, broad-shouldered Gypsy.

His mother had her own calculations. "Now that my son is a Cossack," she said, "and wears his pretty uniform, he'll marry a girl with a rich dowry." The son laughed, but his mother angrily insisted he would marry only a girl with a rich dowry.

The few Jews who lived in *stanitsas* could likewise call themselves Cossacks, as could Armenians, Georgians, and others.

In 1936 I visited the village of Troitskaya and called on a Cossack family named Striha. I had come to interview the daughter who was widely famed as the champion *dzhigitka* (contestant in Cossack war games) in the county. Galloping on horseback, she had cut down with her saber more saplings in a row than anyone else, including all the men who competed in the match.

The mother set the table under a thick-limbed apple tree, cut a huge, newly picked watermelon, brought out biscuits and honey, and invited me to partake of her humble Cossack *ugoshtshenye;* she would go off to the field where her daughter was working and bring her home.

Soon she returned with a diminutive, golden-haired, frecklefaced eighteen-year-old girl. So embarrassed was the girl that at first she would not say much of herself or of the championship she had won in one of the most strenuous and exciting Cossack war games.

I had a camera with me, and with the help of her mother I persuaded her to don her uniform and weapons, bring out her horse and saddle, and pose for a photograph. When she finally came into the courtyard on a white horse in her scarlet-crowned Kubanka and the flowing scarlet-lined *cherkesska* with the red hood on her shoulders and a sword at her side, she was no longer a timid young girl but a stately Cossack warrior.

For the first time in Russian history Cossack girls were encouraged to take up cavalry on a basis of equality with men, though they were not drafted into the regular army . . .

When I revisited the village of Troitskaya in August 1944, I asked about the champion girl *dzhigitka.* "Oh, Striha, you mean," said the Party secretary. "When the war broke out, she volunteered for service in the Red Army. The kolkhoz gave her a horse and she went off to war. She is now a captain in a Cossack regiment."

All over the Cossack territories the Cossack was a Cossack again, with a uniform and weapons and wherever possible with a horse and saddle. Collective farms everywhere were encouraged to breed cavalry horses. . . . Outwardly the Kuban was beginning to change its color and its spirit.

In the evening of November 6, 1936, the foreign colony in Moscow, diplomats and correspondents, were invited for the first time to attend the annual Party celebration of the anniversary of the October Revolution. It was a significant occasion.

The spirit of that year's anniversary was signalized by a sentence taken from a speech by Stalin, "Life has become easier and more cheerful."

As always the Opera House was crowded with invited guests. The meeting started with speeches, followed by a long program of entertainment. The most impressive feature of the evening was the song-and-dance program of the Kuban and Don Cossack choirs. They were all in uniform, the bearded *stariks*, the young men, the little boys and the young women. . . . The Russians in the audience, all Party people of consequence, greeted their appearance with clamorous applause. To them, as to others who knew the battles and the conflicts that had once raged between Bolsheviks and Cossacks, this was a historic occasion. The presence of Stalin and Voroshilov in a box near the stage accentuated the significance of the event. No other living men in all Russia had fought the Cossacks more ruthlessly during the civil war and again during collectivization. Now they were face to face, no longer as antagonists fighting one another to the death but as leaders and citizens of a vast, fast-growing new country, hallowed again as the fatherland.

There were many songs and dances. Now and then Voroshilov scribbled a note and sent it to the choir leader. It was a request for an encore of a particularly spirited song or for one not on the program.

There were both harmony and rivalry between the Don and the Kuban performers. They were well aware of the glory of that moment and of their great responsibility as artists and as Cossacks. In the dances the bearded *stariks* and the little boys evoked the most tumultuous applause. The ease, the dash, the brilliance with which they executed ancient Cossack dances was an unforgettable experience for all who were at the Opera House that evening. . . .

This concert was a symbol of the reconciliation between Soviets and Cossacks.

PART THREE

The Cossack of Today

CHAPTER XII

"You Are in America Now"

———◆———

IN JULY 1944 I was back in the Kuban.

The plane skidded to a halt in a grass-grown rutted airfield outside the village of Pashkovskaya, a suburb of Krasnodar, capital of the Kuban Cossacks.

All the way from Moscow there was brilliant sunshine. The plane flew low, often barely brushing treetops, a favorite practice of Russia's wartime pilots. Warmth poured into the plane; the overcrowded passengers, sitting or sprawling amidst sacks, packs, and boxes, were hot and uncomfortable. But the moment the journey ended and we came outdoors a cold breeze blew into our faces. Suddenly the sky grew black and a squall of rain burst over us. "Just like the Kuban to catch us so unawares," said a passenger.

We ran for shelter under the wings of the plane—passengers and crew. Then passers-by crowded under the wings, all women, some of them fleeing amidst loud laughter and merry shouts from a nearby cornfield. Rain-soaked though they were, they seemed to be having the time of their lives. They were dressed in white —white kerchiefs, white waists, white skirts or one-piece garments with or without sleeves.

The rain stopped as suddenly as it had started, and the sun came out. We drove by automobile to Krasnodar, about four miles from the meadow airport. It was late afternoon. Offices had already closed for the day; so had the colleges, which, to make up for the time lost during the German occupation, had dispensed with the customary summer vacation. Sidewalks on the main avenue swarmed with people. The few men I saw were mostly wounded soldiers in rumpled uniforms, some on crutches. Most of the women were young; they were clerks, college students, factory workers, or visitors from the country. Their day's work done, they were indulging in the favorite Russian pastime of promenading along the avenue in a leisurely fashion. They too dressed almost exclusively in white.

Wave after wave of white billowed up and down both sides of the broad, tree-shaded avenue. I had never seen so much white, such spotless white, in any Russian city, not even in the gayest summer resorts of prewar days. I could not help speaking of it to Mr. Robakov, the assistant mayor of Krasnodar, who had come to the airport to meet me.

"This is southern influence," he explained, "and Cossack tradition. When you go out to the *stanitsas* you'll see Cossack women wearing white *kasinkas* [three-cornered kerchiefs] even in the harvest fields. People in the Kuban love white in summer."

It spoke eloquently for the pride and energy of the promenaders that in the midst of war, and despite shortages of soap and fuel for hot water, they managed to keep their summer dresses so clean and white. Like the acacias all along the avenue, they made the ugly wreckage of war a less oppressive sight. They gave the old, now faded and battered city an aliveness and brightness which, like the budding leaves of spring, preluded the arrival of new growth and new life.

That day was Sunday, July 30, 1944. The Russian armies were sweeping westward all along the far-flung fronts from the Finnish Gulf to the Black Sea. Victory heartened the spirit of the people. Life became more easy, but not too easy. The previous evening while milling through the crowds past the sprawling, ungainly Moskva Hotel in the capital, I heard the half chant of a phrase which the war had banished from the vocabulary of the people. The phrase was "*yest Eskimo*"—"Eskimo pie for sale." This imported American delicacy was back at last on the streets of Moscow, as was brick ice cream, as were the women vendors in the white kerchiefs and white jackets of prewar times.

Yet Moscow was living on meager and monotonous war rations. New potatoes had not yet made their appearance. New cucumbers, onions, radishes were about the only fresh garden products available. Not a sign of new cabbage, new tomatoes, new apples, new pears, *any* fruit. The Metropole Hotel, once famed for its cuisine, was only too often serving guests tasteless noodle soup with badly cooked macaroni or badly boiled rice as substitutes for vegetables, with the diminutive meat or fish course.

But here in the Kuban, Nature was prodigal. As we drove out of the airport and turned into the highway to Krasnodar, I saw ahead of us a truckload of fresh tomatoes, shining like red rubies in the hot sun. The truck stopped before a gray tumbling Cossack cottage, and the driver beckoned to a boy in the courtyard. The boy, bareheaded and barefooted, dashed into the road, lifted the hem of his dark blouse, and the driver threw down several handfuls of tomatoes. I could not help thinking how happy Muscovites would be to receive so luscious a gift at that time of year.

As we drove on we passed another truckload of tomatoes, then a truckload of large, freshly picked apples, such as I had not seen in Moscow since the war began, not even at receptions of the Foreign Office or the foreign embassies. In the streets of Krasnodar, on corner after corner, women and children were selling baskets of all kinds of fresh vegetables and fruits. In the market place, slovenly now and dilapidated and infested with flies, with none of its prewar order and primness, women were hawking loudly and cheerfully not only new cucumbers, new tomatoes, new onions, but new eggplants, new cabbages, all the fresh fruit and honey anyone with money might care to buy. . . .

I was extraordinarily food conscious. Anyone living in a country at war, particularly a country as vast as Russia, with nearly all its young manhood and much of its young womanhood in combat, with most of its produce from the land and nearly all its output from the factories streaming to the front, cannot help becoming excited at the sight of fresh tomatoes, apples, and honey.

"You seem to have everything here," I said to Robakov, the assistant mayor of Krasnodar.

"You are in the Kuban now." He accented the word "Kuban" as though to impress the meaning not only of its geography, history, and extraordinary bountifulness, but his personal pride in the land.

"I suppose," I said, "you are a native of the country?"

"I am," he answered. "I come from a mountain *stanitsa*, Yaroslavskaya."

Tall, wiry, dark-haired, with large black eyes shadowed by heavy black brows, fine teeth, a strong chin, a neat little mustache, Robakov had about him the appearance more than the manner of the North Caucasus mountaineer. He was too jovial, too witty, too talkative, too informal, too unconscious of dignity and ceremony in the presence of strangers to fit the picture of the somber mountaineer. But there was mountain color in his speech, mountain pride in his humble origin and in the wildness and grandeur of the surroundings in which he had spent his early years.

He was one of a family of eighteen, of whom sixteen had survived.

"Where else," he said quietly, "will you find such old people as in the mountains, so many old people, a hundred years old and older, yet riding horseback, climbing rocky heights, and working? And have you ever been caught in a storm in the mountains? Think of it, you are below the clouds. If you rise a little higher you are above the clouds and above the storm. You can play a game with nature: now you are above and now below the storm." He thought awhile and went on:

"Down in the valley people don't think of it. They can't; they are always below the storm. And lightning in the mountains is not a mere flashing thread of fire, no sooner seen than it vanishes. It's a wall of flame. It lingers, dazzles, frightens. You search for shelter, and if you have your wits about you, you run from rock and tree. Lightning seeks objects of least resistance, and if you are under a rock or tree you may get hit—and good-by! If you are a mountain man, you look for shelter in a cave. You go inside and wait, and you aren't bored. You listen to the thunder, prolonged and explosive. The echoes leap from one wall of rock to another, from one mountain to another. They make you think of an army of men with mighty voices rolling down from one height to another and shouting at the top of their lungs. It's very terrifying and very beautiful, and you never forget it. No, you cannot know what a storm is until you've met it in the *mountains!"*

By profession Robakov is a construction engineer. When the war broke out he was building a factory for the manufacture of electrical measuring instruments. He spoke in a soft, quiet voice, yet with the restraint and the inflection of a man of the world. Despite his science and his worldliness, he was essentially a man of nature, Kuban nature.

I was his guest for dinner, and we went to the restaurant of the city Soviet. I want to emphasize the word "guest." It has a connotation in Russian which its English equivalent barely implies. In Russian the word "guest" suggests a holiday. A guest means good will, camaraderie, good cooking, lavish drinking. In the summer of 1942, when Willkie and Churchill were guests of the Kremlin, they were tendered banquets which were fully reported in the press of the world. The drinking and eating evoked puzzled or cynical comment. Russia, it was said, was fighting with its back to the Volga; the country was down to scanty rations, especially of fats. Yet within the Kremlin halls meats and cakes, fruits and creams, liqueur and champagne flowed from invisible cellars and mysterious kitchens for foreign visitors.

But Russians who heard of these banquets were not perturbed. They were glad that even in dire and frightful times like the summer of 1942, the Kremlin was living up to traditional Russian hospitality in entertaining distinguished foreign guests.

During the same summer I once invited two Moscow college students for dinner. We ate in my room at the Metropole Hotel. The dinner was modest; there was no butter, and only one lump of sugar for each of us. For my guests the meal was a luxury; they said so. In their college dining room they seldom ate meat, and never of so high a quality. Yet one of them, a *komsomolka*, who is supposed to be politically better educated than the average youth, on learning that butter was served to foreign guests only once a day for breakfast and that one lump of sugar was the usual ration per meal, flushed with indignation and said: "They shouldn't do that. We're not so poor that we can't give more butter and sugar to our *guests*."

In all my travels in Russia during the twenty years that I have been periodically visiting the country, I never had a peasant host, however humble, however remote the village in which he lived, who did not insist on offering me the best food he had and the best sleeping place. Often, in spite of all my protests, he would offer me the bed in which he and his wife slept while both went off to spend the night in the hay or make themselves comfortable or uncomfortable on the floor. That is how Russians were, that is how they are now.

The actual definition of the word "guest" as given by Dal, Russia's most celebrated lexicographer, is: "A visitor invited or uninvited who comes to indulge in leisure, in conversation, in feasting."

There are many folk sayings which bear out this singular definition:

"To stint on wine is to see no guests."

"When the Lord sends guests along, the master is better fed."

"Guests after guests and the dishes remain unwashed."

There are countless folk sayings which emphasize, sometimes wittily, sometimes cynically, but always expansively, the epicurean pleasures associated with the word "guest."

Whatever the political motives may be behind a gala feast for a Willkie or a Churchill in the Kremlin, to speak of it merely as a show, or "Asiatic vanity," or "barbaric love of ostentation" is to miss one of the most revealing traits of Russian character and one of the most ancient and deep-seated folk customs of the country.

Now I was in the Kuban, in the capital of the descendants of the doughty Zaporog Cossacks—and here, as I soon learned, hospitality has its own laws.

The people of Krasnodar were receiving meager rations. These they supplemented with purchases in the market place, where prices were from one tenth to one half of what they were in Moscow. No new flour or grain had yet made its appearance. The farms were at the height of the threshing season; they had not yet fulfilled their government deliveries of grain or bread. Only after these deliveries are completed is new grain or flour permitted to be sold in the open market place. The bakeries and breadshops of Krasnodar were selling bread of inferior quality—rather soggy and not too palatable. It was not "Kuban bread," the people said; it was wartime bread.

Yet, war or no war, good times or bad, in the Cossack country even more than anywhere else in Russia, a guest is a guest, whether in the home of a Cossack or in a government dining room. The first thing that caught my eye on the dining table in the restaurant were the trays of large, shiny tomatoes, cucumbers, apples, pears, and plums, and the bottles of champagne.

"Kuban champagne!" said Robakov.

"I didn't know the Kuban manufactured champagne," I said.

"Of course we manufacture champagne, as good as any in Russia," Robakov said with pride.

We first drank vodka, then champagne served in tea glasses with Robakov's usual Russian admonition to drink *do dna*—to the very bottom of the glass. Protests were of no avail. They evoked only warm Cossack rhetoric on the privileges of a host and the obligations of a guest.

Yet the assistant mayor of Krasnodar was a temperate man. He did not smoke. He did not like vodka; he drank it only when he was host or guest. When he was having meals at home, he seldom partook even of light wine. Now he was a host, and a host must never fail in the observance of the centuries-old code of Cossack hospitality.

"Do you know what Gorki said about champagne?" he said by way of inducing me to empty my glass so he could refill it.

"Does it matter," I said, "what Gorki said about champagne?"

"It should matter. Gorki was a great man, a wise man, a worldly man, a great patriot. He knew how to live. He said, 'Champagne is the crystallized energy of the sun.' So what harm can it do you if you drink another glass of crystallized energy of the sun?"

"Your Kuban," I said, "is a very rich land."

"You are in America now," Robakov said.

"I am?"

"Yes, sir. The people who live in the Kuban are immigrants, like your people in America. They began migrating here about the time your country became independent. They were mostly Cossacks—that is, adventurous people like so many of the western Europeans who at that very time were flocking to the American continent. And this is a rich country, like America. There is not much you have which we haven't got here in the Kuban."

"Isn't there?" I said. My skepticism must have been evident.

"Very well, let's make comparisons. Let's compare the Kuban with California. Take wheat. We are one of the greatest wheat-lands in the world."

"California," I said, "grows excellent wheat and lots of it."

"Good. We grow barley, rice, oats, corn, sugar beet."

"California grows these crops."

"We grow cotton."

"California is a great cotton country."

"We grow apples, pears, plums, apricots, peaches, and we raise the finest honey in the Soviet Union."

"California can match all these."

"We grow three fourths of the tobacco of the Soviet Union."

Evasively, I said: "California is one of the greatest citrus countries in the world."

"Ah, but along the Black Sea coast we grow tangerines, and does California grow sunflowers for oil?"

"California grows olives for oil."

"We don't grow olives, and California doesn't grow sunflowers, so we are even."

"But California has some of the richest mineral oil fields in the world," I said.

"Have you heard of Maikop?" said Robakov. "Is there any oil pumped anywhere out of the earth better than our Maikop oil?"

"California grows dates, figs—lots and lots of figs."

Robakov was stumped. He meditated and said: "No, we don't grow figs and dates in the Kuban. But we are starting to grow peanuts."

"Very well," I said. "Do you grow coffee?"

Again he was stumped, almost disconsolate. "No, we import coffee."

"So does California," I said, and we both laughed.

"But we grow tea!" he said exultantly. "The finest in the world."

"California doesn't grow tea," I admitted.

"There you are! And has California good hunting? Big game hunting?"

"Certainly."

"But you should see the hunting in the Kuban. We have deer, wild goat, fox, big black bear, and the finest boar in the world— a sleek, swift-stepping boar, with a long head, long tusks, long needlelike bristles, and the tenderest meat you ever tasted. It lives in the mountains and feeds on acorns and wild fruit, and this time of the year, with corn earing out, it comes down in droves from the mountain forests into the valleys. It raises havoc with our corn, for there's nothing the boar loves more than our Kuban corn. Cossacks hunt lots of boar, and there is no more delicious meat anywhere in the world—that's Kuban boar for you. Has California anything like it?"

I was not disposed to let him run away with his triumph. So

I asked if he had seen Sonja Henie in *Sun Valley Serenade*, then showing in Krasnodar's leading movie house.

The assistant mayor's eyes dilated with pleasure.

"Of course I've seen it! A wonderful picture. Our people love it. We don't see much snow in the Kuban. Our climate is mild, and the skiing and skating in the picture is a spectacle we love. What a picture!"

"It was made in California!" I said, quite jubilantly.

"A wonderful place, California," he said, "almost as wonderful as the Kuban."

"But you don't have motion-picture studios."

"We don't, that's true—not yet, anyway."

"And that's not all," I pressed my advantage. "California is famous for its beautiful women—the most beautiful——"

"Ah, aha!" he interrupted, lifting his hand. "This subject we shall discuss when you return from your journey in the *stanitsas*, after you have seen our *kazachki* [Cossack girls]."

I could not help telling the assistant mayor of the Cossack capital that as a booster of Kuban glories he could outmatch any Californian. The booster spirit is growing in the Russian land. It is encouraged from above and below. It is becoming more and more an integral part of Russian psychology and Russian speech.

Not even the Siberian can match natives of the Kuban in the eloquence of their local patriotism. They are the Californians of Russia.

> *Kuban, our motherland,*
> *Our age-old knight*

runs an old folk ditty. The history of the country is as rich in adventure as its land is in natural scenery and natural riches. When the Germans occupied it, Hitler boasted that one of the greatest wheat and fruit lands of the world was German forever. The "forever" was a dream now dead, but the boast of wheat and fruit was justified.

The Kuban can never be the great oil and fruit land and the

great mountain country that California is. But Robakov was not exaggerating when he boasted of its natural riches, its mountains and steppes, rivers and ponds, forests and sea, wild life—and wild fruit—apples, pears, nuts. Kuban forests abound in wild game. The waters, salt and fresh, abound in all kinds of fish. No Cossack in old times ever mounted a horse and went off to war or to cavalry maneuvers without packing pressed caviar into his baggage sack. Long before the world had ever heard of vitamins, the Cossack, as sturdy a man as ever lived, knew the health-giving qualities of caviar. There is no record of a scurvy epidemic in the Kuban. Centuries before the Cossacks came there, the ancient Greeks, who did a thriving barter with the Kuban natives, in appreciation of its rich fishing waters, spoke of it as *antiketes*—a river rich in sturgeon.

Proximity to mountain and sea has made the climate of the country mild and invigorating. Its annual rainfall is seldom less than 400 millimeters. The average is from 500 to 800 millimeters. The days are hot, the nights are cool. September and October, which in Moscow are ordinarily raw and cold, murky with drizzle and rain, are known in the Kuban as "the golden autumn." There is no rain, or very little, during these months. There are sun and warmth. There are balm and fragrance. There is many-colored beauty in turning leaves, withering meadows, rust-colored stubble. It is a time for work and, if leisure permits, of adventure—hunting, fishing, nut picking in the forest, duck-shooting in the steppe, galloping on horseback. There is scarcely any winter in the Kuban. Snow melts soon after it falls. The Kuban River seldom freezes thick enough for skating. "We don't need *shubas* [fur coats] here," people in the Kuban say. A spring overcoat is warm enough. The chief use of the sheepskin is for the Kubanka. Nor, save along the seacoast, are there any gales or hurricanes.

The spring starts in February, is accompanied by mist, rain, mud as deep and sticky and heavy as anywhere in the Ukraine. It is the most unpleasant season of the year. But it doesn't last long. Flowers come early. Garden produce grows fast. Bees start their house cleaning with the arrival of the warm breezes. In April the weather clears. In May it is hot, and with welcome relief people take to their white clothes.

The soil is as black and "fat" as any in the world, and the black earth reaches down to a depth of nearly five feet.

"Put a bare stick into our black earth," say the natives, "and it'll grow fruit."

The folk sayings emphasize the extraordinary fertility of the land. It grows all the crops Robakov so proudly listed and many others, among them the castor bean, the soya bean, Italian hemp, and an importation from California known in Latin as *Chascolus lunadus.*

"The Kuban is the botanical garden of the world," Professor Novatowsky, a well-known plant expert in Krasnodar, said to me. Not quite, of course; but it is rich in trees, plants, flowers. This is the birthplace of Russian champagne. In 1944, despite all German destruction of vineyards and wine factories, the Kuban bottled one hundred thousand quarts of champagne and about six million quarts of various brands of wine. This in addition to the homemade wine and brandies which the Cossack customarily stocks up for his own personal use. . . .

In area the Kuban is as large as all of Holland, Belgium, and half of Switzerland combined, but its population is only one seventh of theirs. It has neither the cities nor the industries of Belgium or Holland. It is still overwhelmingly agricultural. It has space in which not only to breathe but to gallop around and to spend violent emotion in physical effort and adventure. Except in the critical political years of the civil war and the early period of collectivization, when the Kuban was swollen with acrimony and hate, and the fat steppe lay largely untilled, growing wild grass and thick-stemmed weeds, the Kuban has known an abundance which no other part of Russia has rivaled.

Here Cossack love of food and drink is, in peacetime, seldom unappeased. Here was none of the severe poverty of the northern village. "*Shtshui ee kasha, pishtsha nasha* [Cabbage soup and porridge are our food]"—this centuries-old humble chant of the northern peasant never became part of Cossack vocabulary. The Cossack here did not know the experience out of which it grew. "Cossack borsch," said Robakov, "is so thick that if you stick a spoon into the plate it'll stand as upright as an oak."

In the Kuban man seldom is a victim of Nature, rarely fails to be its master. Sea and sun, beauty and wildness, space and riches are only a part of its glories. Here the earth is the kindliest Little Mother.

No wonder that when he went to war the Kuban Cossack tied a little sack of black Kuban earth around his neck. He wore it next to his skin like a charm. When he fell in battle and was laid to rest, the first handful of earth that covered his body came out of the little sack.

CHAPTER XIII

"The Gift of Catherine"

IN AUGUST 1944 the Kuban had already been liberated from the German-Rumanian occupation for a year and a half. The front had moved so far west and north that no echo of gunfire was heard. Save for a blackout more dense than Moscow's, Krasnodar had lost all aspect of siege, of military bustle, and, outwardly, of military vigilance. There were few soldiers in the street. Civilians again dominated the scene. Robust girls directed traffic and did most of the policing.

The Kuban's capital was at peace. The sun was hot and white, whiter than it ever gets in Moscow; the young, thickly foliaged trees with their sweeping umbrella-shaped tops, trimmed low to keep them from touching the electric wires overhead, were a refreshing sight. As I talked to the people of Krasnodar, I was impressed with their love of the city. Their speech rang with phrases like "our beloved Krasnodar," "our valorous Krasnodar," "our glorious Krasnodar," "our beautiful Krasnodar." The trials they had suffered during the German occupation had stirred new depths of emotion and a new devotion to their city. They had almost lost it! They had seen much of it go up in fire and smoke, blood and death. Now the knowledge that it was theirs again—this Krasnodar where they were born and grew up, where they had studied and worked, loved happily and unhappily, suffered defeat and triumph—invested it with a new halo and a new sanctity.

Yet the rise of Krasnodar to eminence was slow and in pre-Soviet days singularly undramatic. The first party of Cossacks arrived there on June 6, 1773. The place was a wilderness of marsh and oak forest, rank grass and thick brush. There was no human habitation; no settler had yet penetrated its rich blacklands. Hardy men inured to action and strife, seasoned to pioneering in wild, uninhabited country, the Cossacks proceeded to cut the timber and erect forty *kureni*—regimental barracks. They built a Cossack community dedicated to military exploits. The architecture of the *kureni* and the community's way of life were patterned after those of the Zaporog *setch* from which the men had originally come. As in the *setch*, the community in its beginning was exclusively masculine.

But some of them had families, and the families and outsiders settled in the northern part of the wilderness. Until the 1860s a span of ground about a hundred steps wide separated the new settlement from the gates of the military community. The population grew slowly. The place was remote, inaccessible. The people of the North knew nothing of it or the promise it held for the pioneer. In 1796 it had only 1,685 inhabitants. Only in the 1850s did the figure rise to 10,000. A primitive, isolated, self-sufficient outpost of civilization, with scarcely a hint of cultural advance, such was the original city for several generations, with mud and swamp, wood and wild vegetation all around, and with not a single brick or stone house. The very structure of the city

Cossack girl in battle

Cossack girls specializing in surgery in the Krasnodar Medical School

Cossack father and daughter loading wheat they earned on collective farm

emphasized Cossack indifference to new ideas of housing and Cossack love of primitiveness.

Yet it was the beginning of a new city and the administrative center of all the Cossacks along the far-flung Black Sea territory. It was the capital and chief stronghold of a luxuriant, undeveloped country. On the Cossack living here devolved the task of taming the mountaineers and the other rebellious, bellicose natives, whose Mohammedanism alone made them fiercely hostile to Russian rule and Christian neighbors. War was continuous —incessant and sanguinary guerrilla campaigns.

In 1867 the military community became a city named *Ekaterinodar—*"The Gift of Catherine," in honor of the Czarina in whose reign it was founded. The city was never a fit abode for the Cossack. It stifled his manner, corrupted his discipline, shrank his expansiveness. Unless he was willing to forswear his Cossackhood—which some of them did—and be degraded to the rank of burgher or trader, he must forsake the city and flee to the *stanitsa*, where alone he could be his full unbridled self. So the Kuban became dotted with villages, all alike in style and architecture, with the traditional broad streets and spacious square for the practice of war games and with trees around the houses.

"The Gift of Catherine." remained the administrative headquarters of the Cossack armies. Its geography and sheltered position made that inevitable. After the first railroad was built in 1888, outsiders in ever growing numbers flocked there. But except for officials, the Cossacks were gone. Commerce and industry gave the town a new visage and a new spirit.

With the advent of the Soviet Five-year Plans, the city boomed. In 1917 its population was 106,700; in the 1930s it was almost double that figure. The development followed the usual Soviet pattern, along two main lines—industrial and cultural. Huge chimney stacks towered to the skies. Factory after factory, though not on as grandiose a scale as in Tula or Stalingrad, rose above the one- and two-story homes. Cultural institutions sprang up as swiftly as new buildings could be constructed and new staffs recruited to man them, sometimes swifter. The city boasted two museums, a drama theater, a musical-comedy theater, a symphony orchestra, a vaudeville stage, a summer theater, motion-picture halls, an immense outdoor dance pavilion, sixteen higher, specialized colleges, six scientific institutes, four experimental stations, numerous trade and technical schools, and a large network of elementary and high schools. New buildings mingled with the old—hotels, schools, offices, residences, and of course factories, standing beside ancient hovels.

Under the driving energy of the Plans, Krasnodar streets were broadened, cobbles were coated with asphalt. A new power station loomed up. Rows of trees were planted; they grew so lush with limbs and leaves that on some streets they formed a low-hung canopy which shut out sun in summer and wind in winter.

Once only a Cossack village and fortress in the forest, Krasnodar was now a tumultuous city with all the cultural and industrial attributes of a Soviet metropolis. An outsider learning its history, once slow and placid, then swift and turbulent, could appreciate adjectives like "beloved," "valorous," "glorious," with which the natives speak of it. But it is not a beautiful city and never was, though with the Kuban River near by and the haze of wooded mountain in the distance, it abounds in bits of scenic splendor, more outside than within the city limits.

But neither czarist nor Soviet architecture or city planning have lent it artistic distinction. Nowhere is there a hint of the grandeur of prewar Leningrad, Odessa, Kiev, Russia's most distinguished and most modern cities. Excepting a few private dwellings such as the Italian-style residence of the czarist Cossack ataman which I saw on my previous visit, but which is no more, having been blown up by the Germans, the city grew—as did all provincial Russian cities in the old days, as did Moscow itself—in helter-skelter fashion; and today a bleak primitiveness casts its shadow over streets and buildings. Under the Soviets, with the feverish rush to enthrone the modern machine and to lift quickly the cultural level of the people, there was neither time nor talent to elevate architecture or city planning to an art comparable to that of the Western world.

If Krasnodar was no city beautiful in the prewar years, the city I now saw devastated by war presented a melancholy spectacle. Sidewalks were battered, pavements torn. The old one-story homes, the ones the Germans had spared, though not all of them, were falling apart with age and rust and dilapidation. None of the once towering new buildings remained to remind the visitors of the feverish boom during the Five-year Plans. The achievements of the Plans lay in ashes and rust and rubble. It was as though an evil spirit had deliberately blown them to pieces and reduced to mockery the sweat and blood, the struggle and hope which had gone into their erection and the growth of Krasnodar. The drama theater, the Pioneer Home, the bank, the Teachers' Institute, the medical and other colleges, the public schools, the public offices were mountains of debris or shattered walls. So, too, was the once tall and teeming department store, into which, as one of its former clerks said, a citizen could enter only in trunks and come out dressed from head to foot in work clothes or holiday attire. Everything was shattered brick and twisted steel, or mere shells without windows or doors, with no partitions or floors, with everything gutted, burned, or blown up. This was the first liberated Russian city in which I could browse around at will and at leisure, and here more than Sebastopol, Kharkov, I saw at every turn the deliberate, scientifically planned devastation of an entire era of history—the era of the machine age, old and new, and all the power and promise that it signalized.

There was no hotel in Krasnodar, and I stayed in a private home, one of the solidest and most comfortable one-story brick houses in the city, with shade trees in front, a water pump, a flower garden, fruit trees in the courtyard. My hostess was a woman in her early forties. She was dark-haired, dark-eyed, with broad features and a light complexion. Her husband, a colonel in the Red Army, was at the front, and she shared the house with her sister and an old mother. A woman of culture and refinement, she talked with the simplicity and frankness typical of Russian speech. She was a native of the Kuban, she said, and had spent all her life there. She had never visited Moscow, Leningrad, or Kiev.

"I am only a provincial woman," she said, "and I hope you will excuse the simplicity of my house and the lack of comfort."

Yet the furniture and furnishings in the parlor where I slept were superior to anything I had seen in any of the Moscow hotels. I was especially impressed with the glassware, silverware, rugs, mirrors—all ancient family heirlooms—the shelves of books, Russian and foreign classics, Soviet college textbooks. There was even a small bottle of perfume on the mantelpiece. I did not expect to see such a home in a city that had suffered such cruel devastation.

"The Germans," I said, "must have treated you exceptionally well."

"Do you suppose," she replied, "they saw any of these things? Of course not. If they had, this would be an empty room. We buried everything deep in the ground and covered the furniture with withered sacks and made it look old and ugly." Her story of how she saved her home and all that it held told much of Russian shrewdness and of German obtuseness.

I asked how many Germans lived in her house, and she said none. Reading surprise in my expression, she laughed and explained, "We fought the Germans and Rumanians with cunning. We had to, because they had all the power. How did we do it? Well, the first thing we learned was that Germans hated the Rumanians only a little more than the Rumanians hated them. We never saw them walking together or sitting at the same table in restaurants. We saw them quarrel and fight. The Rumanians kept telling us that if it wasn't for them, the Gestapo would have killed us all. The Germans assured us if it was not for them the Rumanians would have slaughtered all of us. This gave me plenty of ideas on how to act. I played in my own way on this mutual enmity of the Axis partners. When a German came to my door and asked for a room, I said, 'Two Rumanians are already living here!' He would immediately turn up his nose and walk away. When a Rumanian came and asked for a room, I said, 'A German officer is living here.' He would immediately turn up his nose and walk away. If they had stopped to investigate, it would have been too bad for me. I mightn't have been alive now. But I took my chances."

Neither she nor her sister nor her mother worked for the Germans. They resolved from the first day of the occupation that they would keep to themselves. The less attention they attracted, the better were the chances not only of survival but of saving their home and all the household possessions they had hidden and camouflaged. They would not be seen coming in and out of the house any more than necessary. They would not call on neighbors or visit friends. The less they were seen, the less they would be thought about by the enemy. They did not mind forgoing the meager bread ration which the Germans allowed those who worked for them.

"How did you live?" I asked.

"We sold clothes—our own, my husband's—and bought wheat or corn. We soaked the wheat in water for three days. Then we ran it through a meat cutter and fried the mush into griddle cakes. We did the same with the corn. . . . It is the fried mush of wheat and corn that kept us alive."

Her face became grave.

"I'm lucky they never learned my husband is a Red Army colonel. If they had, I would not have been here now. That's another reason I kept out of sight. Fortunately for me, no neighbor denounced me. And would you believe it? The Gestapo was only a few steps away—right around the corner! I saw a lot of Gestapo men coming and going with the people they marched under guard into their building. I shuddered when I saw these people. I knew they were going to their death. Once I saw a friend of mine go by, a Jewish physician. Her name was Dr. Klashnikova. She was very popular in the city. Two of her patients, Gentile women, volunteered to go along and testify she was innocent of any wrong and that there was no reason for arresting her. Neither the doctor nor her friends have since been seen."

Every evening when I came back from walks or interviews we sat in the parlor and talked. We often talked about America, always a topic of unending interest to the untraveled Russians, especially in the provinces. But no matter what we started talking about, my hostess would invariably revert to her experiences under the occupation. The memory haunted her:

"I never, never imagined I'd know what it means to be alive and yet in the shadow of death. There was so much death all around, and always the question kept hammering through my mind: 'Is it your turn next? Will you be alive this time tomorrow?'"

To live under lock and key with curtains drawn over the windows, to live alone, away from friends, and as little as possible in touch with the outside—that was their one purpose in life. They were like hibernating animals bent solely on physical survival. What few warm garments they had, they wore by turns. Many families in the city did the same. No one dared wear presentable clothes—no one except the collaborators and the loose girls who accepted chocolates from enemy officers, walked and danced with them, slept with them. There were such girls in Krasnodar, and the Rumanians and Germans vied with one another in winning them. They had gifts for these girls—chocolate, perfume, bracelets, wrist watches, silks. They flattered these girls, bowed to them, saluted them, got down on their knees before them, trying to make themselves appear romantic, the Rumanians more than the Germans.

"But here am I," my hostess said one evening. "I am no longer young. I am a middle-aged woman, and often it was agony for me to get even a pail of water. They shut off the city supply, and only at certain hours in certain places could we draw water from outdoor taps. A German soldier was always at the tap. The young girls he let fill their pails at once. It made no difference how late they came and whether they were in the middle or at the end of the queue. The soldier beckoned to them, helped them fit the pail over or under the tap. . . . If there were no young girls around, he often shut off the water and yelled: 'Go home, you old hags.' Pleading was no good. A woman like me had to stand and wait and boil with rage and eat her heart out and yet be silent. Once an old woman started weeping and said, 'There's a sick child in my family. I must have water immediately, please, mister.' The soldier made no answer, sat there lighting a cigarette, and kept the tap shut. 'Please, mister,' she begged. He got so mad he chased her to the end of the queue. She cried and cried, and when he finished his cigarette he opened the tap but would not let her fill her pail until the very end. They were always doing mean little things like that to torment us older women—they always played up to the young girls."

From other residents of the city I learned that the hunt for young girls—girls of high-school age, fifteen, sixteen, or seventeen—was an obsession with the German and Rumanian officers. The gifts they had for these girls were loot they had seized in France, Poland, Holland, Belgium, and other countries. "They had the phonographs and records of nearly all our Kuban," said a mother. "And some girls . . . are just girls, female animals. There were no Russian young men around, so they took up with enemy officers. Some of them are still going to venereal clinics."

The Germans posted announcements all along the main avenues and squares that Russian war prisoners, many of them natives of Krasnodar, would parade along the main street. They invited the people to come out and welcome them. The response was overwhelming. Women and children poured out in the hope of recognizing a father, husband, son, or brother. They brought parcels of food to give to the prisoners. They waited and waited, but there was no parade. Suddenly Germans began to mingle with the crowd. They were friendly and talkative. Russians wondered what it meant—Germans actually smiling at them, waving, like old, devoted friends. Germans had never been like that before.

Finally a procession of German Red Cross cars rolled along the avenue. In the front seats next to the chauffeurs sat German soldiers with bandaged heads. In the rear seats were more German soldiers with bandaged heads. No one in Krasnodar had ever seen so many men with bandaged heads. The cars drove back and forth, around and around, always with the same passengers, all except the chauffeurs had bandaged heads. The Germans among the crowds became more and more talkative and friendly. Then Russians saw on the roofs of houses near by German cameramen grinding motion-picture cameras. They were filming the parade and the crowds, showing the apparent peace and friendliness between Germans in uniform and Russian civilians. Now the Russians understood what it meant. The Germans were taking documentary films intended to show that the Russian civilian population was bringing gifts for wounded German soldiers, though they didn't understand why all were "wounded" in the head, not a single one of them with a bandage on any other part of the body. The Russians went home bitterly cursing the German deception.

A second time the Germans announced a parade of Russian war prisoners. Again people came. Perhaps this time the Germans would live up to their promises. Again people brought little parcels of food. Again children kept asking their mothers: "Why isn't Papa coming?" or "Will he be here soon? Will you let me give him the parcel, Mamma?" Again they were deceived. . . . They went home more and more incensed than before.

A third time the Germans posted announcements of a procession of Russian war prisoners. Krasnodar was important to them. It was the capital of the Kuban Cossacks. They needed these films to show in the Kuban villages, the villages of the Don and other conquered territory, and to the people in Germany. They could not have enough of such films to boost morale at home and break down morale in occupied countries. . . . Cossacks welcoming wounded Germans with parcels of food—Cossacks, symbols of Russian patriotism and Russian fighting valor.

But this time the deception worked no longer. From one end

of Krasnodar to the other the word was passed instructing citizens to boycott the procession. No one came out.

The Germans were enraged. They posted more placards announcing another parade and still another. But the boycott was firm. The streets and parks were empty. The people of Krasnodar remained at home.

On February 2, 1943, at eight in the morning, a Russian physician said good-by to his wife and left for his day's work. An hour later his wife started for the market place to buy food. Approaching a telephone pole, she was startled to see a body hanging from it. She recognized the body. It was her husband. She burst into tears and begged passers-by to help her take down the body. No one dared help her. All around were Germans and their collaborators with tommy guns.

She ran home and returned with her sister. The two women wanted to take down the body for burial. The Germans shouted, "Verboten!" The body hung there for two days. The two women cried and pleaded. The Germans glowered and shouted, "Verboten!" They refused to tell why they had hanged the doctor. They just hanged him. The reason was obvious. The Red Army was drawing close, but they were still masters of Krasnodar, and they wanted the Russians to know it.

Finally they allowed the wife and her sister to take down the body. They offered no help, and with the armed police near by, passers-by were too scared to help. So the wife and her sister climbed the telephone pole on a ladder, cut the rope, loaded the body into a cart, took it to the cemetery and buried it.

News secretly swept the city that the Red Army was about twenty miles from Krasnodar. People started whispering. They were hopeful. Deliverance only twenty miles away! If only the Red Army would hurry! More and more Germans were leaving. The Rumanians had already left. The Germans did not want them any more in Krasnodar. The Germans started blowing up and burning the big buildings.

More and more Russians were hanged. Their bodies dangled from trees and telephone poles. No one was permitted to take them down. In the market place people who came to sell or buy food were roped off and ordered to stay in their places. Those who did not run were loaded into trucks and hauled away. They have not been heard of since.

The city was in flames. Germans were burning their own supplies. Food, clothes, footwear, bedding were piled into stacks in courtyards and in the streets and set afire. German cars drove up to storehouses. Officers, including generals, stepped out, helped themselves to new uniforms, rolled the old ones together, flung them into the burning pyre, and resumed the journey into their rear.

The city grew redder and redder with flame, blacker and blacker with smoke, louder and louder with explosions. Russian houses were burning. German automobiles were burning. Germans blew up the Gestapo building. The basement was jammed with Russians. Not one Russian remained alive.

My hostess, her mother and sister were frightened. They locked all doors, darkened all windows, tied up bundles of food, and waited in the cellar. They did not dare to sleep. A bomb might be hurled into the house. A mine might be planted under it. They might be blown to pieces. They might be asphyxiated. They might burn to death. They did not know what was happening in the city. They dared not come out to learn. Hours passed. Night came. Explosions thundered, the earth rocked. It was a night of fire and horror. The world seemed falling to pieces.

Morning came. There was a knock at the door. None of the women would open it. They were too frightened. The knock was repeated over and over, louder and louder. My hostess tiptoed over to the door and whispered feebly, as though she were too ill to speak:

"Who is it?"

"Open up," came a neighbor's triumphant voice, "the Red Army is here!"

"If you had your way about it, what would you do with the Germans?" I said to my hostess.

She thought a moment and answered:

"I don't know. I am not a diplomat. I don't want to think about it. I know only one thing—I never want to see Germans again. Never!"

Water
Light
Bread
Health
Transportation
Schools
Theater
Movies

This is the order in which Krasnodar proceeded to rehabilitate itself as soon as it was liberated. Party workers, government officials, if they survived guerrilla warfare and were released by the Red Army for civilian pursuits, came back on the heels of the Army and started rehabilitation. Sleznev, Party secretary of Krasnodar, who was in command of all Kuban guerrilla fighting, was at his desk while the city still burned. The engineer Litvinov, now mayor of the city, was also back. So was Robakov, the assistant mayor. College professors, scientists, factory managers, physicians, engineers returned in rapid succession.

There was no time for rest, for talk, not even for grief. There was no time for debating and dreaming, for personal living and personal enjoyment. There was time only for work. Nothing else mattered, nothing else was of any consequence. Work builds and heals, cheers and elevates. Work purges man of sorrow and pain, enriches and sanctifies life. Work above all!—above civil liberties, above any and all rights of man, above any and all values in life, for without work nothing happens, even as without sun nothing grows. Such is and has been Soviet gospel and Soviet goal. Kursk, Oryol, Kiev, Minsk, Leningrad, Odessa, Stalingrad, Krasnodar, in all these cities, as in the most faraway hamlet as soon as it is liberated, work transcends all personal desire, all individual aim, all the havoc and horror anyone may have been facing.

Moscow diplomacy may be in the midst of one stormy crisis after another. Power politics in Russia lives its own life, fights its own way. The rest of the country, except when war threatens, remains unshaken and unruffled. It toils and toils. Never is a plan in process of realization but a new one is already in process of formation. There is no letup on work. No one is exempt from his or her part in the consummation of a plan, especially now when there is so much ruin to be restored. Physical incapacity is the only excuse that counts, and woe to the man or woman who gives the least heed to the ancient Russian saying: "Work is no wolf, it will not run off to the woods."

Yet there are moments when even the busiest man pauses for contemplation. "On my return to my apartment," said Robakov, the assistant mayor, "I found a letter from my son. Miraculously it had escaped detection and destruction during the German occupation. My son was sixteen when the war broke out. I was so overjoyed to see the letter that my hands shook when I opened it:

" 'Father! I've gone off to fight. When you were my age, you did the same. I can do no less. I'm sure you understand.' Of course I understood. But a son is a son, and he was only sixteen."

I went to the Medical Institute in the heart of the city. During the occupation it had been evacuated to Tumen, Siberia. It came back to Krasnodar at the end of 1943. The huge solid brick building rambling over two blocks was in ruins. The Germans mined it and set it afire a few days before they retreated. Inside it was a mass of broken brick, twisted steel, rain-soaked plaster. All the floors were burned. All doors and windows were gone. Weeds crept out of the heaps of debris. Birds made their nests inside the large cracks of the thick brick walls. Unafraid of man, they flitted in and out, flocks of them, filling the vast desolate emptiness with merry chirping. Nothing remained of the laboratories, the classrooms, the equipment that was left behind when the college had rushed off to Siberia.

"Where do you hold your classes?" I asked Daniel Kalinko, the stocky, mild-mannered director of the college. He is a native of the Kuban, from the Cossack village of Novo-Selchevskaya, and like his wife he is a practicing physician, a specialist in gynecology.

"I'll show you," he said.

He led the way down a dimly lighted stairway into a cellar. Following a dark, narrow, circuitous hallway, we came to a door. The director knocked, but there was no reply. He opened it and entered a small, low room with two windows which rose out of the earth on the outside, filtering scanty light inside. It made me think of the cellar on the New York farm where I was once a hired man and in which we stored away for the winter beehives, barrels of cider, squash, pumpkins, and apples. It was spacious but no better lighted than the cellar on the farm, but it was cleanly swept and furnished with benches, chairs, a desk, a wood stove with a pipe running along the ceiling and through a hole in the thick wall to the street. In the corner, out of a mass of shadows, loomed a white human skeleton.

"This is where we study," said the director.

The other classrooms were as cavernous and dingy. When students and professors returned from their enforced exile in faraway Siberia and saw the broken walls, the heaps of rubble covered with weeds, the rain-packed stacks of ashes and charcoal into which the college had been reduced, they were angry and grief-stricken and cursed the Germans, and some of them wept with wrath and despair.

"But we did not yield to despair," said the director. "Despair never builds anything, and we are a nation of builders. There was no labor available for cleaning up the cellar and other undercover space for classrooms and laboratories. So we got together, students and professors, took up shovels and spades, picks and hammers, and went to work. Day and night we labored until we cleared up the cellar and some of the smaller buildings on the campus. We had no furniture—the Germans had burned or stolen everything we had left behind—so we searched around and with the help of our trade unions and the Soviets we rounded up benches, chairs, tables—and started our studies. . . . Science cannot wait—least of all medicine—and we're doing the best we can."

The campus was overgrown with weeds and brush; a fitful breeze was stirring up little clouds of dust. Girls, now and then a man, on a crutch or limping, obviously a war veteran, were walking, standing around, or sitting on the grass in the shade of a tree, with textbooks or notebooks in their laps, writing and talking. These were study groups. They were doing assigned lessons in groups. There were not enough textbooks for individual study.

The girls looked quite young, in their late teens or early twenties. Most of them were dressed in white, with a ribbon or a flower in the hair. They were all barelegged and bareheaded, and without any trace of make-up.

There were eleven hundred students in the college, two thirds of them Cossack girls. I could not help thinking how far was the road the Cossack woman has traversed through the centuries since the days of Taras Bulba and the Dnieper republic. Here were Cossack girls by the hundreds studying medicine, whereas in the old days, even in the immediate pre-Soviet era, few Cossack girls thought of college. What was even more astounding, every other girl I talked to wanted to be a surgeon. I know of no other girls in Russia for whom surgery holds such an overpowering lure as for the Cossack girls.

"Why do you want to be a surgeon?" I asked a blue-eyed girl with shimmering, wind-blown light hair.

"Why can't a girl manipulate a scalpel like a man?" was her reply.

Behind her words lay Cossack history and Cossack culture.

Physically and emotionally these girls, because of their superb heritage, are well equipped for their chosen profession. They are alert and energetic. There is an ease and a grace about their movements that is pleasant to behold. Though none of them would deem slenderness a virtue or would think of cultivating it, they resemble the American girl more than any others I had seen in Russia. They are gay, witty, magnificently self-possessed. They are never lost for a retort whether gentle, sly, or capriciously good-humored.

Besides, living in an environment permeated with a traditional warrior spirit, hearing tales of the Cossack's fighting past, watching or participating in *dzhigitovkas*—horse races and war games—they do not shiver at the sight of wounds or blood. Also, from their fathers and mothers they acquire a special reverence for the very word "surgeon." In his day the Cossack has known magicians and miracle workers and witch doctors. In the Kuban there were no physicians until 1803, when the first medically educated practitioner made his appearance there. Until that year and for some time afterward, not barbers, as in other parts of the world, but cooks tended the sick. They treated wounds with ointments extracted from herbs and plants. Broken bits of bone they hunted out with a horsehair. When gangrene or *Anton fire*, as they spoke of it, formed, they cut it off with an ordinary kitchen knife. Anesthetics were unknown. If the patient proved unruly, friends stood at his head, beat drums and sang songs to distract his attention from the manipulations of the cook.

But as more and more physicians came, the cooks went back to the kitchens and stayed there. Now when a Cossack fell off a horse, broke an arm, a leg, a shoulder, a rib, or mangled his limbs, the surgeon tended him, set his bones, sewed up his wounds, restored his health. With the years the prestige of the surgeon mounted higher and higher. He was the miracle man, the hero of the village. The veneration of the surgeon has not vanished. Hence one more reason for the popularity of surgery among Cossack girls.

Here is a singular example of the fusion of tradition and

science, of custom and revolution, of past and present, which underlies so much of the new Cossack culture and the new Cossack life in the Kuban.

The city seethed with life. After work hours crowds promenaded the streets, the parks, the boulevards. Hungry for entertainment, they flocked to the motion-picture halls, the band concerts, the immense outdoor dance pavilion, the lone theater in the city. The theater building was blown up, and the company of professional actors gave performances in a back-yard hall that had been used by amateur theatrical and singing societies.

The lighting was incredibly poor. The seats were hard and squeaky benches. The stage was small, the equipment old-fashioned. The play, *Davnym Davno* (Long, Long Ago) is one of the duller offerings in the repertoire of the Russian theater. Yet not a seat was vacant, and there were several rows of standees in the rear. Though the performance lasted four hours, not a soul left, and in between acts the audience poured into the open and refreshed itself with soft drinks, ice cream, and the choicest apples and pears I had seen in Russia. Few men were in the audience, and as I watched the women promenade around, I observed only a few of them smoking. All over Russia, but especially in the provinces, smoking is losing its lure for women.

The acting of the company was spirited, the costumes were rich in fashion and in color. There were moments when the dialogue sparkled with wit, and the audience responded with loud and spontaneous laughter. No actors could wish for a more responsive or a more appreciative audience. Watching this audience, hearing it laugh and applaud, and remembering the city in which they lived, the woe and privation they had endured, were still enduring, I could not help marveling at the vitality and the sheer lust for living in the Russian of today.

CHAPTER XIV

The Man Who Was Dead

Two of the most interesting men I met in Krasnodar were Ivan Ivanovitch Kotov, a former superintendent of housing, and Pyotr Karpovitch Ignatov, a retired college president. I shall tell their stories, as they related them to me, in separate chapters.

Ivan Ivanovitch Kotov is the only man in Russia, in all territory the Germans had held, who had been flung into a *dushegubka*—murder van or gas wagon—and has survived the ordeal. That is why the people in the city speak of him as "the man who was dead."

The Germans started using the new weapon in the autumn of 1942, shortly after they occupied Krasnodar. People saw the van moving about the city, but for some time they did not know what it was. It looked innocent enough. It might have been a huge gray van with refrigerating equipment for transporting food or drugs that needed to be kept at freezing temperature. But soon the people learned the real purpose it served and shuddered at its sight.

The van was a five- or seven-ton truck equipped with a Diesel engine. Inside it had neither seats nor windows. It had only one door in the rear, a double door. In the floor was a grating, under it a pipe attached to the exhaust tube of the engine. As soon as the engine started, concentrated carbon-dioxide gas was transmitted through the pipe to the grating and to the interior of the car. When the door was slammed the car was hermetically sealed. The gas had no avenue of escape. It grew thicker and thicker. The people inside were asphyxiated.

Anyone who had been inside such an execution chamber and remained alive had an extraordinary story. He was as if resurrected from the dead. So when I learned that Ivan Ivanovitch Kotov was in Krasnodar I set out to find him. He was not easy to locate. He avoided people. He did not like to talk. He wanted to be left alone.

With the aid of Robakov, I finally found him. He was fifty years old but looked younger. He was of medium height, stocky, with an oval face and large dark eyes. The only unhealthy feature about him was his puffy red cheeks. They were very puffy, as though ready to burst, and very red. The moment I began speaking to him I realized he was a sick man. I asked him a question. He did not answer at once, but stared at me with blank, wide-open eyes, as though in wonder at what I had said or wondering what I wanted of him. I had to repeat my questions over and over. Then he would say a few words and suddenly stop. He seemed unable to finish a sentence, as though something inside of him automatically cut off his power of speech. After a long pause he would repeat the few words he had spoken, shake his head, fidget around with his broad, thick-fingered hands, slap his lofty forehead as though in disgust with himself, and blurt out:

"It's no use—no use."

"What's no use?" I would ask.

After a protracted pause he would look at me, stammer, then gurgle like a child that was just beginning to speak and say:

"I cannot talk. I don't remember."

After another lengthy pause his face would light up, he would lift his hand in an expressive gesture and gulp out the sentence he had originally begun. It was obvious that his powers of speech, thought, and memory were seriously impaired. During the first hour of our conversation I managed to wring out of him no more than about a hundred words.

"I never was like that," he burst out in the one somewhat connected sentence he uttered in the course of the entire interview. "I was a bookkeeper—a wood turner—my wife is dead—

my son and daughter are in the Red Army—in Krasnodar people knew me—I had friends—I was superintendent of housing—doctors can do nothing for me—it's no use."

"What's no use? Why do you talk like that?" I said.

He rested his forehead in his hands and remained silent. He looked bored and lost to the world.

It took no end of questioning and of coaxing to obtain from him the story of his experiences inside the *dushegubka*.

Late one afternoon he went to a city hospital where he had had medical treatment to obtain a clearance certificate. The doctor was busy, and he waited for two hours before the certificate was handed to him. When he walked out of the hospital it was already twilight. In the yard he saw a huge gray van, and men and women in pajamas were being loaded inside. He wondered what was happening, and as he was passing by a German officer seized him by the coat collar and without saying a word flung him inside through the open double door in the rear. The car was already jammed with people—men, women, two or three children. They were so tightly packed they could not move. They shrieked, wailed, cried. The Germans paid no attention to them. Six or seven more persons were pushed inside. Then the heavy door slammed and Kotov found himself locked in the van.

The engine started to hum. The car began to move. Suddenly he felt a choking sensation and realized he was being gassed. He thought fast and acted promptly. He had fought in the first World War and knew something about gas warfare. As superintendent of housing in Krasnodar, he had attended lectures on the subject of protecting oneself from a gas attack. He knew that the first thing to do in the emergency was to moisten a cloth in water and quickly apply it to the nose and mouth. But there was no water in the murder van. There was nothing there but a crowd of people screaming wildly and streams of gas pouring out of the rough grating in the floor. Swiftly he pulled out his shirt, wet it with his urine, pressed it close to the nose and the mouth. Then he lost consciousness.

When he awoke he found himself lying in an antitank ditch in a field. All around were corpses, some covered with a thin layer of earth, others unburied. He did not remember how long he had been in the van or how long he had lain in the ditch. Soon he realized what had happened to him. He looked around to see if anyone was near. Seeing no one, he clambered to his feet. He was shaky and groggy, his head was bursting with pain. Through fields and bushes he staggered and groped his way to Krasnodar.

The Germans were still in the city. Fearing a repetition of the experience which might not end so fortunately, he remained in hiding until the city was liberated.

He had been under treatment by eminent psychiatrists and neurologists. But his case seemed hopeless.

"No one can do anything for me—it's no use—I'm no good any more," were the last words I heard him say.

CHAPTER XV

The College President and His Sons

BEFORE THE WAR, Pyotr Karpovitch Ignatov was a college president. He directed the education of six hundred students in a newly opened school which trained experts for the food industry. Only one third of the students were men; the others were women. Most of the graduates went to work in Siberia, where the rich fishing waters in the rivers, lakes, gulfs, and seas started a boom in fishing canneries. Pyotr Karpovitch kept up a correspondence with his students and continued to be their friend and counselor in their work and in their private lives. The challenge, the difficulties, the adventures incident to pioneering in a new field of education kept the schoolmaster busy and happy.

He is now fifty years old; he looks older but acts younger. He is alert, with a chivalric manner, a gracious smile, a boyish undertone in his rapid-fire style of speech. He speaks so quickly it is often difficult to understand him. He is tall, lean, broadboned, with light brown hair, gray eyes, and a sharp face. In his demeanor he seems the soul of meekness and proverbial Russian simplicity. Hearing him talk, laugh—he loves to laugh—watching him bow his way in or out of a room, one would never imagine he had ever shouldered a gun, killed anyone, or plotted and commanded the audacious guerrilla raids with which his name is associated not only in the Kuban but all over Russia.

Yelena Ivanovna, his wife, is two years younger than he. They fell in love soon after they met many years ago in old St. Petersburg. She is a pale-faced handsome woman with dark wide-open, contemplative eyes. Neither the privations she has known nor the tragedies she has suffered have silvered her dark wavy hair or lined her brow. Only the shadows under her eyes give her face a careworn expression. In contrast to her husband, she speaks in a low, deliberate voice, sometimes pausing long for reflection. In her youth she studied medicine and practiced the profession in Krasnodar, devoting herself to work in the Mother and Child Institute.

We were sitting in the enclosed porch of the Ignatov home in Krasnodar. The glass in the windows was largely gone, smashed or stolen during the German occupation. There was no new glass as yet to replace it. Insects buzzed in and out of the porch, circled about the bright lights and fell to the floor. A warm breeze rustled the tall trees that shadowed the porch. Crickets chirped. It was an evening of quiet, of warmth, with a full moon, "strong air" as Cossacks say, meaning rich in the aroma of flowers, ripening fruit, and green vegetation. It was an evening for play, gaiety, camaraderie. Yet the tale the college president told was one of the saddest and most heroic I had heard in Russia.

In November 1941 Rostov fell for the first time. Rostov,

capital of the Don Cossacks, is the gateway to Krasnodar and the Kuban. On hearing of the city's fall, the college president said to his wife:

"It's about time, my dear, we took to our guns again."

Yelena Ivanovna made no reply, and her husband knew she shared his thoughts. Under the Czar, soon after they became acquainted, they had worked together in an underground society in the former capital of Russia. When gendarmes seized him, exiled him to faraway, ancient Nevyansk on the Nevya River in the Urals, she followed. When revolution swept Russia and civil war rocked the land, they fought together in the same guerrilla detachment, she as Red Cross nurse, he as scout, gunner, anything that was demanded of him. Peace came, and they completed their education, settled in Krasnodar, he as an engineer, she as a medical officer.

They had three children, all sons. Valentin, the oldest, was an engineer. Yevgeny or Zhenya, the next, was also an engineer. Genandy, the youngest, was a junior in high school. Like their father, all the sons had a passion for mechanics. At the age of ten the youngest had learned to drive a car. He loved to prowl around garages and often came home with his hands and clothes soiled with dust and grease.

In November 1941 Genandy was sixteen. He was spending much time among tanks and tankmen outside the city. He was the most joy-loving member of the family and one of the more popular boys in his school and in the city.

The catastrophe that came to Russia shook the Ignatovs. Pyotr Karpovitch and his wife were not young any more. But when Rostov fell his mind was made up. So was Yelena Ivanovna's. They would not seek security in evacuation in faraway Siberia or Central Asia. They would fight. That evening when the fall of Rostov was announced and he said they must take again to their guns, their son Yevgeny made a sudden call. He brought the father exciting news. At the giant margarine factory in which he was an executive, the intelligentsia had formed a guerrilla squad. He, Yevgeny, was chosen chief of staff, and unanimously the members decided to invite the college president to be their commander in chief. Without a moment's hesitation Pyotr Karpovitch accepted; his wife said she would go along and be the surgeon of the outfit. Immediately they decided that his assumed name would be Batya and that the men who were to go with him would be known as Batya's guerrillas.

August 8, 1942, while Krasnodar was in flames and the Germans were pouring into the city, Ignatov's detachment moved into the mountains and built its camp in a well-sheltered gorge. Excepting the oldest son, Valentin, who was already in the regular Red Army, the entire Ignatov family was in the camp.

In all Russia there was no guerrilla squad like the one led by the college president. It was made up of university graduates—college presidents, factory directors, engineers, economists, chemists, and other specialists. The number was limited to fifty, all carefully chosen, many of them direct descendants of the famed Zaporog Cossacks who had conquered and settled the Kuban. The background of these men made it inevitable that they should prepare themselves scientifically for their tasks, anticipating all possible situations and developing adequate means to meet them. "We left nothing to chance or accident," said the college professor.

Before they went into the mountains, they had undergone assiduous and many-sided training. They learned to grunt like boars, croak like frogs, chirp like jay birds, crackle like cicadas. When on scouting or raiding expeditions they would communicate with one another as do Cossack *plastuns*, by means of these bird and animal sounds.

They learned special trades. Litvinov, today mayor of Krasnodar, became a driver of oxen. The director of the nationally known margarine factory learned shoemaking so that he could mend shoes and harnesses. A well-known engineer became a blacksmith so that he could repair guns and tools. Other men of science and education learned other trades—carpentering, bricklaying, road building.

While still in Krasnodar they had also mastered firearms—the tommy gun, the shotgun, the machine gun, the hand grenade. Yelena Ivanovna was no exception. She too became a sniper, a machine-gunner, a grenade thrower. All could ride horses; all learned to build fires without attracting enemy attention; all knew how to climb mountains, orient themselves in the most faraway passes and in the heaviest forest, identify tracks on the ground, however faint, of animals and men. All could crawl or creep on their bellies in traditional Kuban Cossack fashion—*po plastunski*—"as noiselessly and invisibly as a snake." All knew something about make-up, so they could skillfully disguise themselves, make their way through heavily guarded German positions and fulfill trusted missions in villages or towns. All were prepared for hunger and cold, danger and death.

Though qualified for any action that would hurt the enemy, this detachment specialized in mine laying and blowing up bridges, power stations, storehouses, railroads, tanks, other motor transport—anything. It did more. It opened a school deep in the enemy's rear for training guerrilla squads. In the wilderness of the Caucasian Mountains it laid out and put up an elaborate camp with a kitchen, dining room, machine shop, hospital, dormitories, clubhouse, repair shops, and a laboratory. It kept in close communication with neighboring and faraway guerrilla squads and aided them in keeping their clothes, tools, and weapons in fit condition. It co-ordinated its own plans and raids with those of the others. It was at once a fighting organization, a laboratory, and a school for perfecting the most destructive methods of guerrilla warfare.

Above all, it set for itself the task of smashing any German scheme for sending reinforcements to Novorossiisk on the Black Sea. If this city and naval port became German, the Reichswehr would secure a firm hold on the coastline.

"It would then seek to push its way down to Turkey," explained the college president, pointing out on the map the route the Germans had planned to follow, "coax or goad the

The college president and his wife in their guerrilla camp

Monument to the Ignatov brothers in Krasnodar

Turks into fighting on its side, make a swift demarche on Iran, Iraq, penetrate India, and join forces with the Japanese."

In the summer of 1942, at the time Winston Churchill was visiting Moscow, Russians were convinced the Turks were waiting to see what happened in Novorossiisk and other battlefields in the North Caucasus. If the Germans won their campaigns there, Turkey was certain to join Hitler, so Russians were freely saying.

But at Novorossiisk the Germans were halted. They could not get beyond the "October" cement factory in which the Russians had entrenched themselves. They needed fresh troops and supplies with which to overpower the Russians. That was why they were concentrating both in immense quantities in the Kuban. They were planning to transport them to Novorossiisk over the railroad and the fine highways connecting Krasnodar with the Black Sea port only seventy-two miles away.

The Red Army had ordered the guerrillas all over the Kuban, and especially Batya's detachment, to prevent at all costs the consummation of the German plan.

Meanwhile, with winter advancing in the mountains, the guerrillas felt the need of acquiring a herd of cattle for food and of additional horses for travel and scouting. The lowlands of the Kuban were in German hands. The Germans therefore had complete control of all Kuban agriculture. The only food in the mountains was wild apples, pears, nuts, game, now and then wild honey. The only place to acquire cattle or horses was in German-held territory. Ignatov ordered the younger members of the camp, including his own son Genandy, to go and "hunt" for both in the lowlands.

Mounting well-trained Cossack horses, the youths dashed away. From behind trees and bushes which sheltered them from German observation, they saw ten Germans driving a herd of about two hundred head of cattle. Their plan of attack was to leap on the Germans by surprise. Galloping full speed into the road, they opened fire. Five Germans took to their heels. The others returned the fire, but they were no match for the guerrilla snipers who were mounted on well-trained Cossack horses. Soon all the fighting Germans were dead. Then the cattle were divided into two herds. Genandy and a friend named Pavlik proceeded to drive one herd of twenty head at full speed along the main highway. The other herd was turned in the opposite direction toward a well-concealed glade in the mountains. The purpose of this maneuver was to fool the Germans into thinking that Genandy's twenty head along the main road was the main herd, so that they would start in pursuit of it; meantime most of the cattle would be driven to a well-sheltered place in the mountains. To make the deception more credible, Genandy and his friend chased their cattle fast so as to stir up immense clouds of dust, and make it appear it was the main herd. The more dense the clouds of dust, the more easily the Germans would be lured into hot pursuit.

The deception worked. German cavalry started after Genandy and Pavlik. Both kept on driving their cattle without any sign of fear, as if they might be working for the Germans. But when the Nazi cavalry was clearing into sight, the two youths swiftly swerved their horses off the highways, dashed into the forest and disappeared. The other herd, which included most of the cattle, was brought safely to the designated glade. Now the Ignatov detachment had milk and dairy products and an occasional meal of fresh meat.

The hunt for horses was no less successful, though it involved more desperate action. The young guerrillas rode down the mountain and reached the Cossack village of Makaret. There, outside a melon patch, they saw a small drove of tethered horses. The horsemen were in the patch picking melons. Their arms loaded with melons, the Germans started for the village. Only two remained on guard. So oblivious were they of impending danger that they lolled about on the grass, ate melon and talked. Genandy and Pavlik saw their chance. On their bellies *po plastunski*, they crept close to these guards. Drawing their *finkas*—Finnish knives without which no guerrilla ever ventures anywhere—they plunged them swiftly below the left shoulder blades of the enemy soldiers. They died quietly. Quickly tying the horses together by their halters, the young Cossacks rode away to the mountains.

Despite his youth, Genandy was perhaps the most adventurous fighter in the guerrilla squad. He never tired of action, was always ready for the most hazardous missions. Once, together with his older brother Zhenya, he seized a German baby tank. Concealed inside, they drove the tank into the German-held *stanitsa* of Smolenskaya, straight to German staff headquarters. Without lifting the metal cap, Genandy blew the siren long and loud. German officers rushed outdoors. Never suspecting guerrillas were inside the tank, a crowd of the officers had gathered to see what the siren signalled. Zhenya opened the machine gun on the officers, and Genandy drove straight into them and crushed some of them. From German headquarters came a hand grenade, then another, and another. Zhenya Ignatov poured machine-gun fire into the window, and no more hand grenades came out of it. "Full speed ahead, Genandy," Zhenya shouted. Genandy stepped on the gas and raced through the *stanitsa*. On the outskirts of the village the tank was ambushed. A heavy German machine gun plastered it with bullets, and the tank caught fire. It was smoky inside. Genandy drove on at full speed, hoping the wind would extinguish the fire, but the wind made it worse. Their clothes caught fire. It was no use trying to escape in the tank: they might burn to death. So the two brothers jumped out, rolled around in the grass to put out the flames in their clothes, and managed miraculously to get away. "I guess luck was with them," said the father. "That's the only way I can explain their inexplicable escape this time."

This was not their only hairbreadth race with death. To describe at length the battles and adventures, the raids and expeditions in which Zhenya and Genandy Ignatov alone participated would require a book. The father is writing two books, he said, one for children, another for adults.

Hardly a day passed but the life of everyone in the camp was replete with danger and excitement, with action and sometimes with horror. They all knew hunger and cold, aloneness and desolation. Some were killed. Some fell desperately ill. But so effectively had they terrorized the enemy that whenever a German ventured into the open road at night or by day, he kept firing tommy guns at random to protect himself against possible attack. The Germans imagined guerrillas everywhere, even in the shadows of night.

The two Ignatov boys were deeply attached to each other. Genandy always wanted to follow Zhenya on any expedition on which he embarked, but he was not always permitted to do so. Now and then, in leisure moments, the two brothers would lie on the grass and talk and tell each other all that was on their minds and hearts. One night Genandy said:

"I love to dream, brother. There was a time when I thought it was a disgrace to give oneself to dreaming. But I notice that the more I dream the better I feel. Do you know what I am dreaming of now? When the war ends I'll give up the spade, the fishing rod, and even my pigeons. I'll become an engineer like you, Zhenya. And I'll try to invent a machine that'll go anywhere on land, on water, under water, in the air, over marshes, over the Sahara—anywhere, everywhere."

The time now came for the most decisive act of the Batya guerrillas. Three engineers, including Zhenya Ignatov, had at last invented a new mine. No guerrillas anywhere had been using such a mine for the simple reason that none was in existence. It was called the automatic mine. There was not a grain of metal in it. It was made of wood and dynamite and was detonated by the weight of the object that pressed against the earth in which it was buried. It was so constructed that an ordinary peasant cart could ride over the road in which it lay without causing it to explode. But the weight of a truck would set it off. If buried to a proper depth, the tramcar that usually preceded a German train on the railroad would not detonate it. But the locomotive would. And so would a freight or passenger car. This was a *secret weapon*, a prize weapon, and it was invented just in time.

Agents brought the news that at the station of Georgia

Afipskaya the Germans had assembled about two thirds of all their Kuban movable transport. They were to use it for the transportation of troops and supplies to Novorossiisk. The news excited but did not alarm the guerrilla intellectuals. They now had the weapon with which to foil the German maneuver. Taking fourteen men with him, including Zhenya, his older son, the college president Ignatov started in the direction of the railroad. Genandy, the younger son, remained in the camp to repair a brick oven. Excepting the men directly engaged in the mission, no one in camp knew of it. Absolute secrecy was the law of the camp. Yet the amount of supplies and the number of men that went with his father roused Genandy's suspicion that they were departing on an especially important mission, and he decided not to miss it even if it meant violating camp discipline. He caught up with the detail and said to his father:

"You have no right to leave me out of this. Zhenya and I have agreed that we'd always be together on important missions."

"Very well," the father said, and they resumed their journey.

They decided to lay their mines along a two-mile track outside the village of Severskaya, at the point where two highways and the railroad run close and parallel to each other. They would blow up not only the train, but the motor transport, which they knew was also bound for Novorossiisk.

Coming close to the scene of operation, the guerrillas lay down. Ahead were scouts making a final checkup. The night was dark as only dark nights can be in the Kuban. From far away came the faint sound of a train whistle. The time was short, but they had not yet heard from their scouts, giving them the all-clear signal. Soon a frog croaked. This was the signal. The guerrillas rose and hastened to the tasks their commander had assigned them.

They dug holes for the mines on the railroad track and on the two parallel highways. Meanwhile the train was drawing closer and closer. Most of the mines were already in the holes. But the tiny safety pins had not yet been pulled. Now it was too late to pull them. The train was almost upon them. If the train passed this spot it would reach Novorossiisk. Nothing and nobody on the way could stop it, and the Red Army battling for its life in the Novorossiisk cement factory might be overpowered.

Zhenya Ignatov, a skilled engineer, thought fast. He told his younger brother they could detonate the mines by throwing hand grenades at them. Pulling grenades from their belts, they flung them under the locomotive. The explosion was so violent it threw the father far back into the grass. The boiler heaved high, crashed to pieces. Car after car tumbled over the tracks. Fires started, lighting up the dark night. The cries of the dying and wounded Germans filled the night. The air was hot and suffocating; it scorched the face, the hands; it burned the throat. Over on the highway the mines were as active as on the railroad. Trucks were blowing up, and the German attempt to send reinforcements to Novorossiisk was frustrated. This was the first wrecked train in the Kuban. "But not the last," said the college president.

But where were the Ignatov boys? The father and the others searched for them. Zhenya, the older one, they found pinned down by fragments of debris. He was dead. Guerrillas picked up the body and carried it off into the bushes. They searched for the younger son and found him blown away into the grass. He too was dead. The body was still warm. The father lifted it in his arms, carried it into the bushes, and laid it beside the body of his older son.

Working with their *finkas*, the guerrillas proceeded to dig a grave. Bullets whizzed overhead. The Germans who had recovered from their panic were shooting in every direction. It was dangerous to remain longer in the vicinity of the wreckage. So the bodies of the Ignatov brothers were hastily laid in a shallow grave and covered with dirt. The father could not leave. He was on his knees, saying to himself over and over: "No sons any more, no sons any more." He was oblivious of bullets. He thought only of his dead sons. Only a quarter of an hour earlier he had heard them talk, had seen them run; now they were no more. Suddenly he felt someone's powerful hand. It was Pavlik.

"The Germans are drawing a cordon around us," he said. "Quick, let's run!"

He seized Ignatov by the arm and led him away.

For some days no one dared tell the mother of the death of the two sons. The father faked a telegram informing her that Zhenya and Genandy were seriously wounded. He faked another telegram stating one was dead, the other in critical condition. Anxious and apprehensive, the mother slung a sniper's rifle over her shoulder and started for the hospital where her sons were supposed to be. She was a surgeon. With her skill she might save the living son from death. Then Ignatov told her the truth.

Heavyhearted though they were, the Ignatovs remained at their posts to the very end, until the Germans were forced out of the Kuban. Then they returned to Krasnodar to an empty home, full of memories and grief. Valentin, their oldest son, had lost his life fighting with the Red Army on the Kerch Peninsula. They were all alone in the world.

The loneliness was too much for them, and they adopted two grown children, a niece and a friend of Genandy's, a boy named Valery. The niece is now a freshman at the Krasnodar medical school. Valery is completing his studies in a Siberian aviation school.

In May 1944, after the raw Kuban spring gave way to summer weather, the father and some of his friends went to find the bodies of the dead sons. They wanted to bring them to Krasnodar and give them a fitting burial in the city cemetery.

The ground was so overgrown with fresh grass and foliage that the identification marks they had hastily left on nearby bushes and on the grave were gone. After twenty-four hours the search yielded no results. But Ignatov persisted. Finally he stumbled on withered pieces of clothing. He recognized them as belonging to one of his sons. Spurred into hope, he continued the search, and finally the grave was uncovered. The bodies were disinterred and brought to Krasnodar.

The Ignatovs planned a private funeral. But Krasnodar authorities insisted on making it an occasion of public mourning. The events associated with the death of the Ignatov brothers and the manner in which they died made them the outstanding war heroes of the Kuban, and the Supreme Soviet in Moscow had proclaimed them posthumously "heroes of the Soviet Union."

Draped in red bunting and surrounded by rows on rows of flowers—roses, chrysanthemums, poppies; "all the flowers of the Kuban, it would seem," the father said—the two coffins lay in state at the city hall for two days. From all over the Kuban, Cossacks, young and old, came to pay tribute to the sons of the college president. Zhenya was twenty-seven, Genandy was seventeen when they died.

The bodies were laid to rest, not in the city cemetery, but in the Sverdlov Square park in the heart of Krasnodar.

I went to see the grave. There is a monument over it—a high obelisk of dark shiny Labrador granite. Shadowed by a bushy silver maple and a finely trimmed oleander, it is the most impressive and most beautiful monument in the city. On it in gilded letters is engraved the citation of the Supreme Soviet. Flanking the citation are portraits of Zhenya and Genandy dressed in dark Sunday suits, with collar and tie.

An iron railing surrounds the burial plot. Flowers in red earthen pots or planted in the ground adorn the grave—white and red roses, chrysanthemums, pink carnations, others. It was the most luxurious flower patch I saw in the Kuban. Some of the flowers are inside, some outside of the iron railings.

Every morning and evening the college president and his wife come here on a pilgrimage. They water the flowers, sweep the grounds, wipe the dust off the railings and the obelisk.

"We shall do this to the end of our lives," said Pyotr Karpovitch Ignatov.

CHAPTER XVI

The Two Russias

I sent a note to Mikhail Mikhailovitch Bessonov, chairman of the Kuban territorial Soviet, the governor of the province, requesting an opportunity to talk with him. He replied by inviting me to come the following evening. At the appointed hour I climbed the broad creaking stairway of the old building in which Bessonov had his office. I had walked through the dark streets, and the brilliance of the light in the window-blackened office was as startling as it was welcome.

Bessonov introduced himself, then presented a group of men gathered around the long conference table. They were "the experts" of the country—college professors, scientists, engineers; specialists in grain, livestock, fruits, and other crops; specialists in education, health, the arts. Among them was the youthful blue-eyed and contemplative Professor Pokrovski and the director of the medical college, both of whom I had already met. All the men were clean-shaven, dressed in summer suits, with collars and ties, very much like men in similar positions in England or the United States.

Bessonov himself, a stocky man of medium height with massive shoulders, a broad, sunburned, and mobile face, and thick black hair combed straight back, wore a dark business suit, a soft white collar, and dark tie. He looked very much like an American governor.

"I have invited these gentlemen," said Bessonov, "because they are experts. I learn from them, and there may be questions they can answer better than I can." He was cheerful and informal.

It was all in striking contrast to Moscow, where, at official interviews with a Russian executive or government representative whom one meets for the first time, there is often an air of formality and aloofness. In Moscow the Russian in an official position, who in private life is talkative and comradely, bursting with curiosity about foreign countries and peoples, who loves to ask questions about the lands you have visited, the books you have read, often compels himself, when receiving a foreign visitor, to freeze his inner liveliness and assume a demeanor of chilly correctness. The purges, the war, the presence of large foreign colonies, the largest Moscow has known, and supposed to be out of sympathy with a collectivist society and therefore suspect of hostile intention or of espionage, have made Moscow officials and others who deal with foreigners wary of them. In their presence such Russians maintain an attitude of stiff artificial, often forbidding, reserve.

The foreigner who meets only these Russians, especially if he is ignorant of the Russian language, Russian history, Russian manners, or who has tilts with censors and bureaucrats over this or that issue, this or that request, whether it be for a plumber to repair a bathtub or for a trip to a near or faraway part of the country, never can know or appreciate the social expansiveness and warm camaraderie innate in the Russian and which in moments of ease and relaxation shine out of him with the glow of spring sunlight.

In all my years of travel in Russia I have deliberately stayed away from Moscow as often and as long as desire and circumstances allowed. I know of no other place in Russia where sensational gossip, mordant misinformation, cocksure prophecy, abetted in the war years by the obtuseness and ignorance of the new crop of Soviet bureaucrats, can so ungently upset an understanding of the country and an appreciation of the people. For this disagreeable circumstance Moscow officials must shoulder their share of the blame. But the foreign colony which lives in a world of its own and approaches Russia more in terms of its own social background, its own ideology, its own privileges and predilections, than of Russian reality, past and present, contributes its doleful share. I have always felt that a week in any village, however remote geographically, however backward culturally, is more fruitful of results, more revealing as to the real nature of the country and the people, than a year or a decade spent in the tumultuous and gossip-reeking capital.

But here was the Kuban, far away from Moscow. Here were no foreign colony, no foreign military missions, no play of power politics, no international embroilments, no crowd of uniformed officials whose ignorance of the outside world and of their own country is often enough matched only by their incivility and incompetence. Here was a gathering of the governor of the province and of his experts to enlighten me on the country in which they lived and on the work that they were doing.

The conference table was laid out with a white cloth and set with trays of fruit and pastry, mineral water and wine. Two girls in black dresses and white aprons quietly placed glasses of steaming hot tea before everyone. Yet neither food nor drink proved tempting. It was barely touched by anyone. Since the war had begun, these men had hardly been out of the Kuban. They had been feverishly busy with rebuilding their devastated land. The mere presence of an American writer in their midst seemed as much an adventure to them as their presence was to me. I was bursting with questions and they were bursting with answers. Facts and figures tumbled out of them, like the streams that roar down the Kuban mountain slopes.

I do not wish to clutter these pages with figures. Yet a statistical survey of a country that has been at war, under violent occupation by the enemy, which since its liberation has struggled to rehabilitate its shattered institutional and personal life, speaks with a concreteness and eloquence which are beyond the power of words to convey.

The prewar population of the Kuban was 3,172,674. In 1941 there were 2,200 collective farms, which tilled 8,500,000 acres of land, 3,500,000 acres in winter wheat. Wheat was king in the Kuban.

In no other part of Russia had agriculture been so highly mechanized. Tractors did all the plowing, seeding, cultivating, and hauling. Four fifths of the harvesting was done by 4,208 combines. Horses had lost their earlier importance in agriculture. They were used for short hauls, such as fetching oil and water to tractors, for garden work, above all for riding and for the practice of war games. Every collective had one or more ponds for watering livestock and for fish. The ponds were fed by springs or mountain streams.

The revolution in agriculture since the coming of the Soviets was as complete as the revolution in politics. Excepting individual gardens, there were no privately owned or individually tilled lands. All land was collectivized and worked by the community or was state-owned, the state farms embracing an area of only 750,000 acres.

Many new crops have been successfully acclimated. The most important of these are tangerines, lemons, rice, cotton, soya bean, peanuts, new blends of tobacco, the castor bean, other medical herbs. Grapefruit was doing badly. But the sweet potato was making satisfactory progress.

Especially proud was the Kuban of its inland sea, variously known as "the people's sea" or "the Krasnodar sea," thirty-five miles outside of the city. All Kuban participated in its construction; 65,000 men and women from all the villages and towns, working with 12,000 teams of horses and oxen, 1,000 tractors, completed the excavation within twenty-five days, and for the first time in the history of the country, the unruly swift-flowing Kuban River was tamed. The sea held 400 million cubic meters of water. It drained the river's overflow in the spring, had made floods only a memory, and supplied fresh sources of water for such a water-thirsty crop as rice.

There were fish in the sea. There were walks and boathouses. There were picnic grounds and playgrounds. It was to become the great inland water resort of the Kuban, free to all vacationists and all seekers of healthy outdoor recreation—swimming, boating, fishing, dancing, walking, playing games. It was the proudest

Sixty-four-year-old Don Cossack

Kuban Cossack guerrilla

РАССТРЕЛ МИШИ ПИНКЕНЗОНА

Painting of Musya Pinkenson in the Cossack museum, Krasnodar

achievement of the Kuban, and its success encouraged the Soviets and the people to plan another inland sea elsewhere.

In prewar days the Kuban was Russia's primary source of melon and vegetable seeds; of select alfalfa seeds; the nursery for the magnificent Italo-Hungarian plum tree, and for other fruits.

Because of its rich and varied agriculture the Kuban was maintaining a series of new colleges and experimental stations which Cossacks in the old days had never known: they are for the advancement of the manufacture of vegetable oils; the cultivation of select seeds for vegetables, grains, especially wheat for bread; for tea and rice; for the improvement of berries and subtropical fruits; for select breeds of livestock. Out of these institutions the people of the Kuban and of other regions resembling it in soil and climate have been receiving fresh knowledge on how to make nature yield ever-increasing rewards for man's toil.

"We can grow all the cereals in the world," said the tall, thin, scholarly Professor Novatowsky, "from rye to rice, all textile crops, all the bean crops, and what's more our yield in rice is greater than yours in America, and only Spain and Italy obtain higher yields per acre. But your people are away ahead of us in the cultivation of fruits and berries. We have a lot to learn from America, and someday we'll catch up with you in everything."

"Our Kuban never stands still," interposed the governor with pride.

In the prewar days the Kuban was also the leading center for the canning of vegetables and fruits.

Then the war came and the Germans strove to hurl the flowering and mechanized Kuban to a condition of rank primitiveness.

They put to death 52,518 civilians, 9,022 war prisoners.

They drove 31,700 Kuban citizens to Germany for forced labor.

They devastated 10,000 livestock departments on the collectives, valued at 1,442,000,000 rubles ($280,000,000).

They blew up all the locks in the inland sea, and once more the river was out of control and was flooding the lowlands.

They devoured and shipped to Germany more than three

fourths of the pigs and poultry of the Kuban, more than half the cattle.

They stole and shot about three fourths of the horses, the finest in the country.

They burned and blew up nearly all public buildings—schools, hospitals, libraries, theaters, clubhouses, shops, offices, factories, resorts.

The damage to the collectives alone amounted to seven billion rubles ($1,400,000,000).

In the beautiful Taman Peninsula, a hallowed place to lovers of Russian literature because of its association with some of the choicest prose writing of the poet Lermontov, they razed many a village to the ground.

They devastated most of the tea plantations.

They brought gonorrhea and syphilis to the Kuban. With the reoccupation of the country by the Red Army, clinics were set up to combat these scourges. Before the war such clinics were rare in the Cossack villages.

The enemy troops also looted millions of dollars' worth of clothes, shoes, furniture, kitchenware, bicycles, gramophones, mirrors, sewing machines, pictures, other personal possessions of the people.

A particularly pernicious heritage of the occupation is the neglect of the fields, which in over a fourth of the tillable area are overgrown with tall thistles and other rank weeds.

Since the return of the Soviets the one problem that has been preoccupying the minds and the energies of the Party, the people, the Soviets, is rehabilitation.

Nearly all the elementary and high schools are now functioning. They may be temporarily located in renovated barns, basements, in hastily restored school buildings. But no child in the Kuban need any longer go without elementary or high-school education.

Five colleges have been reopened, with a student body of 3,000, and fifty-one technical schools with an enrollment of 5,600.

Excepting in the Taman Peninsula, which has been the greatest sufferer of the war, all collectives have been re-established. In 1943 they planted three fourths and in 1944 four fifths of the prewar area. In 1944 they managed to bring up the cattle herds to three fifths of the prewar numbers, but horses to only a little over one fifth. Poultry was coming back fast, but progress in pig raising was slow because the enemy had slaughtered the choicest sows and boars.

So much of industry was destroyed that in 1943 the output of factories was only one fifth and in 1944 one third that of prewar.

The most pressing immediate problem was to supply each individual Cossack family with a milch cow, pigs, fowl, sheep, bees, so that, as in prewar times, the family can produce its own dairy foods, eggs, meat, honey. Within two years at most, each Cossack family will regain its quota of livestock. The individual gardens were flourishing, but individual and kolhoz (collective-farm) orchards needed strenuous attention to lift them to their prewar yields in fruit.

Since agriculture is the main source of livelihood in the Kuban, it holds first place in all the plans and all the approximations of the state. Not until 1947 will the full prewar area be in cultivation. . . .

In the summer of 1944 every kolhoz already had its summer nursery.

Farm machinery was an acute problem, though about one half of the prewar combines, droppers, and cutters had been renovated and restored.

"Whatever else the good Lord may or may not have in store for us in the immediate future," said one of the professors, "we shall not suffer for lack of work."

We talked for a long time, Bessonov, the experts, and I. They poured out information on agriculture, industry, education, social life, youth, women, religion, a host of other subjects. Not a single question did they fail to answer. Always there was a specialist who knew the correct answer or made the necessary explanation.

It was long past midnight when I returned to my quarters. The night was dark and cloudy, all the darker for the umbrella-shaped trees rising like awnings over the streets and shutting out the few glimmering stars in the sky. I kept thinking of the meeting, thinking and thinking.

Bessonov and his specialists had neither hedged nor equivocated. Not once did any of them say, as Moscow officials so often do, "Sorry, the war is still on; we cannot answer your questions." Of course I asked for no information involving military security. But then to some Moscow officials figures on livestock, wheat, agriculture, machinery, the birth rate in a village, the death rate in a county, is as much an object of military secrecy as the production of planes and tanks.

But not in the Kuban. After the long evening's talk with these men, the cream of the country's intelligentsia, toiling away with scarcely any recreation or vacation for the reconstruction of their devastated land, I was more than ever convinced that for foreign writers and observers, there are two Russias, at present anyway: the Russia of the official Moscow that is in continuous relationship with foreigners, and the Russia outside of Moscow, the Russia of the people. A gulf as immense as the spaces between Moscow and the Kuban separates these two Russias in mode of thought, in social behavior, in ease and naturalness of manner, in the purely human quality of their person and in the concept of their duty.

Foreign correspondents who went to Odessa shortly after this southern city was liberated will remember with pleasure the representative of the Press Department who was in charge of the trip. Himself a former reporter on the *Red Star*, he understood our needs and did not seek unduly to impose himself on our desires and our movements. We roved around the city and interviewed people everywhere we went. But those of us who made the trip to the American air base in the Ukraine will remember with execration the arrogant and mean-minded official who accompanied us. It took the united efforts of all correspondents to stop him in the first place from killing the trip for some of us and in the second place from killing the story as we wanted it reported. Officials like him have burdened correspondents and other foreigners in Moscow with a load of frustration and fury which will not readily and in some instances will never wear off. But the men of the Kuban—Party men, executives, scientists, dam builders, factory managers, schoolteachers, college presidents, directors of plant and animal experiment stations—all these and others like them are as loyal to the Soviet cause as the officials in Moscow. Yet they seem as if of a race apart. Most of them are natives of the Kuban and boost its virtues and glories with fervent and good-humored eloquence. Dedicated to the mammoth tasks before them, they have the candor of their deeds and convictions, the faith and self-confidence which go with the execution of a specific program of action, the achievement of positive results. They indulge neither in sophistry nor in banality. They can afford neither, for the one or the other thwarts achievement. Their minds are attuned, not to subterfuge or circumlocution, but to reality and fact. They neither fear nor doubt themselves. They walk in the bright light of reality and not in the shadow of abstraction and speculation. They always remember the maxim that a straight line is the shortest distance between two points and swerve neither from the meaning nor the implications of the maxim. To meet such men, to talk to them, to observe them, their ardor and courage, to obtain from them the immense amount of information they freely gave me, to hear them invite me to their homes and meet their families, was one of the most extraordinary and revealing experiences I have had in wartime Russia.

All these men had suffered heavily from the war and the occupation. Many of them had lost someone in the war—a son, a daughter, a mother, a brother. Most of them had their homes looted and sacked. Not one but in his own way, either as guerrilla leader or as a specialist in evacuation, had done his share of fighting. . . .

Yet there was no vein of tragedy in their speech or in their spirit. However deep their personal sorrow, they kept it to themselves or only hinted at it. . . . Busy with the work of today and the plans for tomorrow, they had no time for words of grief. Their minds were fixed on the rehabilitation and recreation of the Kuban, and in coaxing out of Nature more and more of the good things that it holds within its unfathomable embrace. Nothing else mattered as much. Not once did they express concern over the immensity of the task before them. They were determined builders—businessmen in the fullest and truest sense of the word. They were absorbed in business problems, in business achievements, with the businessman's faith in his powers to reach the goal he has mapped out for himself. In mood, temper, and mentality, ages separated them from Soviet and Party functionaries of the twenties or early thirties. Those men had been first and foremost political agitators and crusaders, only secondarily businessmen.

When one meets men like Bessonov and his specialists, one realizes that the initial political radicalism of the Revolution inside Russia has spent itself, at least for the present. Slogans which once rocked Russia and the fanaticism that once seemed like a beacon light of redemption were no part of their code or even their vocabulary. They were done with private enterprise; that was manifest. They were building on a new system of ownership and a new principle of social behavior. For them neither the one nor the other was any longer a theory or an experiment. Both were the new center of gravity in all their thinking, all their being. Not once throughout the long evening did any of them allude to the possible advantages of the old economic system. The subject no longer arose because it no longer existed for them. Now they were bent on conserving and consolidating the gains that the new system, tested in the caldron of war, had proven for Russia solid and stable. All their plans in agriculture, industry, education, all their eloquence about the Kuban of the future, all their enthusiasm—and their local patriotism, so reminiscent of the American booster—derived its inspiration from collectivism.

These men were proud of the Cossackhood of the Kuban. They saw in it the history and the romance of the past. They were resolved to elevate it to a new history and a new romance in tune with the new social dispensations and the new intellectual aspirations, whose fulfillment is vested in the mastery and advancement of the machine age more than in any other circumstance.

At times the talk of these men about Cossacks, especially of the historian, dripped with remembrance and nostalgia. Yet their very appearance, the business suits they wore, bespoke an absence of the former pomp, the former glitter, the former primitiveness. Here were a new Cossack and a new Cossackdom, though the old warrior spirit was as much glorified as in the old days when the destinies of the Kuban were presided over by the picturesquely clad hetmans and *starshinas*—elders.

Before leaving the conference I had asked Mikhail Bessonov how old he was.

"I was born in 1901 in the village of Medvezhye, not far from Krasnodar."

"I suppose," I said, "you're married and have a family."

"Yes, I am married, and as for family, praised be the Lord, I cannot complain. I have five daughters and one son. They are all doing well."

New or old marriage laws, subsidies or no subsidies for large families, the intelligentsia as a rule remains true to its own tradition and its own tastes and contents itself with a small family. But the 43-year-old Bessonov was already the father of six children. Intentionally or not he was emulating the Kuban tradition of the large family.

"Tomorrow," he said, "you may start on your journey." He was putting at my disposal a jeep, a chauffeur, and a guide who happened to be a newspaperman. "Go anywhere you want," he said, "see anything you like, talk to anyone you choose."

No one in Moscow had spoken such language to me, not since the war began.

Young Zorin from Moscow's Press Department was with me in Krasnodar. I said to him:

"See how different these people are from officials in Moscow?"

"Well," he said laughingly, and recited the refrain of the well-known Cossack song:

> *"Kuban, our motherland,*
> *Our age-old knight."*

CHAPTER XVII

The Open Road

THE OUTSKIRTS OF KRASNODAR, as of nearly all Russian cities, especially in the provinces, bear the aspect of a village. Here are low huts, untrimmed trees, a garden or a courtyard or both with each hut, broken fences, chickens squawking around the grounds, a pig wallowing in a ditch by the roadside, a goat tied to a stout post, pigeons sunning themselves on the roof, dogs pouncing on passers-by and barking savagely. Here people walk around in bare feet, children are more diffident, more aloof from strangers, eye them with a curiosity that is compounded of distrust and excitement. Here is an atmosphere of simplicity and ease, and here is more pronounced primitiveness in the surroundings.

Beyond these outskirts in the western part of Krasnodar, from an elevation that commands a sweeping view of the city, begins the highway to Novorossiisk. The distance between the Cossack capital and the Black Sea port and naval base is seventy-two miles; every inch of it is weighted with battle and blood, with history and drama. Once it was barely a footpath, over which Cossacks galloped in pursuit of rebellious natives or natives slyly ambushed Cossacks. During the civil war armies of Whites and Reds swung tidelike back and forth in savage combat. Over this road early in August 1942 the Germans stormed into the Kuban, on their way, as they loudly proclaimed, to Turkey and India. Over it in February 1943, flaccid and morose, they hobbled their way out of the Kuban and to ultimate doom.

Decisive marches, battles, campaigns, victories were lost and won on this road linking the two leading cities of the Kuban.

Now the road was almost deserted. Save here and there for the rusty hulk of a broken tank, the blackened frame of a burned automobile, there was no evidence of battle. Skylarks soared overhead, hundreds of them. The air resounded with their happy warbling. Now and then, when the automobile was almost upon it, a hawk took to its wings, slowly and easily, with no show of haste, as though defiant of hazard, and flying not much higher than the grain stacks in the fields. I had never seen more lazy, self-assured hawks.

Peace and quiet reigned over the land. The air was redolent with the smell of drying hay and the fragrance of wild flowers. There was little traffic, little bustle. The hard dirt highway was repaired, the small bridges rebuilt, only the larger ones still needed to be constructed. Nowhere were there signs regulating the speed of automobiles, as on American highways. One could drive as fast or as slowly as one chose. The waves of air our speeding jeep whipped up now chilled, now warmed the face.

All around was steppe, merging on one side with the wall of blue haze that curtained the foothills and the forests of the Caucasian Mountains, on the other sinking into the sea of mist on the faraway horizon.

The corn was high and green, the long ears, very long, jutting spearlike out of the stalks. The sunflower was resplendent with color, and here were acres and acres of it. The oil that the seed yields is known to every housekeeper in Russia; it is the most common vegetable oil in the country, used in cooking and salads. The heads had already formed, large, round, yellow, and shimmering with a golden luster.

The wheat was cut. It was now stacked, shocked, or bunched like hay after it had been dried. Here and there it was being thrashed. Sheaf binding never had been much in vogue in the Kuban. The coming of the combine had dispensed with all need for it. But in the summer of 1944, because of the shortage of combines a campaign for sheaf binding was launched, so that less of the grain would shell in the handling. Not everywhere was the campaign heeded, as was evidenced by the fields of bunched wheat. There was not enough labor for the task.

The evening before, I had heard Mikhail Bessonov and his experts describe and document the ruin the Germans had left in the Kuban countryside. Now that I was journeying in the countryside I observed that, in the year and a half since its liberation, the land though still scarred was healing its wounds. The bumper crop of wheat, corn, sunflowers, one of the best the Kuban had known, testified to astounding recovery.

But alternating with fields of wheat, sunflowers, and corn were fields of weeds. The stalks were tall and heavy, and thick as grass in a meadow. In one place I tried to walk through and I could not. I might as well have tried to walk through a wall of sand or snow. The seed was ripening. The weeds should have been cut and burned, but there was no time, no labor, no tools to spare. Only about one fourth, or rather twenty-eight per cent, of the prewar animal energy was available for field work. So the weeds remained uncut and were sullying one fourth of the rich Kuban lands. . . . Weeds are one of the saddest consequences of the occupation in the Kuban.

Yet not as sad as another sight which the Kuban never had known in all its history—the cow carts that hauled freight in the countryside. The carts were little, the cows were large, a breed known as the "red steppe," widespread in the Kuban and the Ukraine. They were good for meat and for milk. But neither nature nor man ever intended them to haul freight—certainly not in the Kuban, where distances are immense, where fields are from ten to thirty miles away from villages.

Though large-bodied and well fed, the cows were lazy and slow-paced. The very smallness of the carts to which they were harnessed testified to their limited physical capacity to perform the task imposed on them. But there was nothing else to do. The Germans had slaughtered or stolen the horses and oxen, and there were few trucks. Women were leading the cows by the halter, for none could be driven, still less could be trusted to follow the road of its own accord. The sight of grass would be too alluring, and the roads would be littered with capsized carts and fallen cows.

The cow carts were a striking contrast to what the Kuban knew in prewar days. Nowhere else in Russia was field work so highly mechanized. There was little hand work in the grainfields and in the meadows. Every kolhoz boasted at least three trucks. Grain fresh from the combine was loaded into trucks and carried to elevators, state granaries, or to village storehouses for distribution among members of the collective farm. Unlike other parts of Russia, here women and young people hardly knew the sickle, the scythe, the cradle.

Now the *cheliabinsk*, or sixty-horsepower tractor, was a rare sight. The truck was as scarce. The cow carts dominated the fields and the highways of the Kuban. The pastoral primitiveness they signalized made one think of biblical times, except that in those days the ox and not the cow bore the yoke. Now the cow was supreme, the savior of the Kuban. She gave milk; she plowed, harrowed, cultivated, and she drew the freight of the country. In her new role she looked odd and comical. It was as if the horse and buggy had returned to the streets of New York or London.

Yet the women who led the cows appeared neither impatient nor disconsolate. They ate apples, picked seeds out of freshly cut heads of sunflowers or kept pace with the cow, humming a melody. Some were barefoot, others wore shoes. Not one was without the famous *kasinka*, the three-cornered handkerchief. Sunburned and wind-bitten, they seemed oblivious of distress.

No doubt they would have preferred the tractor, the combine, the truck. But they cheerfully accepted the inevitable. They waved their hands and smiled. They were ready with merry quips. More agile, more energetic, more cultivated than peasant women, they were also more jovial.

At one place we stopped for a change of tires. While the chauffeur was busy with his work, I strolled up the road. Coming toward me was an elderly woman leading a cow cart ladder-high with freshly cut grass. On top of the grass was a flock of gay and loud-voiced children.

"Good day, *mamasha* [little mother]," I said.

"Good day, *papasha* [little father]," she answered.

"I'm no *papasha*," I said.

"Where d'you come from, Moscow?"

"No, *mamasha*, I come from a faraway land, from America."

"Ah." She stopped, surveyed me critically with her deep-sunk, twinkling blue eyes, and said:

"If you lived around here, stranger, you'd be a *papasha* all right. Our *Kazachki* would see to it that you were."

When I repeated the conversation to the chauffeur he said:

"You'll never get the best of them in conversation. Their tongues spit fire like a blacksmith's anvil."

I could not help remembering Tolstoy's tribute to the Cossack women: "They're stronger, wiser, more cultivated and more attractive than Cossack men." Most manifestly they are as independent-minded and far more sharp-tongued.

During the German occupation they had had their share of trial and bereavement. They did their cursing and weeping, their fighting too, with their wits more than with their hands or with weapons. But the occupation was over. The enemy was on his way, not to India, as he had boasted, but to Germany, running fast. He was no longer a threat, not even a haunting shadow. He was only an evil memory. But unlike the peasants, Cossacks have no heritage of serfdom in their souls. They don't moan or mourn like peasants. They have stronger nerves and infinitely greater self-control. They have always been a people not of words but

Trucks gone—Cossack women carry wheat on their backs

Cossack women sowing

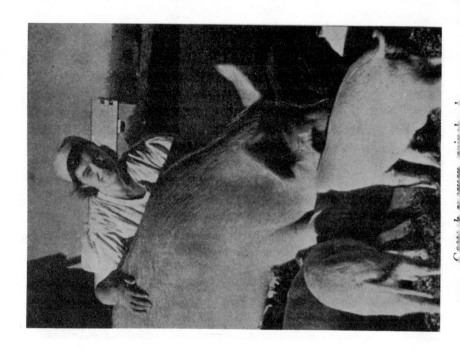

Cossack women animals [...]

Cossack women shucking corn

of deeds, not of meditation but action. In literature as in life they have been, first and foremost, men of audacity and achievement. Their minds are attuned to victory and triumph. Today's failure does not ban tomorrow's success. That is the way they have always felt and thought. Even in their love-making, as evidenced in their songs and stories, they are not given to melancholy and despair. They know the meaning of violent passion, but only seldom of inner collapse. They could always drown disappointment or anguish in drink, in a fist fight, in war exercises, in battle. A rough, tough people, with little inner refinement but much outward dignity, they do not go to pieces over yesterday's sorrows and frustrations. It is impossible to imagine Cossacks in the role of Dostoyevskian Karamazovs and Raskalnikovs or Tolstoyan Pierre Bezukhovs and Levines. They are not and never were that kind of Russians. Hence the expansive, carefree manner of the women walking beside the cow carts.

The richness of the country and the balmy climate have accentuated their naturally jovial disposition.

"If I feel gloomy," I heard a Kuban schoolteacher say, "I go for a walk, breathe deep our Kuban air, take a long look at our Kuban sky and land, and I feel so cheered I wonder how I ever allowed myself to become lonely or depressed."

Ivan Ossipovitch Yudin, editor of *Sovietskaya Kuban* (Soviet Kuban), the leading daily of the country, journeyed with me to Novorossiisk. Though middle-aged, his face was singularly free from lines and his hair, though thinning, was nowhere streaked with gray. Long-legged, broad-shouldered, with a massive head, a thick neck, and sharp features, he looked more the warrior than the editor. He was one of the tallest men I have known.

When he was silent his expression was inscrutable and forbidding, as of a man too wrapped up in himself to say much. When he listened, he looked intently at the speaker, his large plum-shaped eyes dilating as if with disbelief and displeasure. Yet the moment he spoke, his soft low voice, with its deep undertones, revealed an inner gentleness in striking contrast to his outward severity. He was married and had two children, a boy and a girl.

I spoke of the bumper crop in the Kuban and of the cheerful spirit of the Cossack women we had met.

"Cossack women are like that," he said. "They love to live and to sing. When you hear two of them singing some distance away, you'd swear a whole choir was singing. The way they harmonize creates that impression. They are lucky to be that way, and their children are lucky." He paused and added: "The war has done something to our children—to my little girl, for instance. The other night she cried out in her sleep, 'Mamma, Mamma darling, come here quick, the grass is tall, they won't see you.' She was dreaming of running with her mother from an air attack and looking for a place of safety. We waked her and got her quiet, and she went to sleep again. She is often like that."

Yudin is a native of the Don Basin. For eight years he had worked in the coal mines. He had gone to school, read books, attended a journalist institute, become a reporter, then an editor. He knew the Kuban from end to end. He had studied Cossack history, folklore, manners. He had first come to the Kuban for military service in the Kuban cavalry. He knew little about horses, especially Cossack horses. He could not sit properly in the saddle; something always went wrong with his legs, his shoulders, his posture. Cossacks laughed at him as they always do at a person ignorant of horsemanship. They laughed so much that out of sheer hurt he practiced assiduously and in secret first on a wooden horse, then on a live horse. He would go off by himself and ride after dark, so no one would be around to taunt and mock him. At last he mastered the horse, the saddle, and the weapons that went with cavalry. At once the Cossacks changed their attitude toward him; they accepted him as one of themselves.

"To them a man is no real man unless he is a daredevil on horseback," said Yudin.

As we drove along he talked about himself, the Kuban, the landmarks we were passing. At one place he asked the chauffeur to stop.

"There is where the Ignatov boys were killed," he said, pointing to the right. I leaned out of the car and strained my eyes. All I saw was steppe merging into brush, trees, mountains, haze. There was nothing in the outward scene to suggest the deed or the death of the two young sons of the college president.

"Someday," said Yudin, "we shall put up a monument there. We shall put up a lot of monuments on this road."

We stopped for rest beside a tree shaded brook. The sun was hot and parching, and, baring his head, Yudin exposed himself to its full glare. "Sun, sun!" he recited. "Who is there that loves the sun like a miner? Who can love it like a miner? Who can glory in it like a miner? Nobody. To a miner the sun is never too hot, never too oppressive."

But it was hot and oppressive to me, so I started down the bank to dip my head in a flowing brook. "Come back," Yudin shouted. There was alarm in his voice, great alarm. Quickly I returned to the road. For a few moments he looked at me without saying a word; then he said:

"You must never go down a riverbank unless you know it has been cleared of mines. The Germans have sowed our riverbanks with explosives so that unwary pedestrians who might need water or might want to rest and wash their hands and faces would be blown up. . . ."

Eighteen months after liberation, and the wooded bank of a roadside brook might still be infested with mines!

A barefoot man passed by with a load of brush on his shoulders. Another drove along in a little cart drawn by a burro. A woman appeared leading a cow which drew a cartload of dry reeds. A truck clattered into view with a crowd of singing girls. As they drove by they waved their hands and smiled and kept on singing. Yudin recognized the truck—it belonged to a tractor station, and he said:

"That's a thrashing crew going off to a wheat field."

We climbed into our jeep and resumed our journey.

CHAPTER XVIII

"Our Outlet to the Sea"

WE WERE out of the steppe with its rich unending flatlands, its still air, its hot sun. We were climbing the mountains. The sun was as brilliant as in the steppe, but a cool breeze broke up the heat, and the higher we climbed, the cooler was the air. It was like a new country with a new terrain and a new climate. We were out of the rich wheat belt with its paucity of pasture and in the land of rich pastures. Trees were more abundant, especially oak, old and mighty and beautiful. Villages were more rare. But it was all part of the Kuban.

We were drawing closer to Novorossiisk. "Our outlet to the sea," Krasnodar calls this Black Sea port. Enemy armies had swept back and forth over the road we were traveling, armored equipment rolled ahead and behind them, guerrilla squads ventured forth in the night, laid mines, flung hand grenades, ripped and blasted the surface and the subsoil of the road. But it was all repaired now. Broad, smooth, shiny, it looked as if some wizard had blown all trace of damage out of the surface. It invited speed, and, like a spirited horse sensing home, our chauffeur stepped on the gas and the jeep raced forward.

Suddenly the jeep slowed down almost to a stop. We came to a road squeezed into the jaws of towering rock, with a deep canyon below. "This is Wolf's Gateway," said the chauffeur. The sharp, jagged peaks did remotely suggest a wolf's fangs, and because of this rock and the canyon below, the Germans in their retreat from Novorossiisk were caught in a deadly trap. They could not leap into the canyon. Least of all could they run back; the Red Army was close on their heels. They could only press forward, and ahead of them was a rain of Russian fire. They had to breast the fire or fall into a Russian net. Now, no mark of battle was visible at "Wolf's Gateway." The blood had dried, the road was mended, the canyon was freshly grown with grass.

We wound up and down the mountain roads and dropped into the valley that runs to the city and the sea. The closer we drew to Novorossiisk, the more dense were the trees lining the highway—tall, sturdy, and old, like the maples and the elms that shade the roads in upper New York State where I once lived. But here the trees bore the marks of war. A few feet aboveground a broad and deep notch had been chipped out of them, as though a woodsman were making ready to fell them so they would tumble across the road. The Germans had cut these notches. To delay the pursuit of the Red Army they had intended to blow up the trees with dynamite and block the road. But they miscalculated the speed of the Russian advance. They had time to cut notches in many trees, but the dynamite remained unused on the ground.

It was middle afternoon when we drove into Novorossiisk. The mountains that rimmed it on three sides and the bay, shaped like an amphitheater, with not a craft plying its shimmering waters, were a majestic sight. Few seaside cities anywhere command so grandiose and so beautiful a setting.

The beauty of its surroundings has not saved this southern city from a succession of historic tragedies. Its geography invited attack after attack which spelled catastrophe. At the beginning of the Christian era it was a Greek colony. Then the Genoese came and drove out the Greeks. In the eleventh century they built a fortress where the city now stands. There were many battles; the fortress was again and again destroyed and rebuilt. In 1722 the Turks converted it into a powerful military post named Sudzhuk-Kale.

Cossacks began dribbling into the territory in the sixteenth century, as well as fugitives from serfdom or religious persecution, loafers, adventurers, and marauders. They came here to settle or to roam the far-flung valleys and mountains. Here they could freely exercise their unruly impulses or their deep convictions.

Nature was bountiful. The waters never froze. Craft from many parts of the world bringing news and goods reached the harbor, summer and winter. There was fish in the sea and the streams. There was plenty of game. The winds were violent. The mountains did not always offer protection against the treacherous northeasters. But life was easy and free. Not as rich as the steppe of the Kuban, the mountains still afforded rich pasture. In the valleys, cereals could be cultivated. Fruit was abundant. Wine and honey became part of the daily diet.

In her push southward Russia drove out the Turks, hoisted her own banner over the coveted lands and the warm sea. More and more Cossacks were sent to tame the natives and entrench Russian rule. They were the same Cossacks as those that founded Krasnodar—that is, from the Zaporog *setch*. They built a settlement along the bay and called it *stanichka*, little Cossack village. They call it that to this day.

Once Russian, Novorossiisk became a more powerful fortress than it had ever been under the Greeks, the Genoese, or the Turks. But it was not impregnable. During the Crimean War big naval guns of the British fleet blew the fortress to bits. The *stanichka* was wiped out.

A new day came to Novorossiisk with the rise of Russian industry and trade, especially foreign trade. More and more settlers flocked to the city and the surrounding countryside. It grew less and less Cossack, more and more middle-class. A railroad connected it with the North Caucasus and with the rest of the country. The city flourished. It became a leading exporter of grain, an importer of agricultural machinery and other foreign manufactures, and a naval base second only to Sebastopol.

It was rich and gay. Italian, Greek, French, British, American, and Russian sailors loved to go there. It was a sailor's town, a merchant's town, a town of fat men and fat women, of coarse hilarity and flagrant dissoluteness. It was garish and slovenly. Its natural grandeur was dimmed by tawdry architecture. The blinding sandstorms were a calamity, the biting flies an agony. Out of the rock in the mountains, stonecutters now and then fashioned pretty cornices or swanky pillars that arrested attention. But neither the Czar's government nor the *nouveau riche* who ruled it nor the Cossack atamans who guarded its security thought of making it another Odessa or even a Sebastopol, a civilized city with a claim to art and culture.

The Soviet Revolution swept it with the violence of its northeasters. Again tragedy laid its hand upon it. The Black Sea Fleet sought safety in its harbors. The first World War was still on. Stalled in the west, the Germans availed themselves of the military disintegration of Russia and pushed east. They demanded the surrender of the Black Sea Fleet. Lenin knew what that meant—the Germans would use it to fortify their hold of the immense Russian lands along the coastline and deep inland. He ordered the sinking of the fleet. The sailors were perturbed and heartbroken. To sink or not to sink the fleet became a subject of violent and vituperative debates. On June 18, 1918, they sank the fleet. The city raged with battle. Whites and Reds, Cossacks and workers fought for its possession. Denikin swooped down on it, in swift and gory retribution. The Bolsheviks drove him out and had their sanguinary reckoning with their enemies. The port of Novorossiisk was in ruins; the grain export stopped; buildings were blasted and burned. Hardly a home but suffered bereavement. The merchants fled to Turkey, France, and other countries. The Cossack atamans who fought with Denikin were killed or fled with their chief. Poverty and squalor stalked the streets.

Then came the Five-year Plans and the greatest building and business boom the city had known. The port and the naval base rose to new eminence, national and international. As in Krasnodar and other Russian cities, construction flowed along two main lines—cultural and industrial. The export of grain and oil brought Novorossiisk new traffic and new wealth. Ships from all over the world docked in its ice-free harbors. Tourists, Russians and foreigners, crowded its hotels. The gateway to the Crimea and the Caucasus, to the most celebrated resorts in the country, it became a city of crowds and of joy seekers.

Yet it was always disenchanting to come to Novorossiisk from Odessa, its chief trade rival in the Black Sea. Despite the boom during the Five-year Plans, it remained a slovenly city, with nowhere a hint of Odessa's grandeur, its eminence in music and literature, with no trace of Odessa's good taste in architecture, dress and manners, with nothing comparable to Odessa's beautifully terraced boulevards along the waterfront, its palaces and monuments, its world-famous staircase into the sea, its fusion of races and nationalities, its lively, colorful, and witty speech, its pretty women and frivolous men. "Mamma Odessa" always had character and personality, history and witchery, and more cheer and jollity than any other city in all Russia.

Novorossiisk is much smaller than Odessa, though not much younger. Yet save for its incomparable geographic location, its renowned cement factories, rising like gray giants on a mountain across the bay, its bustling port, it was in prewar days an unpretentious, unglamorous city. The streets were broad, with many shade trees. It became a city of schools, clubs, libraries, amateur dramatic and choral societies. But it had not even bothered to pull down the slumlike clutter of shanties along the magnificent bay and what might have been a magnificent bathing beach.

The people of Novorossiisk never apologized for its lack of architectural distinction or cultural polish. Irked when invidious comparisons were made with Odessa, they snapped back hotly, "But Odessa is a city of knaves and pickpockets!" No Odessa-ite would deny that his city sheltered the most rascally pickpockets and the jolliest knaves in Russia. The labyrinth of underground caves offered outlaws superb shelter. But to the Odessa-ite, Odessa is Odessa—"God's own resting place." The citizen of Novorossiisk, in self-defense and self-assurance, boasted of his city's future—when, under new building and industrial plans, it would attain a grandeur worthy of its natural setting.

Tragedy, the grimmest it had known, struck Novorossiisk again in September 1942, when the Germans occupied it.

As I passed through streets I well remembered—Pushkinskaya, Lermontovskaya, Koltsovskaya, all named after poets, or Pervomaiskaya (First of May)—not a trace of the city was left. It was a scene of complete and consummate demolition. Before the war the *stanichka*, or original Cossack settlement, had grown into a suburb of 10,000, with comfortable though unpretentious homes, broad streets and boulevards, parks and schools. Now it looked as if a tornado had hit it. The trees were uprooted or burned of limbs and bark; the homes were shattered or blown away; the earth was churned up.

There were no streets, no people, no life. Except now and then for a truck with soldiers and sailors driving about their duties, there was no traffic. The prewar community was wiped out. Weeds and brush grew over the ruins, hawks and sparrows hovered over them. A sturdy, yellow-headed sunflower plant, a short row of tomatoes or corn which someone had planted, was all the civilization I saw in this once crowded, tumultuous community.

In the business part of the city only one building escaped demolition. It had been the headquarters of the German administration. It was now the headquarters of the city Soviet. Everywhere else homes, offices, factories, clubs were heaps of rubble, often mercifully overgrown with green weeds, or tottering skeletons of buildings which carpenters, bricklayers, plumbers were toiling to hold together and make usable. Of the eleven thousand buildings in the city only 197 small cottages could with small effort be made livable. The twenty-two schoolhouses, the thirteen motion-picture halls, the five hotels, the five churches were in ruins. Nothing was left of the fifteen libraries; of the 300,000 volumes on their shelves only 5,000 have been recovered. The Intourist hotel, in which so many American and British visitors stopped on their way to the Crimea or the Caucasus, was a sprawling mass of ruins. The Germans took apart 1,500 homes for materials they used in fortifications. Pavements from sixteen streets and sidewalks almost everywhere they tore up for a similar purpose. Pillboxes, machine-gun nests, gun emplacements peered out of every brick pile, every wall, out of the very earth.

All the American-made tools from the Red Motor Factory had been seized and shipped to Germany. The best machinery from all the factories went the same way. There was no port any more, no docks. The railroad station was a stack of rubble. There were no trolleys. The wires the Germans had lifted and shipped to Germany, the tracks they took up and laid into fortifications. The medical center with its fifteen buildings, its up-to-date installations, escaped complete destruction, but not a building escaped blasting damage. Nothing was left of the equipment—not even chairs, beds, pillowcases. The Germans shipped everything away.

The Novorossiisk I knew before the war was no more. It was a gargantuan shambles. It made me think of a man with arms amputated, legs chopped up, shoulders wrenched, spine broken, but with the breath of life still in him. The damage was valued in August 1944 at $238,000,000. It would be much larger when two thirds of the population which was still absent returned and announced its claims.

"We mean to collect every kopeck," said Osipov, the bustling mayor of the city. "The Germans shall not escape reparations—not this time!"

In the light of what has happened in Novorossiisk and other cities, it is easy to understand the eagerness and the speed with which Russians have been dismantling German shops and factories in Berlin and other cities in their zone of occupation.

On September 16, 1943, when the Red Army returned to Novorossiisk, it found only one family living there. Of the 106,000 prewar population, of the 63,000 who were there when the Germans had seized it a year and eleven days earlier, only one family had weathered the occupation, a family with not a single man, of only two women, a mother and a grandmother, and four children, the oldest of whom was seventeen, the youngest three. In no other city the Red Army had retaken had it found so few Russian survivors. I had read much about this family when Novorossiisk was first reconquered. When I learned the family was home I went to see them. How did they save themselves when all others perished or were driven away?

They lived on the outskirts in a small cottage. Peasants from the Ukraine, they had moved to Novorossiisk in 1935. The mother's name was Maria Tkachenko. Her husband was a worker. He earned the cash, and she, with the help of her 63-year-old mother, cultivated a garden, looked after a cow and chickens, and raised a family of five children. A sturdy woman of medium height, with luminous blue eyes, golden hair, and a white kerchief on her head, she spoke with the soft voice, the melodious intonation that is so unmistakably and delightfully Ukrainian.

Her husband went to war as soon as it broke out. She had not heard from him since October 1941. Neither she nor the Commissary of War knew what had happened to him. When the Germans reached Novorossiisk she and her mother, with the help of the seventeen-year-old boy and the sixteen-year-old girl, continued to cultivate the garden, care for the cow and the chickens. To avoid the attention of the Germans, she rarely went to the city, and only when she needed to exchange tomatoes, carrots, some other garden produce for salt, matches, other groceries.

She had had many a tilt with the Germans, and, peasant fashion, she always stood her ground against them even when it meant risking their wrath, invoking retribution. When the Germans first came they searched her house. On finding two sacks of potatoes they took them away. They made no payment, offered no explanation. She shouted defiance, but they were stronger than she.

The next spring she again planted her garden. When potatoes were ripe she started digging them. Out of nowhere there appeared a truck before her cottage. Two men in uniform leaped out, forced her into the house, told her to stay there or she would be shot, and themselves proceeded to dig up the potato patch. They loaded the potatoes into the truck and drove away. Again she shouted defiance. She wept and cursed, and even as she was talking the memory of the incident made her weep and gulp.

Later two other men in uniform came. They said they wanted her cow.

"I remember the date," she said. "It was February 23, 1943. I told them they could not have my cow. 'We'll see,' they said. 'We'll see,' I said and grasped the cow's halter and held it tight. 'Let go,' they ordered. 'I shan't,' I said. I wept and begged. 'What'll I do without a cow, with an old mother and five children and myself to feed?' But one of them shouted, 'Let go of the cow, you Russian swine!' I shook my head and shouted back, 'No.' The German grasped my hands, tried to loosen them from the halter, but I held so fast he couldn't. My youngest child cried, 'Mamma, Mamma!' 'Quiet,' I ordered, but the child could not stop. 'Let him cry,' I said to myself, 'I want to save the cow.' I was terribly strong, God poured energy into my hands and they were like steel. The German couldn't unclasp them. My heart too was like steel.

"The German drew out a pocketknife and said, 'If you don't let go, I'll cut your throat.' I said, 'Go ahead, cut my throat.' With a quick motion of the hand he cut the halter. Part of it remained in my hands; the part with the bell fell to the ground. He picked up the rope and the bell on the ground, flung them into my face and shouted, 'You Russian swine!' They drove away and slaughtered the cow—and we got hungrier and hungrier."

Again she wept, this time violently, and again she caught herself and apologized and wiped her eyes and her face and smiled as if in reassurance that she was not losing control of herself. "We got so hungry," she resumed, "my mother and my older son and my little girl went to a village to buy corn. Germans rounded them up, drove them somewhere. My mother and the little girl managed to run away, but the boy never could escape. They took him away, and I don't know where he is." She broke down once more and sobbed aloud, but quickly mastered herself.

"One afternoon a neighbor rushed in and said, 'You'd better go and register, Maria, they threaten to shoot those who don't.' I shook my head, 'I shan't register,' I said. 'Let them shoot. It's better to be dead than to be in their captivity.' My neighbor left, we remained in our cottage. We were not frightened, not even the children. If we were to die, it would be in our own home. But everybody else, all around here, all over the city, reported to the Germans and were shot or driven away, everybody but ourselves, because we wouldn't register.

"In the evening there was heavy shooting all over the city. We knew there was fighting between our little sons in the Red Army and the enemy. I felt shivery and lay down in bed. No one seemed to have noticed us, and I prayed that they wouldn't. We had our curtains drawn, but we kept a lamp burning. Then four Germans armed with tommy guns pushed into the cottage. 'What're you doing here?' one of them shouted. My little boy started to cry. The Germans pointed the gun at him and swore, 'Hush you little swine of a partisan!' The boy got scared, crawled under the bed—and remained as silent as a mouse. Again the German turned to me and shouted, 'What're you doing here!' 'I'm sick,' I said. 'What's wrong with you?' 'Malaria,' I replied. But my mother, bless her soul, had her wits about her. Wonderful mother! I don't know what would have happened to us if it hadn't been for her wits. 'Mister Officer,' she interrupted, 'don't believe her. She's feverish, she doesn't know what she's saying. She's a very sick woman, and it isn't malaria, it's typhus.' On hearing the word 'typhus' the Germans acted as though bombs were aimed at them. They swiftly turned round and fled the cottage. That's how we happened to be the only family in the city when our brothers and sons of the Red Army came here—and how we wept when we saw them—how we wept! O Lord my God!'"

Three hundred thousand mines had already been unearthed in Novorossiisk, and the end wasn't yet. Girl sappers in pantaloons, some with kerchiefs on their heads, others with wreaths of wild flowers, were prowling around the environs of the cement factories, poking the ground with the inevitable wood-handled steel rods. Gay, talkative, unmindful of danger, they dug up daily stacks of mines and other explosives. "They're as thick in Novorossiisk," said one of them, "as grass in a meadow."

"They meant to blow up every tree and every rock around here," said another girl sapper, and proceeded to poke around with the dexterity of a chicken pecking away for food.

I went to the cement factories round which was enacted the most dramatic single incident of the Russo-German war. It was here that the German march southward toward Turkey and India was halted in the longest single battle of the war, and one of the most desperate and most decisive. And it was here the guerrillas achieved one of their most sensational triumphs.

For a year and seven days, with all the weapons and science at their command, the Germans strove madly and volcanically to seize the gray, silo-like "October" cement factory in which the Russians were entrenched. But the Russians never budged.

We stopped on the highway at the base of the mountain on which the factory stands.

"Look," said the mayor, pointing to a twisted mass of rails, the ends of which hung over the steep cliff that sloped into the sea. Tucked into the twisted steel as if grown into it were the steel frames of one passenger and one sleeping car. The rest of the train that was caught in battle had tumbled into the sea. Not a splinter of wood had remained on these frames—all of it was burned. The steel was red with rust, and the parts, though bent and twisted, held firmly together. Tall and straight like trees out of the earth rose the upright steel pieces. They were sieved with holes. So was every other piece of steel in the two cars. It was as though every inch of the metal had been a target for skilled snipers. I attempted to count the holes on one upright piece. My eyes ached, my head whirled. I gave up. I might as well try to count the stars.

"These rusty steel cars give you an idea," said Osipov, the

mayor of the city, "of the incredible amount of shooting that passed back and forth—wild, yet concentrated shooting." He shook his head in incredulity and added, "We shall immortalize these rusty cars. We shall put them into a museum so future generations can see for themselves how desperately their *ances-tors* fought."

We walked up the hill and climbed to the roof of the "October" factory. The director and the chief engineer went up with us. They were young men, one in his twenties, the other in his thirties, but both looked much older; their faces were wind-bitten and grooved with care and stress. They had been in the battle of the cement factories from the beginning to the end. Now they were no longer in uniform but in overalls; their hands held not tommy guns but monkey wrenches.

The engineer pointed to "Sugar Loaf," the mountain immediately to the rear of the factory on which he had spent many months as a guerrilla. The "Proletary," the larger of the two cement factories, which the Germans had held, was in full view. Crosslots it was only half a mile away. A short distance from "October" was the *saraychik*—little barn. It never was a barn, the engineer said, only a powerfully fortified dugout, which the Russians had affectionately named *saraychik*. Endless and bloody were the battles for the possession of the dugout. Now the Russians held it, now the Germans, and now the Russians wrested it back from the enemy. As I looked down on it I saw only heaps of gray sand and broken lumber, brick, and steel. There was no *saraychik* any more. A few days earlier a worker had been prowling around and a mine had blown him up. The director proceeded to narrate the sensational "battle of the cement factories," for that is the way it is known and will be known in history.

Germans were in the more advantageous position. They held the bay, the city, all but twenty-five square kilometers of bay shore which a desperate band of Russian marines had seized and from which the Germans could not dislodge them. "The little land" is the name the marines and all Russia have since given to this little strip of bay-shore valley. But its impregnability would have been precarious had it not been for the control the Russians had of "October." This one fortress stalled the German march southward. Partisans hovered all over the mountains and helped the factory. But without the factory the partisans might harass, but could not halt, the German advance.

Again and again the Germans demanded surrender. Invariably the Russians answered with gunfire. Inside the incredibly thick gray walls there was no thought of surrender. The Germans started attack after attack from the air and from the ground. Their infantry crawled and wriggled into no man's land, but never got close to the factory. Russian power laid them out flat and dead or drove them back with cold steel. The Germans dug themselves into no man's land. So did the Russians. At times they were so near one another that they "treated" each other with hand grenades. The Russians wrapped leaflets around rocks and threw them into the German trenches. The leaflets told the enemy of the German holocaust in Stalingrad. The Russians flew kites stuck with pamphlets over the enemy positions. The Germans did not lag behind. They, too, threw pamphlets at the Russians. But "October" remained in Russian hands, inaccessible and impregnable.

The nearest Russian base was five miles away. No vehicle, no horse could traverse the distance with safety. Only human beings could make their way across. With the fall of darkness a caravan of officers and soldiers started on foot for the "October" factory. Bent to the waist or crawling on hands and feet, the caravan wriggled its way through tunnels and trenches and delivered food and ammunition to the besieged and besieging factory-fortress. The men who were inside on the firing line behind thick-walled ramparts of cement and brick or mammoth furnaces never ran short of food or ammunition.

Every day with the coming of darkness the Germans threw up flares, searchlights, started firing with tommy guns, machine guns, artillery. The "October" factory, the bay, the surrounding mountains which were infested with guerrillas was their target. The firing and the flares, the searchlights and the shelling, kept up all night. But the Germans remained where they were in the "Proletary" factory. "October" held. The furnaces behind which the Russians had their beds, their kitchens, their rest rooms, their hospital, did not collapse. Floors burned. Windows blew away, doors crashed. Wood everywhere went up in fire and smoke. Tin and steel were coiled and blasted. But the brick and the cement held. Nothing the German war manuals prescribed, nothing their generals or field marshals conjured forth produced the plan or the weapon with which to demolish or seize the cement factory, by frontal attack or by encirclement, by any tactic whatsoever. They could not get near or around it. They were stopped dead.

To me the most dramatic monument of the fantastic battle of the cement factories was the towering brick chimney stacks. Shells and bombs pounded them from every direction, yet not one fell, not one was even cracked. Holes gaped out of them on all sides, but they stood unbowed. Like bewitched monsters, they had fought off the volcanoes of destruction man had flung at them. Mighty and upright, they reared their lofty peaks skyward, the rims scarcely scathed by fire or shell. I felt like bowing to them out of reverence for their haughty defiance of the fury of man.

I went swimming in the bay with Nikolay Zaitsev, the assistant mayor of Novorossiisk and the most celebrated guerrilla leader in the city. He is over thirty, but looks much younger. He is jovial and talkative. His deep blue eyes, handsome features, strong chin, soft light hair, and gay manner make one instantly aware of a striking, buoyant personality. He seemed born to happiness.

I have neither met nor heard of a guerrilla anywhere who so blithely courted danger and death. Once Zaitsev had to make his way to the cement factory from the top of Sugar Loaf. His colleagues protested. Flares and searchlights swept the mountain. Machine guns roared ceaselessly. Heavy guns boomed. The journey, his colleagues warned, meant certain death. If the searchlights missed him and a shell or bullet did not strike him down, a mine was certain to blow him to shreds. He admitted to his colleagues he was not bulletproof—he had been hit too many times—but he insisted that he was deathproof. Gaily, as though he were leaving for a picnic or a dance, he started out. Searchlights caught him again and again. Guns fired. Mines were all over the ground he was passing. But he never turned back.

"I slid down the ridge," he said, pointing at Sugar Loaf, "quickly, over the thickest mine field—and I got to the factory all right." Eight times he was seriously wounded. No one expected him to recover. Yet he always did and went back to battle.

We swam out into the bay, and soon we heard a voice shouting at us from shore:

"Hey there, don't swim any farther, there're still lots of mines in the bay."

Zaitsev laughed.

"Are there mines around here?" I asked uneasily.

"Certainly," he said. "We haven't fished them all out yet."

With a lithe breast stroke he continued to swim, with no more thought of danger than if he were in a bathtub at home.

"Perhaps," I said, "we had better turn back?"

He chuckled, sprang fishlike out of the water, and turned around like an acrobat.

"See how many wounds I have on me?" Again he turned so I could take a good look at the scars on his body. "Whew," he exclaimed, and instead of turning back he splashed his head into the water and glided on invisibly. When he came to the surface, he beckoned to me to swim toward him, and when I was beside him he said, "Did you ever swim in such wonderful water?"

The man on shore once more called to us to come back.

"Have no fear," Zaitsev assured me, "I'll protect you. I am bewitched. The Germans said so, too. I bewitch everything and everybody around me, even the mines in the bay." Laughing gaily, he splashed onward with swift overhead strokes.

There is to be a new Novorossiisk. Moscow will stint neither funds nor talent to make it a city beautiful with monuments in brick, rock, and bronze, to commemorate the battles of "the little land" and of the "cement factories" and of the bands of guerrillas that prowled ghostlike by day and by night in the valleys and in the mountains.

Novorossiisk is to be a planned city, and for once, if present plans do not miscarry, is to fit itself in line and in color, in stature and design, into the natural beauty of its surroundings. It will ape neither Leningrad nor Kiev, whose climate, history, traditions, culture are different. A southern city, it will seek its inspiration from its chief rival, Odessa, and from Venice. For one thing, it will no longer stand with its back to the sea. It will be turned round so that, like Odessa and Venice, it will face the sea. The waterfront will be cleared of the clutter of shanties and misshaped bathing pavilions that give it a slumlike ugliness and shut its view from the arriving visitor. It will unfold itself in a panorama of boulevards, bathing beaches, blocks of public buildings—the new terminal for ships and trains and busses, the city hall, the town hall, the city library, the post office, the leading theater, the museum, the athletic stadium. There are to be no tall buildings, not one skyscraper, nothing to obscure from view the residential sections or the surrounding countryside with its hills and trees and mountains. No building will be higher than four stories. Apartment houses will not even be that high, no higher than three stories, and most of the dwellings will be one- or two-family cottages, so that each family can have all the privacy it desires. Neither in external appearance nor in internal decoration is any building to suggest somberness or solemnity. Despite its tragic history—the wars, the devastations, the mass murders—Novorossiisk is to have "a smiling face"—as one of its planners expressed himself, "like Odessa, which, no matter how great its afflictions, never forgets its songs and its laughter."

"How long," I said to the mayor, "will it take to rebuild Novorossiisk and make it a city beautiful?"

He shrugged. "If you come back in ten or fifteen years you

will find a new Novorossiisk, perhaps not completed, but well on its way to completion."

CHAPTER XIX

A Village Revisited

WE DROVE into Slavenskaya late in the evening. There was a full and brilliant moon, and the *stanitsa* was as if decked with a silver mantle. From the broad river near by a cool breeze was blowing, and rising above the noises of night—the chirping of crickets, the whine of a faraway animal, the rustle of trees, were the strains of dance music, an unmistakable American jazz tune. Somewhere there was a dance or festival.

When our car stopped, two passing women dressed in white came over to learn who had arrived.

"Is there a celebration here?" I asked.

"No celebration," one of them replied, "just the usual nightly dance."

Harvest was at its height. The women and girls who were gathering it worked from dawn until dark or all night, depending on which shift they were. At no other time in the year is field work in the Kuban so strenuous, especially when there is a bumper crop as there was in 1944. Yet like a foreordained ritual the usual nightly dance remained a part of the daily life of the community. It signalized Cossack enterprise and Cossack joymindedness.

Eight years had passed since I had first visited this old and populous Cossack village, the oldest and the most populous in the Kuban and the one that I knew best. On my previous trip

I had come from Krasnodar by boat over the swift-flowing and teeming Kuban River. Now the river was as clear of traffic as though it coursed through some faraway and uninhabited wilderness. Not a craft plied its swift waters. No craft could pass the broken bridges that lay coiled and twisted and half sunk in the stream. Besides, few boats were left. They had been blown up or burned.

On my trip in 1936, immediately after my registration in the hotel I had gone walking along the main avenue, and the first sounds I had heard were likewise dance music. The playing came from a many-windowed building with large flashing lights at the entrance. The sign over the door bore the imposing name of "Home of Culture." I stepped inside and found myself face to face with a scene which I had never associated with Cossack life. It was too sensationally modern to fit into the picture of primitive romance, which because of my reading of Cossack history the word "Cossack" had spelled to my mind. In the middle of the floor a young man in shirt sleeves, dance slippers, and with light brown hair tumbling over his forehead was demonstrating to a crowd of eager-faced and sunburned young people, especially girls, the steps of an American fox trot.

I stood aside and watched. "One-two-three, one-two-three, one-two-three," recited aloud the earnest young man as he kept pacing around in tune with the music and his own words. "One-two-three, one-two-three, one-two-three," repeated in whispers or half whispers the attentive young people as they too stepped around in imitation of their teacher. On inquiry I learned that the young man was a physical-culture instructor from Krasnodar and had been invited to Slavenskaya to teach Cossack youths the latest sensation in the Russian dance world—the "Boston," or American waltz, and the fox trot. Some of the boys and a few of the girls were barefoot. Yet when the instructor called on them to pair up and dance, they danced anyway. . . .

The coincidence of hearing dance music on my arrival in Slavenskaya eight years earlier and now was like a cheerful greeting, all the more welcome because of the war which I knew had raged with special violence in this village. It testified as nothing else I knew to the irrepressible love of sheer living in the Cossack youth. War or no war, harvest or no harvest, day work, night work, they would have their dancing.

I could not help thinking of the village as I knew it in 1936. The stern struggle of collectivization had been over for about four years. The tractor and the combine as much as political authority and police force had vanquished all opposition. The new agricultural system, swept along by the wheels of the modern machine, had triumphed. An end had come to the age-old and untempered Cossack economic individualism. The wealthiest of individual farmers outside of the landed gentry, not one now boasted a farm of his own. So well was the Cossack fitting himself into the new dispensation that his Cossackhood, which since their rise to power the Soviets had outlawed, he had again recovered. He was not merely a Soviet citizen but once more a Cossack. He was permitted to sport his *cherkesska* with its scarlet breastpiece and his dagger. Again he was, in his leisure moments, the romantic figure of a warrior on horseback. Purged of czarist implementation, cleansed of tribal egoism, sundered from individual landholding, an energetic and highly competent member of collectivist enterprise, he could vaunt once more his pride in his origin, his historic achievement in helping make Russia the immense land that it was; he could take to heart once more the centuries-old traditions and glories of his warrior ancestors. Special farms were started all over the Kuban for the breeding of riding horses, and Cossack youths, under the guidance and inspiration of instructors, fathers, grandfathers, could as in the old days indulge in the ancient *dzhigitovkas*—war games—which the Soviets had originally forbidden.

Despite the fighting during the civil war and the more recent battle of collectivization, both in their time destructive not only of good humor and good will but of property and life, Slavenskaya in 1936 was once more shiny with prosperity. The shops were heaped with goods. The dry-goods section of the leading state department store was weighted with fabrics of as high a quality as Russian textile factories were weaving. There was no shortage of silk. Moscow was nowhere nearly as well supplied with textiles, and here, unlike the bureaucracy-ridden capital, salesmen and saleswomen were polite and attentive. Nowhere did I see any queues. Embroidered shirts and bath towels which I could not buy in Moscow, or could purchase only by wasting several hours in a queue, I purchased here by merely asking for them. In the liquor shops and food stores there was as fine a display of bottled and labeled liquors as in the best Moscow shops. It seemed as if the Soviets on the heels of their political triumph over the Cossack were making a special effort to bring him the material rewards which in their drive for collectivization they had promised him.

The market place was teeming with traffic. Here were stacks of melons, cartloads of fruits, with the largest, cleanest-skinned apples I had seen in Russia, tubfuls of honey, dairy foods, meats, white breads, cakes, vegetables, everything to satisfy the most exacting and the most gluttonous appetite. The fruits and the vegetables were so large and so shiny with quality that they made me think of the old Flemish masters and their paintings of market scenes. Here was a land flowing with milk and honey. No more bountiful a land had I seen anywhere in Russia. All the more remarkable was this new prosperity because only five years earlier, because of sabotage of tillage, slaughter of livestock, incident to the collectivization campaign, the village was prostrate with want. Immense were the recuperative powers of the Cossack Kuban.

At the edge of the river close to the pier where the boats docked was a new hotel, a two-story brick structure with excellent rooms and execrable plumbing. I stopped in this hotel and left my passport with the clerk. The next morning I was waked by a persistent knocking at my door. I opened it and found myself face to face with the chief of police. I wondered what I had done or what had happened to bring him so early in the morning to my room. He was not long in telling me. He had never seen an American passport. He had never met an American. So he came to tell me he was glad to have a good look at an American passport and to get acquainted with me. That was all he came for, he said; he had nothing to do anyway in his office.

He was a little man with a thin, sharp-featured face. He spoke good Russian, without the mixture of Ukrainian which flavors the speech and the intonation of the Kuban Cossacks. He said he was born in Minsk, capital of White Russia. He was Jewish and had had extensive experience in police work. His job in Slavenskaya was the easiest he had ever held. Cossacks, with all their liveliness, were supremely orderly people. They did not steal, not even vegetables from each other's gardens or fruits from one another's orchards. They were family-minded, family-loving. A father was a father and a mother was a mother and children obeyed both. There was hardly any hooliganism, and when it occurred the families did their own disciplining. There were no community scandals requiring the attention of the police. There was in fact so little social disturbance in the village that the Soviet closed the local jail and turned over the building to the power station, which needed extra indoor space. The only real lawbreakers he had ever caught were floating pickpockets and swindlers who had stopped off between trains to ply their trade among unsuspecting Cossacks. But he didn't bother with them. He arrested them and sent them under guard to Temruk or Krasnodar for the police in those cities to look after them. Yes, the Kuban country was as peaceful as it was rich and beautiful, the garden spot of Russia.

In 1936 the Kuban was even more of a revelation to me than to this little Jewish chief of police from White Russia. It was a world of its own absorbed in itself to the exclusion of momentous events in the outside world. The purge which signalized a new epoch in the Soviet Revolution had begun. Zinovyev and Kamenev, once eminent and powerful figures in the Revolution, had already been tried, had made their melodramatic confessions, had been executed. The radio had broadcast the trial, the court sentence. The newpapers had printed long, violent denunciations of the defendants. In Sochi, whence I had come to Krasnodar, vacationists, chiefly intellectuals, while in no mood to discuss the event openly, were shaken with concern. Just at a moment when the country, after weathering so much struggle and adversity, so much terror and death, was settling down to a rising standard of living, a fresh political crisis had broken out. Communists in power were executing Communists out of power precisely as, in the French Revolution, Republicans in power had guillotined Republicans out of power.

Yet in Slavenskaya no one seemed concerned about the purge. Except in certain political circles, I did not hear people discuss it. It did not involve Cossacks. It meant no break in their life, no interference in their plans or their pleasures. It belonged to the realm of high politics. It took place in faraway Moscow. Besides, the young generation had barely heard of Zinovyev, Kamenev, and the other men on trial with them. The village was swept along by its own stream of life—the good harvest, the manufactured goods in the state shops, the rehabilitation of Cossackhood, the dancing teacher from Krasnodar. There were poor people in Slavenskaya, people who earned little either because of physical incapacity or subjective incompatibility. There were older Cossacks who nurtured irrevocable bitterness because of what had happened to them personally or to close friends or to members of their families during the civil war and collectivization. These people were sullen and inarticulate. But others, the young people especially, were busy with their work and their social gaieties. . . .

Now that I was back in Slavenskaya and caught my first glimpse of the village by moonlight, I could not help thinking of the sharp contrast I had observed eight years earlier between the sweep of the machine age over fields and the untouched primitiveness of the village itself. The streets were as broad and unpaved as under the Czar, with hardly any sidewalks. There was no escaping the dense clouds of dust which a passing truck or oxcart whipped up. It fell on fences, on buildings, on pedestrians. It ate into the eyes, the nose, the mouth. Whenever I was caught in it I could hardly breathe and hastened a handkerchief to the nose and the mouth.

With their fresh and neat whitewash, the low one-story cottages were a pretty sight. There is nothing the Cossack woman loves more than to tidy her cottage inside and outside, giving it a fresh coat of whitewash as soon as dust or rain has sullied the old one. The interior was always clean and cool. Larger and more comfortable than peasant houses, the Cossack cottages were also more decorative, with more icons and more family photographs. Sheltered by trees and thick-walled, they were cool in summer, warm in winter. To keep out the hot sun and the flies, the wooden shutters were closed during the day. Nothing was more refreshing than to enter a Cossack cottage after a long walk in the streets.

Yet aside from the trees which grow more or less wild, the rows of poppies, geraniums, other flowers in the gardens, the village was void of the external refinements which give an English village so beautiful and majestic an appearance. There were no lawns. The courtyards were littered with fallen twigs. Chickens strutted around and squawked everywhere. Weeds were uncut, even the thick-stemmed, blooming, pernicious thistles. Fences were unmended and unpainted. Pigs wallowed in mud puddles or in the cool bottom of tree-shaded ditches. There was no sewage. There was no plumbing. Water was drawn by pail from old-fashioned open wells. The only modern acquisition was electric lights. Nothing more. The Plans brought a building boom, not of homes but of public institutions, of which there were few in pre-Soviet days—clubhouses, shops, manufacturing establishments, nurseries, and especially schools. The modernization of housing would have to bide its time.

The dance music I now heard, the brilliant moon, the many trees made me forget for the moment the primitiveness of the village as I knew it eight years earlier and the war with all the ravages it had wrought. Little of it was visible where the car first stopped. The people who passed by on the way from a movie or who were just promenading appeared well dressed and cheerful. They were eating apples, shelling sunflower seeds, talking animatedly.

Only when I went walking along the river front did I become aware of the ruin that had come to Slavenskaya. I looked and looked for the two-story brick hotel in which I had stopped. There was no hotel. The building was as if lifted from its foundations and flung or blown into the nearby river; only the black outline of the foundation was left. There was no dock: there were only solitary pillars jutting ghostlike out of the river. The water had risen out of the banks. There was the gurgle of water striking against an obstacle. Now and then a fish made a splash. Somewhere along midstream was a red light for the guidance of fishermen. There were no barges, no steamers, no canoes with chattering and singing young people as in 1936, when all night long the river was astir with life and movement. Once the prettiest and gayest part of the village, the waterfront was now the most silent and most desolate.

"Not a cock crowed in our village," said a Cossack woman. "Think of it, not one cock crowed in our big and rich Slavenskaya!" The Germans had eaten up or shipped to Germany all the poultry in the village, 25,000 birds. Of the 9,000 heads of cattle only 242 milch cows remained alive. Cossacks had contrived to hide them in dugouts and in woods, and the Germans never saw them. All the pigs were gone, 18,000 of them, all the sheep, 7,000 head, all the horses, 3,000! Those the Germans failed in their hasty withdrawal to drive away, they shot dead. "Mountains of animal corpses lay all around here," said an elderly Cossack.

I had my first meal in Slavenskaya with Goncharov, the Party secretary. Throughout the eight months of German occupation he had commanded a tough, fighting guerrilla brigade within the neighborhood of the village. About forty years old, slightly cross-eyed and round-shouldered, Goncharov was a sturdy man with a broad back, powerful hands, and the voice and manner of a schoolmaster. His wife was a tall handsome woman with luminous dark eyes, thick and wavy dark hair, and the faculty of making a guest feel immediately at home in her house. When she set the table I was amazed. Though I had already become accustomed to Cossack meals with their lavish display of fruits and vegetables, dairy foods and cakes, I had not been away from Moscow long enough to cease contrasting the luscious abundance here with the scarcity of fresh food in Moscow and the laxity of cooks and chefs in the hotels in which foreign correspondents lived. Here on Goncharov's table were fresh milk, homemade butter, apples and pears freshly picked from trees in the yard, tomatoes and cucumbers freshly plucked from the garden. . . . I could not help reaching out for an apple even before we sat down to table. "I am so starved for fruit and fresh vegetables," I said by way of excuse, "that just hearing the crunch of an apple or cucumber is like music to my ears."

"Come to the Kuban," said Goncharov's wife. "You'll soon lose that feeling."

We sat down to the meal and talked.

"What," I asked Goncharov, "is the most memorable experience you had during your guerrilla career?"

He reflected and said: "I had so many experiences that I hardly know which is the most memorable. They are all memorable. But I can tell you what made me as mad as anything I bucked up against in the months I was hunting for Germans. One day, with weapons which we had wrested from them, we ambushed a caravan of horse carts. Quickly we disposed of the Germans and proceeded to examine the goods in the carts. It was all ours, looted from our homes—boots, feather bedding, cotton-padded blankets, rugs, furniture, children's clothes, children's toys, mirrors, chairs, divans, beds—very many beds. Germans were particularly partial to brass and other metal beds. We knew they were going to ship our 'family happiness' to their cursed homeland, and you should have heard us swear. We vowed, all of us, that we'd fight them harder than ever. We would shoot them every chance we had. We stopped thinking of them as human beings. They were beasts, the most cruel that

ever trod this earth. Think of them stealing children's clothes
and toys and women's dresses! We had some pretty bad times in
our hideouts. Often enough we were ragged, cold, hungry, and
sick, shaking with fever and chills. But no matter what our
physical condition was, when scouts reported the prospect of
a good hunt for Germans we leaped up from our cots or from
the beds of twigs on which we were convalescing or suffering
pain and went out to fight. It gave us keen pleasure to ambush
them from behind a tree or hill and see them fall bullet-ridden
to the ground or tumble with their heads down into their horse
carts or automobiles."

His wife said cheerfully: "Now that they're gone, let's drink
to our freedom!"

We rose, clinked glasses, and as we started to drink Goncharov
raised his head to stop us and said, "Yes, and to the friendship
of your people in America with ours in the Soviet Union."

I walked around the village. By daylight, in the absence of
the magic of a full moon, not even the trees and the rich vegetation could conceal the bleakness and the devastation the Germans had left in the wake of their retreat. Not a brick building
escaped burning or destruction. Blocks of buildings put up
mostly since my previous visit were heaps of rain-packed rubble. New schools, clubhouses, one with a theatrical stage and an
auditorium with a seating capacity of 650, the Home of Culture,
the jam factory which annually put out 25,000 tons of choice
fruit and berry jams, the two wine-making establishments, the
cotton gin, the flour mills, the eighteen kindergartens, all the
nurseries—in other words, the building program of the three
Five-year Plans were leveled to the ground or were mere shells.

Scarcely a cottage was newly whitewashed. Broken panes
were replaced with plywood, boards, sacks of straw. Rank
weeds grew everywhere around the houses, the courtyards, the
streets, the squares. I had never seen such lusty crops of weeds
in any village. Fences were gone or smashed beyond repair.
Smoke was curling out of the summer ovens in the courtyards,
fine blue smoke that glistened in the sun as it wove its way,

snakelike, through the limbs of trees and dissolved in the air. Many trees were cut and blasted. Many were barren of limbs and bark. The village looked as though it had been at the mercy of winds, dust, storm, and the fury and neglect of man.

Gone were the bounteous shops I had seen in 1936. Save salt, stray pieces of hardware, a few dusty bottles of cosmetics, they were empty of goods. No new textiles, no new shoes, no jams, no canned fruits, not a trace of the opulence at which I had marveled eight years earlier. The market place was the most flourishing I had observed since my departure from Moscow. The fruits and vegetables alone made it, in wartime Russia, almost a show place. Yet it was only a dark shadow of what it had been on my earlier visit—little jars instead of tubs of honey, little rolls instead of pails of butter, thin slabs instead of large chunks of pork and beef. The German-Rumanian slaughter of livestock, the destruction of beehives, left a ghostly void which only time could fill.

In their work clothes the people looked ragged and slovenly. There had been no new clothes, no new shoes since the war began. Because it was the most prosperous village in the Kuban, the looting of wardrobes by German and Rumanian officers and soldiers was more rampant and more violent. Yet in the streets, in the market place, in the weed-choked public square, children played with hilarity and zest. Some of them had wooden guns, and a few sported real muskets of ancient make, and the little girls seemed as joyfully eager to march and crawl and run as the boys. It was fascinating to watch these children—they seemed so freehearted, so healthy, so buoyant. Whatever else the occupation may have done to Slavenskaya, it had not stifled in children the irrepressible yearning for play and fun and adventure that is so innate in children everywhere. It was one of the most cheering sights in the now impoverished and dilapidated Cossack village.

I went to see Dmitry Ivanovitch Vlasov. He was sixty years old and looked at least ten years older. His large, dark brown eyes were sunk and lusterless. His white hair was closely cropped, and only his neatly trimmed bristly mustache gave his lugubrious face an aspect of dignity. He sat on a bench with his hands pressed against it and trembling visibly. He spoke in a slow throbbing voice.

"Have you ever known any Rumanians?" he asked.

"Very few," I replied.

"I haven't known very many," he said, "but I shan't forget them—in my grave I shall remember them."

The Rumanians, he said, entered Slavenskaya at four thirty in the afternoon on August 11, 1942. In the morning of the twelfth they came to his cottage. "With the butt of a gun they hit me in the breast and demanded my weapons. I said I had none. They didn't believe me, and started searching my house. They found no machine guns, no rifles, no weapons at all. But they helped themselves to a bicycle, to kitchenware, to my underwear, my wife's underwear, my razor, to all the soap they found, to every nail, every piece of crockery they saw. I never knew such petty, greedy thieves. They arrested me and my fifteen-year-old son and led us under guard to a schoolhouse. They crowded the basement of the school with prisoners, among them boys and a few women. My son and the other boys managed to run away, but the rest of us remained.

"In the morning they separated intellectuals from the others. Since I was working in the jam factory as mechanic, I was classed as an intellectual. They marched us off to a gully about two kilometers from the village, two hundred of us, the pick of the intelligentsia that hadn't fled into the rear. They lined us up in two rows and ordered us to sit down with our legs crossed and our faces toward them. Revolver in hand, a Rumanian officer walked back and forth, looking at us. Now and then he shot and killed someone. Then he told seven of the older people to step aside. We did. The others remained sitting on the ground with their legs crossed. They were the flower of our intelligentsia—physicians, agricultural experts, engineers. Knowing they were going to be shot, we older men turned our heads: we did not want to see the shooting. But the Rumanian officer came over and shouted at us and ordered us to turn round and look so we would see the murder of our friends and acquaintances. Then he shouted: 'Fire!' The guns went off and the double row of Russians fell dead before our eyes. Rumanians did that."

He paused and stared at me with glassy eyes. Recovering, he went on: "I have a daughter, just twenty-one years old. Her name is Antonia. Now she is in the Red Army, but during the occupation she was here. Very late one night Rumanians knocked at the door of our house. My daughter suspected trouble and swiftly rolled out of the back window into the darkness of night. I opened the door. The Rumanians swaggered in. 'Where is your daughter?' they asked. 'Gone,' I replied. 'Where?' 'I don't know.' They searched the house, searched and swore and threatened. But my daughter was not there, so they had to leave. Afterward my daughter didn't stay home nights. When the Rumanians left and the Germans came, they too started prowling around our homes at night in search of young girls. My daughter was lucky. They never found her. But other girls in Slavenskaya were not so lucky. We have a venereal clinic here. We never had one in all the history of our village. We never needed it."

During the eight months of the occupation, the Germans and Rumanians put to death over one thousand civilians in Slavenskaya.

"But Slavenskaya never lost its spirit," said Goncharov's pretty wife. "As soon as my husband and the other officials came back, we all started working. . . . Our first task, of course, was to plant our lands and put in as much of a spring crop as we could. But there was no seed in the village. The Germans had eaten it or shipped it to Germany or burned it. Our bins, always bursting with grain, were empty. The nearest place where we could get grain was Annihilinskaya, forty kilometers [twenty-five miles] away. The railroads were shattered, the bridges were broken, and no freight could come by train. We had few horses, no trucks, no oxen, and only a few feeble, emaciated cows. . . . So our Cossack women said they'd go on foot to Annihilinskaya and bring the grain on their backs. They started off like a caravan, there were so many of them, with empty sacks on their backs. The roads were muddy; the weather was bad, raw and rainy. But they walked to Annihilinskaya and came back on foot, each one of them carrying on her shoulders a sack of grain. . . . In all, they brought on their backs 375 tons of seed! And d'you think they grumbled or wept or grew bitter? Not at all. Not our Cossack women. Oh, there were exceptions, but not many. They laughed and jested and sang. They took it all in fun, not as a chore, but as an adventure. . . . That's the kind of high-spirited folk they are, our *kazachki*."

"God bless them," said an elderly Cossack standing near by. "God grant them health and happiness—our wonderful and valorous *kazachki*."

"They do everything so well," I said, "I am wondering what's going to happen to the men here when the war is over?"

"The men will be afraid of them—aye, they will," said the older man, winking slyly and nodding as if in emphasis of the meaning of his words.

"Kuban men have never been afraid of anybody or anything," another man remarked boastfully.

"We'll see, you'll see," the older man persisted.

"The men will have stiff competition, that's certain," said the mayor.

"Who will win?" I asked.

"The person who has the greater competence and can show the better results will win," said the Party secretary. "What we want is results, and if the women can produce them better than the men, more power to them."

"There's nothing our women cannot do," said the secretary's wife. "A tractor breaks down and they crawl under it, on top of it, look at its insides, bang away with a hammer, twist back and forth with a monkey wrench, and it starts going again. A combine stalls and they get off, putter around, and—whew!—off it goes again as though nothing had ever happened to it. They've never been like that in our Kuban, never."

"The only thing our Cossack women cannot do," said the secretary, "is turn themselves into men."

CHAPTER XX

Cossack Girls

IN SLAVENSKAYA a committee of girls called and invited me to attend a gathering of young people. They wanted to talk about the war, the Germans, America, Russia, and kindred subjects. It was so seldom, they said, that they had a chance to exchange opinions with someone from the outside world. The Kuban was so far away from the main traveled roads of the world that Americans rarely came to Slavenskaya. I was the first since the start of the war.

Only four boys were present at the gathering. All the others were girls, some still in high school, others graduates, freshly matriculated in some college, a few were professional social workers. It was obvious that they were the young intelligentsia of the village, the newest young Cossack generation, or rather the leaders of this generation, therefore a minority among the youth of the village. They would reflect, I thought, the best that Cossack youth at its highest intellectual and political level was or aspired to be.

They had worked all day in the harvest fields, but now they were festively dressed, with not a hint of the soiled and ragged work outfits in which I had seen girls and women bustling about during the day. They were so well dressed, better than any girls

I had yet seen anywhere, including Krasnodar, that I asked them how they had managed to save their good clothes from the prowling and thieving Rumanian and German officers and soldiers.

"Our wits helped us," said a short girl with a broad face, a deep bosom, and large glowing dark eyes.

At once girl after girl told the story of how she had contrived to rescue a part of her wardrobe by hiding it in a box in the ground in their back yard or in the woods. One girl had hidden a silk dress behind an icon, "and every time one of *them* entered our house, Mother and I trembled with fear, but they never touched our icons, and so I saved my dress."

"You should have been here before the war," said another girl with coal-black eyes, coal-black hair woven into two long glistening braids that fell over her bosom to the waistline. "I had seven Sunday dresses."

"Many of us had that many Sunday dresses."

"I had eight," said another girl; her hair was severely brushed back, giving her face a broad, open, somewhat solemn expression.

"We had lots of nice clothes," said another girl, tall, with flaxen hair, and a birthmark running tonguelike from the right cheek to the throat.

"We all had at least one silk dress," said the girl with the long black braids.

"Silk was no luxury, not here in Slavenskaya."

There was a buzz of talk, loud and earnest, as girl after girl proudly informed me of the Sunday dresses she and her friends had before the war. They assured me that not a girl in Slavenskaya but was the proud possessor of at least five Sunday dresses.

I must have looked and acted as though I doubted their words. It did seem incredible. Never had I been in any other part of Russia where girls even in the best of prewar days boasted of so many Sunday dresses. I told them I could hardly believe it. My words must have irritated one of the young men, secretary of the Comsomol. With a touch of resentment he said:

"Why d'you think our girls should be poorly dressed? They work hard. They earn wheat and corn and other products for their labor days. They sell these products to the state at the low state prices, and the state sells them, at low state prices, cloth and silk and shoes."

The girl with the braids glanced at the youth with flirtatious eyes, as though in approval of what he said, and, turning to me, remarked, "We love pretty clothes."

"Who makes them for you?" I asked.

"Ourselves," replied the girl with the birthmark.

"All Cossack girls can sew," said the Comsomol secretary. He grinned and added, "Cossack girls learn well the things women should be doing." Tradition was manifestly strong here even with respect to mothers passing on to their daughters, career-minded daughters, the knowledge of homemaking and of other purely feminine activities.

I asked if any of them smoked.

"No," came the loud and many-voiced reply.

"We don't think girls or women should smoke," said the girl with the birthmark.

"D'you approve of boys smoking?" I asked.

"I don't," said the girl with the birthmark.

"Boys can do as they please," said another girl, "but girls should be girls." This must be the attitude everywhere I have traveled in villages, for not once had I seen a Cossack girl or a Cossack woman smoking.

"What about drinking?" I asked.

"If there is a celebration, of course girls should be a part of it."

"But supposing there is no celebration," I said, "supposing you feel a drink would liven up an occasion?"

The Comsomol secretary laughed but said nothing.

"It depends on the occasion," said the girl with the coal-black eyes.

"In Moscow," I said, "right around the corner from the hotel in which I live, at the doorway of a motion-picture house, I see quite a few boys and girls smoking."

"Moscow is Moscow," said the girl with the birthmark, "and this is Slavenskaya."

It was their turn to ask questions, and they came in a deluge. What kind of a life did American girls live? Did they have many Sunday dresses? Did they approve of smoking and drinking? Were they social-minded? Did fathers and mothers ever interfere in the selection of the men they wanted to marry? Did they work in the harvest fields with tractors, combines, other machines, just as Cossack girls were doing? Did they dance much? What were the new American dances? Were there many men in America now to dance with? Question after question intended to bring out similarities or contrasts between themselves, their way of life, and that of American girls. . . .

Then we talked of books. I asked which American authors they preferred. I expected to hear the usual answer: "Jack London," whose popularity in Russia, as well as everywhere else on the European continent, has attained legendary proportions. But I did not. Mark Twain was the favorite author here. The good-humored adventures of Mark Twain's heroes appealed to them more than the violent exploits and the inflated romance of Jack London's.

Their favorite Russian author was Tolstoy. All of them had read *Anna Karenina* and *War and Peace*. They preferred *War and Peace*. It roused love of the fatherland. It pictured the Russian people as simple, heroic, unconquerable. Not only did they drive Napoleon out of Moscow but pursued him to Paris, even as the Red Army was pursuing the Germans to Berlin. As for Tolstoy's women, they adored Natasha and pitied Anna. No girl could be more charming than Natasha, more kind, more lively, more to be emulated as a person and as a woman. But after she marries, what becomes of her? She becomes so wrapped up in her babies, her household, her nursery that she is oblivious of the outside world.

"She settles down," said one girl, "as no woman should settle down. A woman should always study and do social work."

"That's right, motherhood and social work, that's the ideal life for a woman," said another. They all agreed. The boys agreed to this formula of self-realization for women.

On and on they talked with good humor, with animation, with complete acceptance of the Soviet doctrine of a woman's position in society. . . .

"Why did Anna Karenina commit suicide?" began the girl with the long braids. "Because outside her home, her ballroom life, her masquerades, her men, she has nothing to live for, and when she leaves her husband and becomes absorbed in Vronsky, she thinks that she has found her real ultimate happiness. But when she loses Vronsky, she sees her happiness at. an end and she ends her life."

"Life is never at an end," said the diminutive girl with the severe hairdress. "Life always goes on, and there is always a purpose in life."

"Life doesn't end with a man or a woman," said the girl with the birthmark.

The maturity of these girls was astounding, and yet not unnatural when one remembers that in Russia, under czarism as well as now, the educated girl attained intellectual maturity at an early age, earlier than in Anglo-Saxon countries. Let the reader recall Chekhov's and even more Turgenev's heroines. There is nothing adolescent and immature about them. There is in them a sense of life and hope and promise which the men about them, young and old, seldom share. They have greater clarity of purpose and greater emotional consistency. When the world tumbles at the feet and over the heads of the Ranevsky family in *The Cherry Orchard*, it is the seventeen-year-old Anya who says to her mother:

"The cherry orchard is sold; it's gone; it's quite true, quite true. But don't weep, Mamma, you've still got your life before you, you've still got your pure and lovely soul. Come with me, darling; come away from here. We'll plant a new garden, lovelier than this, you will see it and understand, and happiness, deep and tranquil, will sink down on your soul, like the sun at dusk, and you'll smile, Mamma. Come, darling, come with me."

What was especially illuminating about these Cossack girls and their view of life is the swiftness with which the new social gospel was permeating even these remote Cossack villages with their sturdy old family traditions and their once equally sturdy concept of the purely domestic destiny of women. The war, the occupation, had neither shaken nor weakened the hold of this gospel on the young mind, the mind of the boy and girl of high-school and college age. The words of these boys and girls, especially of the girls, the firmness with which they spoke, was a denial of the suspicions and presumptions which one encounters in the foreign press that the new marriage laws, the encouragement of large families, the exaltation of motherhood, the segregation of the sexes in the public schools, presage a return of the Russian women to a purely domestic environment and a purely domestic destiny.

With all the background of domesticity on their side—cooking, sewing, housekeeping, field work precisely as in the days of their grandmothers—and with all the family feeling and tradition in their blood, reinforced by the new teachings they were absorbing, these girls were yet looking beyond the personal glamor and the social horizon of Tolstoy's Natashas and Annas.

As I listened to them I could not help thinking of the women in the great Russian novels on Cossack life. The authors are partial to the physical grace and the feminine appeal of Cossack girls. Tolstoy's Beletzky is so enraptured with them that he speaks of them as "magnificent women." Tolstoy's Cossack heroine Maryanka captivates the reader the moment the author introduces her and holds him fascinated to the last words the author writes of her. Sholokhov's heroine, in *Quiet Flows the Don,* is one of the most moving characters in all Russian literature. Yet neither in Tolstoy nor in Sholokhov, whose novel deals with the Cossack in pre-Soviet days or during the civil war, is there a suggestion of the intellectual stature of the girls to whom I had been listening. "Learning," as Cossacks say, was not a part of the tradition or the ambition of the Cossack girl, hardly even of the Cossack man. Now it is. The flood of books —chiefly classical literature, Russian and foreign—that has poured into the Cosack villages and the new schools that have been built there have created a new type of young woman whose very presence in the Cossack country marks one of the great revolutions in Cossack civilization. One may deplore and denounce as earnestly and profoundly as one chooses the lack of civil liberties in Russia, the cruelty with which political offenders are still treated, their helplessness once they are in the clutch of the NKVD, Russia's political police, yet the intellectual stature to which Sovietism in its Russian mold has lifted the young girls I heard in Slavenskaya marks a towering landmark in the transformation of Cossack humanity and in the advancement of Cossack civilization.

Loaded with apples and pears, we left Slavenskaya. We were again in the open sun-drenched steppe. Wheat stubble, corn, golden sunflowers swept the landscape as far as the eye could see. Here were no heaps of rain-packed rubble, no battered, smoke-blackened chimney stacks. Nature was filling up the trenches, the gun emplacements, even the craters. Fast-growing grass and brush were hiding or healing the wanton slits and slashes in the earth. Only the fields of weeds, thick and dense and shoulder or head high, and the almost comical slow-paced cow carts, evoking the image of biblical times, made one aware of the war and of its evil consequences.

We came to a break in the road. A bridge over a small stream had not yet been repaired. A crowd of women were digging with long-handled shovels and rolling logs, getting ready to lay the bridge over the stream. Before turning off into the nearby field where the stream was shallow and passable, the chauffeur slowed the jeep. Suddenly two women in kerchiefs came over, peered at us sharply, as though they were seeking to identify us. With a loud laugh they drew away.

"No, girls," said one of them turning to the crowd, "they have no apples." We held our breath and said nothing. As he was clearing the stream, the chauffeur said teasingly:

"What would you do if we had apples?"

"What's the use of talking when you haven't any?" snapped the woman with disgust in her voice. "You are only *nachalstvo* [officials], anyway."

"Come back when you have apples," someone cried out.

There was loud, ringing laughter.

"They're always like that," said the chauffeur as we struck the road again, "never too busy or too tired to have a bit of fun, and don't for a moment imagine they'd have hesitated to take the apples away from us if they thought we had them."

He stepped on the gas, and we whirled away to our next destination.

CHAPTER XXI

The Boy with the Fiddle

IN PREWAR DAYS Ust Labinskaya was famous in the Kuban as one of the liveliest and most progressive *stanitsas*. It had its own power plant and its own broadcasting stations. It prided itself on some of the finest schools in the Kuban and the most talented amateur theatrical and choral societies. Though its population was only 15,000, it was subdivided into nine collectives, eight for agriculture, one for fishing. On the completion of the civil war it had planted a new park on an immense grass-grown square in the heart of the community. Now with the trees full grown the park had become the center of all social life in summer, and

Cossacks from other villages, especially young people, came there for their amusement.

Hardly any *stanitsa* in the Kuban could vie with Ust Labinskaya in the flourish of its new culture, not even Slavenskaya. Without losing its traditionally pastoral atmosphere, it was bringing to its own doors more and more of urban civilization. The park boasted a new and spacious summer theater. Despite strenuous work on the land, members of the *stanitsa's* highly talented company of amateur theatricals frequently put on plays, including musical comedies with much choral singing and dancing. Less frequently professional actors from Krasnodar or Rostov gave performances in the summer theater. The park also boasted an outdoor dancing pavilion.

With the money they earned on the collective farms and the new education they were acquiring, the Cossack girls, unlike their mothers and grandmothers in czarist times, were acquiring city tastes in dress and manners. They made their own clothes from patterns created by city designers. When they went to a shoe store for a new pair of Sunday footwear, they disdainfully passed up old models and purchased only the latest city styles. They were learning the fox trot, the Boston (American waltz), the tango, the rumba, and they were hilariously partial to American jazz music for their dances. Ust Labinskaya was making its mark in the rich and rising Cossack Kuban.

Then the war came. Renowned for its Cossack fighters, the *stanitsa* mustered its own Cossack regiment. Dropping all their other work, men and women under the guidance of the *stariks* (old people) set about grinding the ancient sabers, mending saddles and harnesses, overhauling uniforms and blankets or sewing new ones, preparing biscuits, dried fruit, other foods for the departing regiment. As is the custom in Cossack villages, the regiment bore the name of its own *stanitsa*—that is, Ust Labinskaya. More than once it distinguished itself in action on the battlefield.

I had never been in this *stanitsa*, but after hearing of its achievements in Krasnodar and in Slavenskaya, I decided to go there. Especially eager was I to make the trip because I wanted to hear eyewitnesses tell the story of "the boy with the fiddle," which I first heard from Fyokla Navozova, the young woman director of the Krasnodar Cossack Museum. She showed me the art exhibits she had gathered as part of the historical record of the story. "Go to Ust Labinskaya," she said. "The boy's teachers and playmates are there. They know the story better than I can tell it to you."

Osip Yudin, the editor of the Krasnodar daily newspaper, showed me the story. he had written about "the boy with the fiddle." He too said, "You must go to Ust Labinskaya."

It was late Sunday afternoon when we drove into the *stanitsa*. As the jeep bounced along the broad rutted dust-swept main avenue, I observed a lively procession of young people, chiefly girls. Walking arm in arm, in pairs, in threes, in fours, in fives and sixes, they were surging from all directions toward a brick building which bore the external marks of hasty renovation, including a spatter of whitewash. A large hand-printed poster announced a motion picture and a dance. Nowhere else in Russia had I observed such a love of dancing as in the Kuban.

The girls wore Sunday clothes with nothing distinctive in style or fashion. Their dresses did not fit the picture of the lush up-to-dateness of which I had heard so much about Ust Labinskaya. But then the *stanitsa* had been under German occupation. Not one of the girls sported a hat. Women's hats had barely penetrated the Cossack country. Millinery is still an attainment of the future, when Soviet light industry can earnestly devote itself to it. The somber beginnings it has made, samples of which in prewar days were on display in metropolitan window shops and are beginning to reappear in Moscow, would hardly tempt the gay-spirited color-loving girl in the Cossack *stanitsa*. Instead of hats the girls wound round their hair or heads bright-colored ribbons. Most of them wore their hair short, with purely feminine styles of hairdress. Though daily engaged in doing the work of men or training for professions that one often associates with the prerogatives and talents of men, these girls evinced neither in dress nor manner any hint of masculinity. No one wore slacks. No one sported a boyish bob. No people in the world are more masculine-minded than Cossacks or more sternly devoted to masculine deeds and pastimes; yet nowhere else is feminine behavior more highly esteemed or emulated than among Kuban women.

In external appearance Ust Labinskaya was as battered and shabby as Slavenskaya. The wreckage of war, the heaps of rubble, the shattered public buildings were everywhere in evidence. Seldom was a cottage whitewashed. Again and again glass in the windows was missing. With all its vaunted prewar progressiveness, Ust Labinskaya still unfolded itself in a picturesque but ancient primitiveness. The dust and mud in the streets, the absence of sewage and running water, the presence everywhere of individual deep-dug wells, the pigs and chickens strutting about streets and courtyards were here as everywhere in striking contrast to the age of the machine that the Plans had enthroned in agriculture. In the Soviet scheme of things, it must be emphasized, production always comes first; and housing, especially in the village, is awaiting the time—however remote it may be—when the planner, the slogan maker, the mass impetus, the mass emotion, the mass energy, the mass will that invariably accompany community campaigns for a radical change in the way of living or working are free to give themselves to the more personal aspects of individual and community self-expression.

We passed the park of which I had heard so much. From the street it looked dense with trees, like a stretch of young and wild forest. Here were American maples, a favorite shade tree in the Kuban now, silver pines, white acacias, poplars. But the park was deserted; the gateway was barred, bolted, locked. The once tumultuous playground of the *stanitsa* was as silent as a graveyard.

I asked Pavel Prokofyevitch Alexeyev, the tall, broad-shouldered mayor of the village, why the park was closed. "The Germans have ruined it," he said. "They cut trees for firewood and fortifications. They burned the summer theater and the dance pavilion. It is overgrown with weeds and brush, and we haven't had time to clean it up. Until we do, we prefer to keep it closed." With feeling he spoke of the damage the Germans had done to the trees not only in the park but in the streets and around the homes of the people. "They cut thousands of them," he said, "and you know how Cossacks love trees. To a Cossack a *stanitsa* without trees is like a woman without hair. So one of the first things we did was to plant new trees. We have already set out sixty thousand saplings. Every household in Ust Labinskaya has young trees in the courtyard or the street."

Once started on the subject of German devastation, the mayor could hardly stop. It preyed on his mind as it did on the mind of every official I met in the Kuban. Particularly grieved was he that the public buildings, those constructed during the Plans, have been wantonly demolished. As in other places and unlike officials in Moscow, he had no hesitancy in producing figures, all the figures I chose to know, and more. Of the 7,500 milch cows in the county collectives, only 1,300 were left after the Germans had gone. Of the 4,500 horses, only 1,200 remained; of the 9,000 pigs, only 85; of the 7,500 sheep, only 600; of the 112,000 hens, only 2,000. The damage the Germans caused to the county amounted to more than $200,000,000.

"We shall get reparations, of course," said the mayor. "Of course we shall. We can use German engines for power plants. We shall welcome German tractors, combines, mowing machines, trucks, and passenger cars. We can use German typewriters, textiles, bicycles, and radios. We can use a lot of German goods."

Rehabilitation, said the mayor, was in full swing. It had started on the very day the Germans vacated the village. The few men that were home, old men usually, but still firm of body and strong of will, and the magnificent women were toiling away to retrieve everything. The cattle herds on the collectives already numbered 4,000 head. They had not done so well with horses and pigs. There were only 1,500 of the former and 450 of the latter. But their sheep were coming up, and so were the hens: there were now 4,820 of the former, 42,000 of the latter.

Beehives were multiplying rapidly. Most encouraging was the restoration of the family cow and the family pig. Most families were already in possession of the one and the other. What a good life they would have had, what a really prosperous community Ust Labinskaya would have been, what a high state of culture it would have boasted, had not the Germans and Rumanians devoured their riches and abandoned to fire and dynamite what they could neither devour nor take with them.

I stopped for the night with a Cossack family. At supper I became acquainted with a lieutenant quartered there. He was superintendent of an army hospital in Ust Labinskaya. He was a dark-eyed, dark-haired man of about thirty with a contracted brow and an almost sullen expression. Yet there was nothing sullen about his manner. He had traveled all over the Soviet Union. In the Kuban he was a newcomer.

"Nowhere else in our land," he said, "do people live so well as here. It's a glorious land."

At dinner I sat beside the lieutenant. We discussed guerrilla warfare and the best way of killing an enemy without making any noise or giving him a chance to sound the alarm.

"Here we are," he said, "you an American, I a Russian, both of us men of college education. We are feasting, making merry, and what are we talking about? Murder! How to kill a human being so he won't even emit a groan. What a time we're living in! What they have done to all of us, these evil Germans!" He did not say "Nazis." He said "Germans."

He had just come from Siberia, he said. "I went there to prove to my wife that I wasn't a corpse."

At the outbreak of the war, he said, he had joined the Red Army. His wife and three children remained in Saratov, on the Volga. When the Germans made their push toward the Volga his family was evacuated. But he did not know anything about it. For two years he was without any news from his wife and children. His letters brought no replies. His inquiries in Saratov brought "don't know" answers.

"My family disappeared without leaving a trace, as though it never had lived," he said. "Worried and anxious, I wrote to the Moscow Radio Committee. They make regular broadcasts for lost and missing persons. They wrote back that my wife had left Saratov for Siberia, but where she was in Siberia they did not know.

"Pained and alarmed, I wrote to Kalinin, President of the Soviet Union. Sometime later he replied he had made inquiries of the organizations that look after évacuées, but none knew anything about my family. I was really frightened, and in desperation I wrote to Stalin. I said that I took the liberty to address him because he was the leader and the father of all of us. It was a long and personal letter. A month passed and no reply came, so I concluded the Marshal was too busy or no more successful in finding my family than was Kalinin. I had resigned myself to the thought that I had no family any more, that my wife and children had perished in an accident or from an enemy bomb. Then one day I received a telegram. It was from Stalin. He informed me that he had found my family. They were in Siberia, and he gave me the address. Immediately I telegraphed my wife, and as soon as I could arrange it I left for Siberia.

"What a reunion we had. Here was I—convinced that she and the children were dead, and here was she—with two communications from official army quarters notifying her that I was dead. One communication said I had 'died the death of the brave' in Stalingrad, the other that I had met my 'valorous end at Mariupol.' I fought in both places, and I was supposed to have been killed in both of them! But here I was my own 'brave, valorous' self without a scratch, and here were my wife and my three children, all alive and well."

The next morning I set out to get the story of "the boy with the fiddle."

The name of the boy was Musya Pinkenson. He was twelve years old, and in all its history Ust Labinskaya had not heard a fiddle player like him. He was not a native of the Kuban. His father was a noted Jewish gynecologist from Kishinev, Bessarabia. In August 1941 the Pinkenson family was evacuated to Ust Labinskaya. A schoolteacher met them at the railroad station, registered them, and directed them to the house where they were to live. The father went to work in a hospital; the boy entered school.

Marya Voblova, a light-haired, blue-eyed Cossack young woman who was Musya's botany teacher, told me that Musya had been in her class, one of the most likable pupils.

"He was always so polite," she said. "If you met him in the street, he bowed, smiled, he greeted you by your name and patronymic just as if he were a grown person and your very best friend. Whenever an inspector came to school, Musya's teachers called on him to recite. They knew he would make an excellent showing. He was kind, too, very kind. Often when a boy or girl in his class was behind in the work, Musya volunteered to stay after school hours and help them out."

Later I spoke to Yekaterina Kononenko, curriculum director of the school which Musya had attended. She is a dark-haired, dark-eyed woman in the forties and spoke with a firm, resonant voice. Musya, she said, had been one of her favorites in the school.

"He was very neat in appearance. He was a healthy boy, with full red cheeks, red lips, taller than the average boy of his age. He had hazel eyes and dark hair which was cut, 'fox-trot' [pompadour] style. He spoke excellent Russian, and he played the violin divinely. . . . The whole *stanitsa* loved him for his playing."

No one in Ust Labinskaya knew Musya as intimately as Zoya Shuliak, a pretty, dark-haired girl barely twenty, now a freshman at the Krasnodar medical school. She and Musya had attended the same ten-year school. She was a senior when he was only in the fourth class. She was leader of the Pioneer Squad of which he was a member. She often went to his home, and he frequently came to hers. She knew his father and mother well, his aunt, who was his mother's sister, and her little girl, his

83-year-old grandfather and 80-year-old grandmother. They had all been evacuated together to Ust Labinskaya.

"Our Cossack women," said Zoya, "worshiped Musya's father, Dr. Pinkenson. He was never too busy or too tired to receive them and cure them of their sicknesses. But the boy was everybody's favorite. Saturday evenings, when our school put on a public entertainment, he and his fiddle were the chief attraction. If for some reason he was not on the program, the audience demanded his appearance. 'Musya, where is Musya, give us Musya Pinkenson!' people shouted, and when he came out on the stage the hall rocked with applause. Whenever any organization here gave a party or entertainment, Musya invariably was on the program. He thrilled us with his playing of folk tunes, especially Ukrainian, of which he had an unusually rich repertoire. He could also play Beethoven. But it was his folk tunes that won him the heartiest applause."

In August 1942, the year after the Pinkensons had arrived in Ust Labinskaya, the Germans occupied the *stanitsa*. For five months they did not molest the father or any other member of the Pinkenson family. They permitted one school to be open, a four-year elementary school, but children of suspected partisans, Communists, Soviet officials, and Jews were barred. So Musya could not attend school any more.

Yet school lured him, and Yurii Shevtchenko, one of Musya's closest chums, told me that Musya often came to the school yard, walked around the building, waited for the boys to come out so he could be with them, talk to them, find out what they were studying, what school life was like under the Germans. Often he came with his fiddle and would go off with his chums to a corner of the school yard and play for them "Katusha" and other favorites.

Once the boys coaxed him into going up with them to a classroom. When the new schoolmaster, a Russian collaborator, heard of it he turned Musya over to the *starosta*—elder—another Russian collaborator, and the *starosta* arrested him and led him off to the German commandant. But the commandant set him free. The school was soon closed.

There had never been many Jews in the Kuban. Under the Czar they were barred from Cossack territory. Under the Soviets not many came to live there. But there were a few, and these in December 1942 the Germans began to round up. They brought them in cartloads to Ust Labinskaya and shut them up in the local jail.

The Pinkenson family was still free, but the doctor realized that their turn was coming.

One evening, to cheer his mother and father, Musya took out his violin and started to play. Neighbors flocked in to hear him. They always did when they heard Musya play. He played long and with enthusiasm. Among those present was Maria Ivanovna, the woman in whose house the Pinkensons were living.

When the playing ended, the neighbors left. Only Maria Ivanovna remained.

"In the presence of this woman," said Zoya Shuliak, "Dr. Pinkenson said to his family: 'My dears, it's no use fooling ourselves. All over the country, all over the Kuban, they are rounding up our people. Our turn is coming. We cannot escape it, and it cannot be far off. So I propose that we do not wait for them. We can pass out of life quietly, painlessly, in our own way. I am a doctor, I can easily arrange it. We'll just go to sleep and never wake up.'

" 'You're right, Father,' Musya said. 'It's the only thing to do.' "

But Maria Ivanovna was so broken up she wept and begged the doctor not to proceed with the desperate act. It was impossible, she said, that the Germans would want to put to death so eminent a doctor and his family.

Her tears and pleas did not dissuade the doctor from his decision. After Maria Ivanovna left, the doctor opened his medical kit, took out a hypodermic needle, sucked into it a drug, and stepped over to Musya. The boy was standing with his back to the table. He rolled up his sleeve and reached out his arm to the father. The doctor was on the point of sticking the needle into the son's arm when the mother fainted.

The doctor dropped the needle, rushed to resuscitate his wife. When she came to she said:

"No, darling, you mustn't do it. You must not be the murderer of your own family."

The doctor put away the needle. The family stayed up all night talking, cheering itself with false hope.

The next morning the police came and arrested the Pinkensons. Their personal property was confiscated, and they were led out into the street and told to get into a cart. All of them did as told —the father, mother, Musya, the 83-year-old grandfather, the 80-year-old grandmother, the mother's sister and her little girl. They drove along Demyan Bedny Street.

"I live on this street," Zoya Shuliak proceeded with her story, "and I saw them sitting in the cart, Musya hugging his fiddle. The police allowed him to keep it. I wanted to follow along, so did others, but guards pointed tommy guns at us and ordered us away. . . . So we watched and wept and looked after the cart until we saw it no more."

But Yurii Shevtchenko and some other boys outsmarted the guards. They knew where the cart was going—to the old fortress by the Kuban River. They had seen other carts go that way, carts loaded with people brought in from the outside, Jews and non-Jews, women and children, the children invariably barefoot. So the boys climbed up the slope of a hill overlooking the fortress and the deep ravine which skirted it. Here, without being seen, they could observe the scene in the fortress and the ravine. The people who lived in the neighborhood were told to close their wooden shutters. But they, too, could observe the ravine and the fortress through the cracks in the shutters.

"Later," said Zoya Shuliak, "a policeman who had participated in the event was subsequently seized and tried. He told the court all that had happened to the Pinkensons, so now we have all the facts authoritatively documented."

The Pinkensons were brought to the fortress and told to step into the ravine. About 250 people were there, Jews and non-Jews. The Pinkensons were in the front line. Turning to the German gendarme, the father begged that the son be spared.

"We've lived our lives, my wife and I, and the others, but the boy is only twelve and he is so talented."

The gendarme shook his head and said: "*Nein, nein.*"

Turning to his father, Musya said: "No, Papa, I want to be here with you and Mother."

The doctor spoke again: "I wish you'd allow my son to play before we die."

"*Nein!*" the gendarme snapped out.

"Please, mein Herr," pleaded Musya.

There was no reply.

"Just once more—a little bit," the boy begged.

There was something in the boy's voice that made the gendarme look up and reflect. He said: "Very well, go ahead."

The boy opened the case, took out the violin, tuned it, placed it under his chin. Then, lifting the bow over the strings, he started to play the Russian national hymn.

"It was the only way," said Zoya Shuliak, "he could express his protest against all that the gendarme represented."

The gendarme was enraged.

"Fire!" he commanded.

The guns went off. The Pinkensons fell to the ground, Musya on the top of his fiddle.

In the city museum of Krasnodar, on the wall dedicated to war heroes, there is now a painting of Musya Pinkenson playing the violin in the last moments of his life.

CHAPTER XXII

"We Were So Wild, So Wild"

"ONE HUNDRED COSSACKS, one hundred horses, one hundred beards."

This old saying, like so many others, has the defect of its eloquence. It overglamorizes truth. Yet in pre-Soviet days the beard was to the Cossack an ornament and a distinction, the mustaches no less so, the bushy mustaches trailing sickle-like down the chin or gleaming dagger fashion over the mouth. A Cossack *starik*—old man—without beard, mustaches, or both was as unthinkable as a Cossack girl without braids. Both were fashion and fulfillment.

Now both are in discard, the beard more than the braids. Like women the world over, Cossack girls do not disdain the revival of a past fashion if only it enhances personal attractiveness and adds to pleasurable sensation. Hence the reappearance here and there of the girl with braids and pigtails. But not so with Cossack men. When a thing is old-fashioned, it stays old-fashioned. Cossack youth is impatient of beards. It is even suspicious of the mustaches. Rarely nowadays does one see a Cossack youth or man with beard or mustache.

When therefore I came to the village of Novo Velichkovskaya and met the stariks I was not surprised to see them clean-shaven, though most of them still clung to dwarfed and neatly twirled mustaches. It was Sunday anyway—a day for shaving and for embroidered shirts.

In the old days the word starik spelled authority, inspired reverence, evoked fear. The starik was a man of wisdom, of righteousness, of power. Father or grandfather, his word was law. No one in the household dared challenge or disobey it.

"In my own home," said Arkady Perventsev, a Kuban Cossack and one of Russia's more eminent young novelists, "the supreme authority of the family was Grandfather. No one ever sat down to a meal until he was in his seat. After he had sat down and brushed his mustaches and said, 'Be seated,' the rest of us took our places at the table. During the meal, if any of us wished to leave for whatever reason, we might do so only with his permission. On the finish of the meal no one stirred from his seat until after Grandfather had left his."

If a son disobeyed his father, even if the son was himself married and with a family, the father might order him to lie down for a chastisement, and the son, however valiant a warrior, dared not disobey. If the father wished to make the punishment particularly humiliating, he invited the son to follow him to the market place and administered the chastisement there in the presence of other stariks. There were exceptions, of course, but they were neither too frequent nor too flagrant.

At weddings, mass meetings, other public functions, the stariks were always the leaders.

Cossacks usually do not steal from one another, and thievery never was a serious problem in a Cossack village. When it did occur, and if it was serious enough, it caused public commotion. Church bells were rung, and the stariks assembled, questioned the thief and, if he was guilty, sentenced him to a Cossack beating. Invariably they struck the first blows with their fists, and the beating might be severe enough to cause death.

The civil war had shattered the authority of the stariks. More conservative-minded than youth, they fought the Revolution more stubbornly. With the restoration of social tranquillity in the Cossack village and with the revival of Cossackhood, they won back in part the old position of authority, though not in political affairs. Young men exercise political authority. But in the everyday life of the community there are problems which, because of their seasoned competence and their greater experience, the stariks are called upon to solve. When hand labor again became a necessity in agriculture, they taught the women the use of the cradle, the scythe, and other implements. When the war broke out they were the experts in the mending of saddles, in the grinding of sabers. They are masters in the art of horsemanship. Their age is supposed to give them wisdom, and they offer counsel on personal behavior, on personal conflict. Yet the world in which they now live is not the world of their youth, the world their ancestors fashioned and for centuries fought with sword and gun to maintain.

This became eloquently evident when I sat down with the stariks in Novo Velichkovskaya and listened to their spirited and nostalgic, though not uncritical, talk of the old Cossack world and the old Cossack life as they had known it, lived it, loved it.

"In my youth," said Vasily Ivanovitch, a starik with limpid blue eyes and a boyishly boastful manner, "when you were twelve years old, you rode a horse so fast the devil couldn't catch up with you. If you were afraid of the devil you mounted your horse and galloped away at top speed, and you knew the devil couldn't keep up with you, and would drop, exhausted, somewhere by the wayside, on my word you did."

"But we didn't have much book learning," said Andrey Tikhonovitch, a tall upright man with a swarthy complexion and heavy brows over brilliant dark eyes. Despite his sixty-seven years only his forehead and the corners of his mouth were grooved with lines. "After I had three years' schooling," he added, "my father said to me, 'Enough, if you get more book learning you will forget God.'"

"That's the truth," another starik said. "Book learning was not for us Cossacks, neither for our men nor for our women."

"But we had lots of fun," broke in the eye-rolling, effervescent Vasily Ivanovitch. "We drank, we danced, we made love to girls, and we fought."

"Cossacks always loved to fight," said another starik without lifting his head from the stout staff on which it was resting.

"I was leader of the boys in my end of the village," said Andrey. "Being a Cossack, I thought myself superior to the *khokhly* [peasants], and so I'd get the other Cossack youths together and say, 'Come on, boys, let's knock the devil out of the *khokhly*.' 'Let's,' the other boys would say, and so we'd march into the peasant quarters and have a free-for-all fist fight with the *khokhly*. Sometimes we beat them and sometimes they knocked hell out of us. But we had a good time, aye we did."

"We were so wild, so wild," chanted Vasily. "Sometimes we had fist fights, not with the *khokhly*, but with the Cossack youths from the other end of the village. If we got mad enough we picked up sticks and scraps of iron to reinforce our fists. We shouted, we swore, we cursed, and we fought—ah, how we fought—just for the hell of it."

"Sometimes," said the man with his head on the staff, "our fathers and grandfathers came along. They watched and cheered, and if things went badly for our crowd, they flung themselves into the fray, and then the fathers and the grandfathers of our opponents also joined and we had a free-for-all mass fight. We fought as long as our strength held out."

"When we stopped," the loquacious Andrey said, "our heads were full of lumps, our eyes were swollen, our faces bloated, our hands mangled. But we had no regrets. If we lost we vowed vengeance. If we won, we glowed with pride."

"Sometimes," said another starik, "the married folk of the village would challenge the unmarried youths to a fight, and brother might be facing brother, son might be facing father, but no one cared. We fought anyway; an enemy was an enemy, if he was your brother or your son, you walloped him just the same with all your strength."

How reminiscent it all was of Taras Bulba and his fighting days away back in the fifteenth century.

"Have you such fights now?" I asked the boys who had gathered round us.

The boys laughed and said nothing.

"Our sons aren't as wild as we were," said the starik with his head on the staff.

"Sometimes they fight," said Vasily. "I've seen them, but——" He motioned with his hand and left the sentence unfinished.

"They've got too much book learning to fight like we did," said Andrey. "They aren't as untamed as we were. Nobody was as untamed as we were."

"Just look at me," Vasily began again with a happy flourish of the arms. "When I was a boy my father taught me to work, to ride horse, to drink vodka, to fight, to make love, and I passed these teachings on to my sons. But they won't pass it on to theirs, not now any more; they'd be ashamed. But I wasn't ashamed. By God I wasn't. Like son, like father. No sin, either. You should see my oldest son." Flinging his arm high over his head as high as it would reach, he raced on: "That's how tall he is. A giant of a man with arms like steel axles. . . . He's in the Red Army now, and I know that with one stroke of the saber he can mow down any damned Fritz in the world, mow him down like a thistle. No Fritz he ever meets will have a chance to say his prayers." His eyes bulged and glowed with triumph.

"We Cossacks always felt we had to show other nations we were real Cossacks, not just ordinary soldiers, and we're doing it in this war as much as we did in the war against Napoleon, the Turks, the British, the French, the Japanese. The Cossack saber is as sharp as ever. We made it sharp, ground it here in the villages before our boys went off to war."

Contemplatively and with nostalgic fervor, Andrey said:

"We danced a lot in our youth and we sang a lot, and we fought a lot, but we loved horses best. There's nothing like a Cossack horse race. The horse is as spirited and excited as you are. Blood flows into your eyes and into his. Your heart is afire; so is his. You think only of victory, and so does he. Once, I remember, the older people in the village laid out a ring of handkerchiefs around the circular tracks. Each handkerchief was tied into a knot containing three rubles. I had to gallop around the ring and pick up the handkerchief with my hands or my mouth. Every time I picked one up there was a burst of cries and cheers: 'That's the boy, Andrusha, show them your stuff!'—'Glorious Andrusha!' I loved those cheers—oh, how I loved them! —So did the horse, and he galloped around with such skill that all I had to do was to swing down with my body and grasp the handkerchief with my hand or my lips. Not once did I miss. Twelve handkerchiefs each with three rubles in the knot, thirty-six rubles, and all mine, a lot of money in those times."

"The girls," Vasily began as if continuing the story, "always came to the races. They wore their best clothes, and if their boy friends were among the riders they brought a special handkerchief which they laid along the circular race track. With thumping heart they stood and watched, and woe to the boy who missed his girl's handkerchief! Everybody laughed at him. 'You're no Cossack,' people said, 'you're an ox.' The girl might feel so hurt and insulted she wouldn't talk to him. But that seldom happened. A boy would rather lose his arm than miss his sweetheart's handkerchief. Her mere presence did something to him, brought out the best in him, his mind and heart were one, he lived only for the moment of triumph for himself and the girl, a very great moment, I tell you."

Swept on by the memory of old romance, Andrey said reminiscently, "Yes, we danced with our girls, we sang together, we went walking with them, we slept with them——"

"The Lord forgive them!" exclaimed Vasily and chuckled.

"Forgive them for what?" protested the solemn Andrey Tikhonovitch.

Vasily Ivanovitch caught my eyes, winked, smiled, remained silent.

"That was nothing to be ashamed of," resumed Andrey. "If you liked a girl and she liked you, you slept with her. That was the way you courted her. But you never touched her virtue."

"Never?" Vasily interrupted.

"Well, there's a skeleton in every family closet," said Andrey.

"Aye, aye," said the starik with his head on the staff. "Just as there's a spirit in every marsh."

"People do make mistakes, you know," the puckish Vasily interjected with a sly toss of the head.

"If you love the girl, you don't make any mistakes," Andrey remonstrated. "By God you don't. If she loved you enough to allow you to court her and lie beside her in bed, night after night, week after week, month after month, she wouldn't let you make any mistakes." Vasily smiled in obvious disagreement but seemed respectful of his comrade's sentiment and challenged it no more. Andrey continued, "She'd be afraid you'd think her frivolous and lose respect for her and drop her after you'd had your pleasure."

"Right, right," assented Vasily, "and if she allowed a boy to have his pleasure before she was his wife, he'd think she might allow another man to have the same pleasure after she became his wife. That's the truth."

"I slept with a girl for two years," Andrey went on. "We loved each other. We promised we'd belong to each other and to no one else. But her father didn't like me, I wasn't good enough for him. That's why all the time I slept with the girl I had to sneak into her room at night after the family was already in bed, and in the morning I had to sneak out before any of them arose. If I were caught I'd get a terrible beating. But I didn't mind. When you're in love you welcome such risks."

"Aye, aye," interjected the other stariks almost in unison.

"I sent two matchmakers to the girl's father," Andrey resumed, "but the father refused to give his consent. He didn't want me. I was too wild, he said, for such a fine girl as his daughter. Did I quit? No. I went on sleeping with the girl, and we decided I'd send matchmakers a second time. I did. Again the father refused. I sent matchmakers a third time, with no better results. He was a stubborn devil, the girl's father was. But I too was stubborn. I was angry and heartbroken and decided to quit the girl. She too was heartbroken and didn't want me to quit. She wept and begged me to go on sleeping with her—maybe, she said, her father would relent, she would implore him to. But I knew him better than she—a devil of a son of a bitch he was. The saints themselves couldn't change his mind, so I stuck to my decision and told the girl I was through, through, through. Soon afterward I met another girl and I started sleeping with her. I didn't touch her virtue. The Lord strike me dead if I did. Nor would she let me, and I was glad, for here was a girl I could love. We slept together for two weeks and I sent matchmakers to her home. I went with them. They walked into the living room, but I stayed in the vestibule and waited. Of course matchmakers are brazen liars—they have to be, that's their job and their responsibility; and my matchmakers lied plenty about me—they had to, for I had the reputation of being a wild young beast. Well, I didn't have to wait long. The matchmakers called me in. I bowed to the girl's father and said, 'I've come to ask for the hand of your daughter, sir.' He said, 'I have no objections if my daughter hasn't any.' Of course she was willing. So the next Sunday we killed a fat bull and had a feast, and a lot of people came, and we stayed up all night and ate and drank and sang and danced, and one of our guests got so drunk he wanted to start a fight right there in the house, and we had to tie him up so he couldn't move. Then we had our wedding, and we celebrated for a whole week—that's the kind of weddings we had in those days."

"What sort of weddings have you now?" I asked.

Vasily burst into a loud laugh. "There's a wedding in the village now."

I rose to my feet and said, "Let's go and see it."

Vasily motioned with his hand. "It's all over by this time. People don't know any more what a real wedding is."

"It's harvest time, and there's no time for celebrations," said a woman who had come over unobserved and joined in the conversation.

"And how is it in your country?" Vasily asked. "What sort of weddings have you there?"

"We have a reception," I said.

"What's that?"

I explained as best I could, and all of the stariks and the others looked puzzled.

"And we supposed," said one of them, "in a rich country like yours you'd have weddings that last even longer than ours in the old days, at least a month."

I shook my head.

"Ah!"

"So?"

"There now!" Disappointment rang in their voices.

"Don't you even drink a lot of vodka at your weddings in America?" Vasily asked.

"None at all. We're not a vodka-drinking people."

"How uninteresting!" said Vasily. "Now why are you like that?"

"We never developed the habit. We drink whisky instead."

"And what is that?"

I described whisky as best I could, but Vasily Ivanovitch shook his head. He smacked his lips over and over, wiped the shiny beads of sweat on his balding head, again shook his head in grievous disappointment.

"No," he declared, "it cannot be a good drink, this whisky of yours. If it was, we Cossacks would've been drinking it. We'd have discovered it all right. Nobody could possibly have kept us from discovering it. We're not like *babas*, sitting in one place and knowing only this one place. We're wandering folk. Where haven't we been? We rode our horses into Paris, chasing the infidel Napoleon to his lair. We've been in Bagdad, in Turkey, in the Far East. We've been in Berlin, with Alexander Sergey-vitch Suvorov. Nowhere did we see or sniff this whisky of yours, or if we did we turned our noses against it—that is, our glorious ancestors did. They never said anything about whisky. Did they?" He surveyed the other stariks, and they shook their heads. "There now," he raced on. "I have this to say to you, and please write it down, every word I say, and tell it to your people in America. The reason they don't drink vodka is that they don't know how. If they did they would drink it. There's nothing more joy-giving in the world. So this is the way to drink it. Write it down, please. Pour your glass full——"

"A large glass," someone interrupted.

"Naturally, a large glass. Pour it full of vodka, sprinkle it with pepper—lots of pepper—and toss it down, all of it, to the last drop. Then take a large juicy tomato, soak it in sunflower oil, and eat it, and it'll cool your mouth and your insides and you'll feel reborn. By heaven you will." Violently he slapped his hands together.

I shook my head.

"No?"

"We don't like pepper in our liquor."

"Have you ever tried it?"

"No."

"Then don't say you don't like it," Vasily protested with indignation. "Don't contradict a Cossack starik. Try it first, and tell your people in America to try it, just the way I told you, and you'll love it just as we love it. Promise you'll tell them?"

"I promise."

Andrey was not at the moment interested in vodka or in making America vodka-minded. He was void of any missionary zeal. He was absorbed in the story of his romance, which I thought he had finished. There was another chapter which he was eager to narrate, and only the impetuous interruptions of the more prosaic and more convivial Vasily had stopped him. Now that Vasily was enjoying an interval of triumphant exhilaration, Andrey resumed his tale:

"My wife and I had a good life, very good. But I can't say I have a sweet disposition. Sometimes I have it, and sometimes it is as if soaked in pepper. It depends on how much I've had to drink and on how I feel. The truth is I can be a surly cuss, a real son of a bitch, and more so in my younger days than now. There were times when I'd come home growling like a disgruntled pig. I'd find fault with everything around the house, and especially with my wife, and I'd slap her. She bore my beatings for a long time. Our Cossack women are like that. They'll submit to their men, and then they won't. So once I got home late and started shouting and swearing and, lo and behold, my wife shouted back to me. 'Shut up,' I cried. 'You shut up,' she cried even more loudly. I slapped her. She slapped me back. 'What d'you mean?' I said. 'Just that,' she answered. 'You ugly bitch,' I shouted. 'You ugly son of a bitch,' she shouted back. I got so furious I picked up a pot and crashed it against the floor. She picked up another pot and flung it with all her strength against the wall. The pot broke into smithereens. I got still more furious and seized a plate and flung it to the floor with all my strength. She seized another plate and did the same. I banged my elbow against a windowpane and smashed it. She banged her fist against another windowpane and smashed it. 'What're you doing?' I said. 'What're you doing?' she said. 'You're breaking the dishes,' I said. 'I'll break as many as you will,' she answered. I knew she meant it. Her words sobered me, and I said, 'Let's quit.' 'I will if you will,' she replied. I did quit, and so did she. Afterward, no matter what happened I left her and the pottery and the glassware in the house alone. That's the way life is. It's like our Kuban River, now it flows still, now a storm brews over it, and now it flows still again." He grew silent, leaned against the wall and half shut his eyes.

But Vasily's mind was on something else. "You won't forget to tell your people in America how to drink vodka?" he asked.

"I shan't," I answered. He smiled with pleasure.

"Don't forget the tomato soaked in sunflower oil."

"I've got it all down," I said.

"That's excellent," he said.

"D'you ever go to church?" I asked Vasily.

"He doesn't," said the woman who had joined us. "He doesn't even cross himself before the icons when he goes into a house."

"Well," began Vasily, but the starik with his head on the staff interrupted him. Lifting his head, he said, "Once we fought for our Orthodoxy and for the Czar. Now we're confused, and we've lost the habit of going to church."

"The young people," said the woman bitingly, "go to the clubhouse. The first thing they did when the Germans left was to clean it up and rebuild it so they could have their dances and their good times. But what would a woman like me, a *baba*, do in a clubhouse? Who'd look at me? Who'd want to have a good time with me?"

"You don't look as though all fire was gone out of you," the irrepressible Vasily interrupted with a laugh.

"Maybe it has and maybe it hasn't. Why should I tell you? But the clubhouse is no place for me, so I go to church, and others like me feel as I do. Besides, it's better to pray than to have a good time."

"Now take me," Vasily began, philosophically this time. "I was never strong on religion, not even in the old days. Truth is truth, and why deny it? I believe neither in God nor in the devil. But when I die I want a Christian burial."

"You can't have a Christian burial because you're no Christian any more," the woman challenged.

"I didn't say I was a Christian. I only said I want a Christian burial."

"Why?" I asked.

"It would be the decent thing to do. It would give me community standing. After the burial, people would come to my house and have a feast, and they'd drink and eat and remember me and say kind words about me. On the third day after the funeral they'd come together again for another dinner, and they'd talk some more about me, and on the ninth day they'd do the same, and once more on the fortieth, and they'd drink toasts to my memory, and they'd say, 'May he dwell in the kingdom of heaven.' That's what they'd do if I had a Christian burial. Otherwise my flesh and bones would rot away and nobody'd say a word, I'd be forgotten as though I'd never lived. That's the truth, isn't it?"

"What d'you think?" I turned to Andrey. But he only shrugged. He was too absorbed in his own reflections. Perhaps he was thinking of the wild old world of which he and others had reminisced with such fervor and which is dead beyond all hope of resurrection.

CHAPTER XXIII

Sex and Family among Cossacks

"LIFE DICTATES TO MAN its own laws," says Mikhail Sholokhov in his monumental novel on the Cossacks. To his heroes and heroines life *is* a constant struggle between sex and duty, sex and love, sex and respectability, sex and self-interest, sex and good sense. Sex wins, again and again, now vulgarly, now poetically, always overpoweringly. To a man of the Cossack's biological heritage, his expansive nature, his unrepressed emotions, sex, under his conditions of life, marked by long and frequent absences from home, could not but be a source of violent conflict.

Here is Sholokhov's young Darya. Her husband has been away from home only two months, and she says to her sister-in-law: "Just now I could roll around with an old fellow." A married Cossack comes home on furlough. Darya is only too willing to cohabit with him. When her brother-in-law arrives from the Army on leave, she does her utmost to seduce him. Once while in the barn alone with her father-in-law, she throws her arms around him, draws him closer and closer and mumbles, "Here— Father—a soft place." Bewildered, the old man struggles to free himself, but she clings to him, draws his head toward her face and breathes "into his beard with her hot mouth." The old man continues to resist, but she protests: "So you don't want it?" With a blow on the man's breast she pushes him away and says tauntingly: "Maybe you cannot any more? Then don't judge me."

Liza is the merchant's daughter. Pretty and self-willed, fond of bright clothes and gay company, she is attracted to a young Cossack who is an ardent and expert fisherman. She makes friends with him and maneuvers herself into being invited to go fishing with him. Early one morning they go to the river. He has to carry her to the boat, and on the way he stumbles over a rock and her body falls close to his. Brimming over with emotion, she kisses him. They get into the boat and row across. On reaching the other side of the river he lifts her in his arms and carries her into the bushes. "She bit his face, scratched him, screamed stiflingly once or twice; then, feeling herself growing weak, she cried out in anger but without tears." They do their fishing afterward.

On their return home he follows one path, she another. Glancing back at her, he observes a red spot on her dress. He calls her over and tells her about it, and her only regret is that she did not wear a black dress, so the spot would not show. But the young Cossack is resourceful. He picks up a green leaf, rubs it into the spot, and red becomes green.

Axinya is the name of Sholokhov's heroine, and a Soviet critic speaks of her as "one of the most fascinating characters in Russian literature." She is a young woman of great simplicity, great tenderness, great courage, a great capacity for self-sacrifice. At the age of sixteen while out in the field working, her fifty-year-old father rapes her. A year later she marries. Shortly afterwards she meets Grigory, the hero of the novel. She entrances Grigory but rebuffs his advances, boldly, pugnaciously. He gives her no peace, and finally she succumbs. They meet often, their love deepens. His family is outraged and brings pressure on him to marry a pretty, even-tempered girl. But Axinya haunts Grigory. His wife does not make him happy. He tells her that she is like the moon—she neither chills nor warms. He goes back to his mistress, and to escape the taunts of family and friends both leave the village and hire out to a Cossack landlord in a neighboring *stanitsa*.

But Grigory is a Cossack, and the Army claims him. He goes off to service, then to war. Axinya grows lonelier and lonelier.

She loves Grigory, she knows he loves her. But he is away, has been away for months and months, and her violent nature cries out for gratification. When the landlord's son comes home on furlough and approaches her, she yields with scarcely a battle. He comes to her again and again, and she is always ready to receive him. She loves Grigory no less than when she had last seen him, but "life's unwritten law" gets the best of her.

Grigory has his tussle with this "law." His father marvels at his audacious laxity and accounts for it by saying to himself that Grigory is *his* son. "He is like me, the old devil. Perhaps he's even worse than his father, the tail of a bitch."

Grigory's temptress is not the young unmarried girl, but the married young woman, whose husband, like himself, is away from home, in the Army or at war. Once he stops for the night in a Cossack home. The daughter of his Cossack host waits on him. She is a young woman with "groping inquisitive eyes." She can hardly keep her eyes off him. As she makes his bed she says:

"I'll be sleeping by the barn. It is hot in the house, and the fleas bite." He remembers her words, and as soon as he hears the snoring of her father he removes his boots, tiptoes out of the house, finds his way to the barn, lies down beside the girl, and she gladly makes room for him. Wild with passion, they give themselves to one another. In the morning after the cocks have crowed, Grigory rises to leave. He does not want the father to discover him outside the bed in which he was supposed to sleep. But the young woman holds him back, clings to him and pleads, "Lie awhile longer, sweet little berry . . . please."

On a subsequent occasion when he is already a defeated Cossack and a defeated man, he catches a ride with a young woman who is driving a pair of oxen. "How do you get along without your husband?" he asks.

"What do you mean?" she inquires.

"Just that."

"Well, there's plenty of such pleasure around," she says. "The world is not without merciful people . . . it's better now—

young Cossacks have come back home . . . before, it was pretty bad."

After dark they stop for the night in the steppe. She keeps glancing at him, thinking of him and saying to herself, "He is gray, but he is not so old." They build a fire, cook supper, and then retire, she on the cart, he on the ground beside the fire. Sleepless and restless, she says:

"I'm afraid you'll freeze . . . the ground is so cold . . . if you get to feeling too cold, come and join me . . . my overcoat is warm, very warm. Coming, are you?"

He reflects, sighs and says:

"Thanks, girlie, I won't. If this had happened two years earlier . . . Never mind, I shan't freeze." In the two years he speaks of, he has been so mercilessly battered by fate that his mind is too troubled, his soul too wounded, to respond to the coaxing of the woman beside him.

Sholokhov writes of the pre-Soviet Don Cossack, neighbor to the Cossack of the Kuban. There is no perceptible difference in the sex and family life of the two. They are subject to the same laws of nature, the same social attitude, and profess the same religion. Not that Cossack morality and social usage as they have unfolded through the centuries approve sex transgression. Most emphatically they do not. In the old days in the Kuban if a woman whose husband was away from home was known to give herself to another man, someone in the village, young boys or a neighbor, painted black with axle grease the doors or shutters of her home or the courtyard gateway. The village talked about her. She was violating village decorum and village respectability. Her father and mother felt disgraced, scolded her, might even beat her. When her husband returned and learned of her waywardness, he punished her mercilessly. She endured the punishment in silence or amidst tears, always with a sense of guilt and helplessness. Yet when the husband departed again and remained away a long time, neither consciousness of guilt nor the knowledge of imminent punishment on her husband's return was always a powerful enough deterrent from a repetition of the transgression. The desire of the flesh transcended the fear of retribution.

Yet it would be easy to exaggerate the prevalence of sex laxity among Cossacks. The brutal vividness with which Sholokhov depicts it may give the impression that it was a part of Cossack folkways. Its occurrence was frequent and flagrant enough to impress itself powerfully on the author's imagination. But if only to heighten the drama of a situation, a novelist is prone to over-emphasize its reality. No Cossack historian I have read or talked with admits that sex laxity was the rule in the Cossack village. Yet all point to the particular life of the Cossack which invited the bursting of the bonds of convention.

Here is the young Cossack girl in pre-Soviet Russia. She is reared in the concept of the sanctity of virginity. During the period of courtship or "sleeping together," wherever it is the custom, the knowledge that if she yields to the man beside her, she may ruin her chances of marrying him, is ever in her mind. Since marriage is the ultimate triumph and spinsterhood the ultimate frustration, she fights strenuously with words, with tears, with the fist, against all temptation and all persuasion.

There are exceptions. In his novel *The Cossacks*, Tolstoy portrays a girl who joyfully gives herself to a Russian officer. But Maryanka, the heroine of the story, commands sturdy self-control of herself. To the young Cossack who loves her and woos her she says:

"If you love me, I'll marry you, but no foolishness will you get from me." The Cossack girl who yields to such foolishness may have cause to rue it all her life. Though the man who has inveigled her into the act may marry her, in moments of inebriation and aggravation he is likely to remind her of the transgression with harsh epithets or with blows of the fist.

The tussle of the unmarried girl with "life's law" is short-lived. She marries young, at seventeen, eighteen, nineteen. Rarely does she pass her twentieth birthday without being wife and mother. Her difficulties begin after marriage. Being Cossack, she is possessed of superior biological attributes. She is strong and healthy.

She eats good food, in the Kuban and Don especially, milk foods, meat, fruit, vegetables, sweets. She is of a gay and life-loving disposition. Before her marriage she freely mingles with men in her home, in the field, in church, at dances, at festivals.

She is in the pre-Soviet days rigidly Orthodox and a faithful churchgoer. But Russian Orthodoxy never was noted for its puritanism, never invested sex indulgence outside of marital life with the strong sense of sin with which other Christian faiths have weighted it. Besides, deep inside of him there is always something lyrical and earthy in the Cossack's approach to sex. Tolstoy hints at it in the conversation between Olenin, who comes from the north, and the old Cossack Yeroshka, who has always lived in the Cossack wilderness. Olenin asks Yeroshka to introduce him to Maryanka, the beautiful daughter of his landlady. Yeroshka replies he will find him a more beautiful girl, one dressed "in silks and silver." But the moralizing Olenin doesn't mean a mistress. "You old codger," he chides, "it's a sin to talk like that."

The word "sin" neither annoys nor appalls the old Cossack. It only surprises him. "A sin," he says, "where is the sin? A sin to look at a pretty girl? A sin to play with her? A sin to love her? Is that what it is where you come from? No, my good man, that's no sin, that's salvation. God created you, and He also created the girl. He created everything, little father. That's why it's no sin to look at a pretty girl. She is created to be looked at, to be loved, to give rapture. That's the way I look at it, my good man." There is much of Yeroshka in every Cossack, though he may not voice his sentiment as fully and as eloquently as does Tolstoy's "old codger."

What makes the position of the married young woman in the Cossack village particularly difficult, and now and then beyond her powers of self-control, is the fact that her young husband is a professional warrior. At eighteen he starts his term of service in the Czar's army. He serves on and off, here and there, for twenty years. He comes home on furloughs. But during the ripest years of his manhood and his wife's womanhood, he is away for long periods of time. Besides, wars are frequent, now against an internal enemy, now against an external foe. Furloughs may be delayed or denied. . . . Death is frequent. In the course of the prolonged separation man and wife are subject to feverish restlessness and to inevitable temptation. *He* may visit brothels, which were legal and widespread in old Russia, or he may cohabit with the women he meets in his wanderings.

But the wife is at home and alone. She works hard in the field and around the house. But youth and health and romance press for fulfillment and often enough overpower convention and judgment. Yet, however profligate the husband's or the wife's transgressions, rarely does it lead to the breakup of the family. There is no divorce—it is banned by Orthodoxy and by social custom. The thought of it is remote to the mind of the Cossack. In the days of the Dnieper republic, when celibacy was almost a cult, the Cossack who had his wife outside of the *setch* remained loyal to her as a wife. During his absence from home he might cohabit with other women. "Women we shall find," runs the refrain in a Cossack ditty, "lonely we shan't be." But if he remains alive he goes back to the family. Children alone, especially sons, draw him irresistibly to home and hearth. Taras Bulba might boast that the saber was "the Cossack's mother." The scouts who rode around the countryside called on the domiciled men to answer the call of arms with the admonition that it was time for them "to cease fooling around with women and wasting on them their knightly powers." But the family remained unshaken. The word "mother" was invested with reverence, far more than in peasant villages. Even Taras Bulba grows sentimental about the mother of his sons. Before his departure for the *setch* and for the war from which neither he nor his sons return, he calls on her to give the boys her blessing. "A mother's prayers protect a man on land and on water."

The family becomes not only the cornerstone of the Cossack's life, but a sanctity of sanctities. The very word *semya* is hallowed. It gives a man prestige and social position. The coming of a son is always a joy. It means the birth of a new Cossack, of someone to perpetuate not only the race but the valor and the glory of Cossackhood, the spirit and the achievements of ancestors. No other people in Russia were as ancestor-minded as Cossacks. Besides the birth of a son carries material reward, an allotment of free land larger in area than the holding of the average muzhik family. A Cossack without children because of his or his wife's sterility was rare. Rarer still was the unmarried Cossack.

Because the family was so deep-rooted in the old days, the Soviet Revolution even in its early years scarcely shook it. The turbulent and sex-crazed days of the early twenties did not loosen age-old bonds of fealty and discipline, as was the case in so many non-Cossack towns or villages. The older muzhik might divorce his wife and marry a young girl not only because she was more appealing sexually but because she was stronger physically, could do more work on the land and around the house. But not the Cossack. He rarely took advantage of the easy divorce laws. He was too dependent on his wife, too attached to his household, too devoted to the very concept of the family to upset its integrity. Unlettered as he might be, wild with passion as he might be, he upheld the unity of the family. Besides he never had been the repressed man that the muzhik was. He had infinitely greater pride of person, greater stability of character, greater regard for tradition.

There might be violent cleavages in the family. Sons and daughters often enough rebelled against father and mother and lived with them "at daggers' ends." But the family weathered all storms. I do not know of any other people in Russia who went through the storm-and-stress phase of the sex and family revolution with so little maladjustment, so little turmoil, as did the Cossacks. The eloquence of the late Yemelyan Yaroslavsky in the early years of the Soviets in praise of free abortion as the signal of woman's complete emancipation which no bourgeois society would permit or tolerate, an eloquence which would horrify the Bolshevik of today, scarcely ruffled Cossack usage and Cossack practice.

Most illuminating is the attitude of the Cossack toward the

new marriage and divorce laws promulgated on June 27, 1936, and on July 8,' 1944. The law of 1936 bans abortions except for the woman whose health or life may be jeopardized by pregnancy and childbirth. For the first time since the coming of Soviets divorce is beset with legal difficulties, though not especially serious. No longer may a wife or husband obtain it by merely asking for it with or without the knowledge of the other party. Both have to appear at the registration office. The fee for a first divorce is boosted to fifty rubles, for the second to 150, for the third to 300. The law makes no mention of the fee for a fourth divorce. Presumably it would be deemed so abnormal as to call forth a special investigation, perhaps criminal, of the applicant.

In its comment on the new law, *Pravda* wrote editorially: "The woman who has no children deserves our pity; she misses the full joy of her life." Never before had such sentiments been uttered by *Pravda*.

The suddenness with which the law was enacted caused widespread commotion in certain circles in Moscow and other cities. Abortions had become a popular method of birth control, and girls and women who were "caught" with pregnancies were frantic to rid themselves of their condition. They besieged clinics and clamored for the operation. But the law was retroactive, and the time the pregnancy started did not matter. Abortions were outlawed for good and for all except those whom physicians might pronounce physiologically unfit for childbirth. There were suicides among girls and women who were "caught." Others sought the aid of illegal practitioners and often died from blood poisoning.

I was in the Kuban shortly after the law was passed. Cossacks were busy with the harvest. Nowhere did I hear any complaints or wails of the misfortune that the new law was causing. Clinics were not besieged by frantic women clamoring for one more abortion, "the last one." I heard of not a single suicide or a single death from blood poisoning. Cossacks had not torn themselves loose from their old usages to the extent that the cities had done and were under no compulsion to make violent or catastrophic readjustments. If they talked of the law at all it was in praise of the subsidies that mothers of large families were accorded. The mother of a seventh child was granted a gratuity of 2,000 rubles annually for a period of five years. With the birth of the eleventh child the gratuity was raised to 5,000 rubles for the first and 3,000 for each of the following four years. This was welcome news to the older Cossack women.

The law of July 1944 further tightens the bonds of the family and further curtails the liberties of husband and wife to effect a separation. Abortions are banned more completely than under the earlier law. Divorce, as in the United States, may be granted only by the court, and the expense involved makes it prohibitive except to the person of high earning power. Nor is the procedure simple. The applicant must first print an advertisement in the newspaper announcing his desire for a divorce and must pay for the advertisement. He must then file an application with the People's Court and pay 100 rubles for filing it. But the People's Court has no right to grant a divorce. Its function is to hear the arguments of both parties and their witnesses and attempt to effect a reconciliation. If it fails in this attempt, the case goes to a higher court, and only this court may allow the separation. If it does, the fee is from five hundred to two thousand rubles. The law of 1944 strikes a severe blow at a free-love union or "living together"—that is, the common-law marriage as it is known in Anglo-Saxon countries. It does not ban such unions, but it discourages them. The argument is that they tend to loosen the bonds of the family, to impair the validity of monogamy, above all to hurt children. From intellectuals in Moscow and from others, too, who deem the new restriction a severe impingement on personal liberty, I heard melancholy comments. They do not approve of the puritanical compulsions inherent in the law, and some of them are heartbroken that it has come to pass.

The press, reflecting official policy, welcomed the law in all its highly ramified details with rapturous outbursts:

"There is no greater happiness," *Pravda* said editorially, "than the happiness of motherhood. Motherhood is the inexhaustible source of human rapture." It quoted Maxim Gorky's famous tribute to motherhood: "Without sunshine, there are no flowers. Without love, there is no happiness. Without woman, there is no love. Without the mother there is neither poet nor hero."

Echoing the sentiments of *Pravda*, *Izvestia* said: "In human speech there is nothing more pure and exalted, nothing more tender and more holy, than the word 'mother.'" No old-fashioned American revivalist could be more sentimental in his tributes to "mother" and "motherhood."

I happened to be in the Kuban shortly after the law of 1944 was passed, and, as in 1936, I heard no word of complaint, no word of dissension. Except among new settlers who have come to the Kuban to work in the canning or other factories or on special assignments, "factual" or "common-law" marriages were rare. The new and more liberal subsidies to mothers were welcomed with enthusiasm, because they are generous and begin not with the seventh child, as under the law of 1936, but with the third yielding the sum of 400 rubles ($80). On the birth of the fourth child the mother receives 1,300 rubles ($260) and 80 rubles ($16) monthly allowance until the child reaches its fifth birthday. With each additional child the state aid increases until in the case of the eleventh child the subsidy is raised to 5,000 rubles ($1,000) as immediate payment and 400 rubles ($80) monthly allowance until the child attains its fifth birthday. "If only we can soon buy the same amount of goods for our money," said Cossack women, "that we did in the prewar times." Never shaken by serious departure from ancient usage and custom, the family is nowhere more deep-rooted and more stable than among Cossacks. One of the frequent tributes the Soviet press bestows on the Cossacks is in praise of their age-old and steadfast devotion to the family.

The Cossack is still the warrior on horseback. But he is also a farmer, and in time of peace he is far more the farmer than the warrior. His term of army service is no longer twenty years. It is the same as for any other citizen. The lengthy separations of

To the Cossack, Orthodoxy meant more than to the muzhik, if only because he was a free man and a warrior and never dissociated his freedom and his wars from his religion. Long before he ever fought for Russian autocracy, he fought for Russian Orthodoxy. *Za veru*—for the faith—was for centuries as impassioned a battle cry with him as "For Allah" was to the Mohammedan with whom he had so long and so savagely been at war. He battled for Orthodoxy when it was attacked, he battled for it when he needed an excuse to launch an attack. Anyone who was of a different faith was to the Cossack an infidel, and it was never a sin to take the life of an infidel, whether Mohammedan, Jew, or Roman Catholic. Had Poland succeeded in converting the Cossack to Roman Catholicism by the sword or by persuasion, the Cossacks never would have petitioned the Russian Czar to make the Ukraine a part of the Russian nation.

The Cossack was a devout churchgoer, one of the most devout. On Sundays and holidays he attended church in "family droves," as Sholokhov expresses himself. He gloried in the mystical gestures, the magical symbols, the exalted singing. Marriage was no marriage, except when witnessed by the priest. He might deem the priest a boor and a rascal, but he was the servant of the Church. The priest christened the newborn child. The priest shrove the Cossack from sin when he was on his deathbed. The priest laid him to rest in the good earth which he loved and without which there was neither life nor adventure for him.

Orthodoxy meant magic and miracle, pomp and ceremony, beauty and elevation. It transcended all ordinary and extraordinary processes of human thought and human sublimation. It was beyond human doubt and human criticism. Had anyone in pre-Soviet days mumbled a word of aspersion on Orthodoxy or icons, the Cossack in his explosive militancy might draw the saber and avenge the heresy in blood. There was nothing tolerant or flexible, meek or humble, bookish or philosophical in the Cossack's espousal of his faith or in his methods of defending it.

In the course of the centuries he composed special prayers

against all possible mishap and misfortune in war and for all possible protection against the enemy.

"Supreme ruler," runs one of these prayers, "Holy Mother of God and our Jesus Christ. Bless, Lord, Thy slave of God enter-ing battle, and my comrades who are with me. Wrap them in a cloud, with Thy heavenly stony hail protect them. Holy Dmitry Soslutsky, defend me, the slave of God, and my comrades on all four sides; permit not evil men to shoot, nor with spear to pierce, nor with poleax to strike, nor with butt end of ax to smite, nor with ax to hew down, nor with sword to cut down or pierce, nor with knife to pierce or cut; neither old nor young, swarthy or black; neither heretic nor wizard nor any magic worker. All is before me now, the slave of God, orphaned and judged. In the sea, in the ocean, on the island of Buuyan stands an iron post; on the post is an iron man resting on an iron staff, and he charms iron, steel, lead, zinc, and all weapons.

"Go, iron, into your mother earth away from the slave of God and past my comrades and my horse. The arrowshafts into the forest, and the feather to its mother bird, and the glue to the fish. Defend me, the slave of God, with a golden buckler from steel and from bullet, cannon fire and ball, spear and knife. May my body be stronger than armor! Amen."[1]

When the Cossack went to war he wrote out this and other prayers and bound them neatly to the little icon which he wore next to his skin and to the little sack of native earth beside it and felt reinforced in the righteousness of his cause and the supreme protection of the Lord.

No one in Russia observed more devoutly the forms of Orthodoxy; to no one else did they carry more meaning or hold greater appeal and constitute so luridly the essence of the faith.

Sons and daughters were as devout as their fathers and mothers and as unquestioning in the acceptance of the Orthodox in-heritance. One reason for the violence with which the Cossacks, especially the more affluent, fought against the Soviets during

[1] From *Quiet Flows the Don*, by Mikhail Sholokhov. Copyright, 1934, by Alfred A. Knopf, Inc. Published in England by G. Putnam & Co., Ltd.

the civil war and during the campaign of collectivization, is that they associated Sovietism with irreligion and with the enthronement of atheism. In no other parts of rural Russia were priests so actively associated with the civil war and with antagonism to collectivization as in the Cossack country, and nowhere else did they invoke on themselves more fierce retribution.

Now that the Germans are gone from the Kuban, the Soviets are back and fully entrenched. The collectives have been reestablished. The prewar socialized economy is supreme again. Not a vestige is left in village or town of the attempts of Germans to bring back the system of private enterprise. Yet nowhere did I observe or hear on the part of Party men or Soviet officials the least mark of disrespect to religion or to Orthodoxy. Icons as of yore decorate homes. Neither church nor priest is discriminated against in the distribution of the scanty consumers' goods that are available. As everywhere else in Russia churchgoing people have a priority on candles. Sometimes the church is accorded a priority on paint, lumber, glass, other building materials. In the village of Plastunovskaya I saw one of the largest and most ornate churches in rural Russia. Because of its architecture it is spoken of as "our little" St. Isaac's, which is the name of the famous cathedral in Leningrad. Not one of the churches which the Germans had opened has been closed. There is reason to believe that if there should be demand for the opening of more churches than there now are, the demand will not be disregarded.

Remembering the violent atheist campaigns during the first two Plans and the acrimonious language of Soviet and Party workers whenever the subject of church and religion came under discussion in the Kuban as elsewhere, I was astounded at the changed temper with which they now spoke of both or of mysticism or of any allied subject.

One hot afternoon I stopped for a drink of cold water and for a rest in a little grove-sheltered building which was the office of the Party secretary. A number of Party people from all over the county were present. We talked of religion, of Orthodoxy, of Mohammedanism, of icons, of the old superstitions of the Cossack. "In the old days," said a schoolmaster, "Cossacks were better educated than muzhiks, but were no less superstitious. They believed in the *rusalka* [water nymph], in the house goblin, in forest and other spirits. Now you don't hear them talk of these spirits any more, and young people laugh at them. Our schools and the Comsomol have educated them out of the old superstitions. Yet I must tell you that there is something beautiful, not in the belief but in the concept of the *rusalka*."

He spoke so serenely, so objectively, that I said to him, "On my last trip in the Kuban, in 1936, I never heard anyone speak so appreciatively of the concept of the *rusalka*."

"Well," he went on, "times have changed. The belief in the *rusalka*, except among a few of the older people, no longer prevails. It is no longer a source of fear or possible intellectual perversion for our youth. But how did this belief originate? A girl is in love. She knows the joy and the rapture of love. Nothing in the world is so desirable and so beautiful to her as the enjoyment of her love. Then something happens. The man jilts her. Perhaps she is pregnant. She is overcome by the tragedy of her shattered romance and the disgrace of her pregnancy. So she plunges into the river and drowns herself. Then her spirit comes out of the water, and you have the *rusalka*. The river is her home, and now and then she comes out on land, hovers over fields, forest, riverbank, such is the folk belief. She may have sinned against God and society. But she is beautiful because to the folk mind youth and love are beautiful, and it is the mesmerizing power of her beauty that lures people, especially children, into her embrace, the embrace of death. But think of the romance of the concept—a moonlit night, the silvery shimmer of the river, a nude woman, with a beautiful body, lying or sitting on the bank or splashing in the water, her luxuriant hair, long and loose, falling over her back or her breasts, and the full moon upon her. A poetic image testifying to the innate love of the comman man for beauty."

As I listened to him I could not help thinking that ten years earlier a schoolmaster like him would have deemed the language he was now speaking the height of political heresy, the acme of intellectual perversity. He would have been merciless in the denunciation of such language and of those who might give it utterance. Now he himself was speaking it, and with no little appreciation of the romance it conveyed, but only of the romance. Whatever else it may or may not mean, it demonstrates the objectivity with which a man like him now appraises the poetic creations, however mystical, of the Russian or non-Russian folk mind, and he himself offered the explanation for the changed attitude—the belief in the *rusalka* was gone. It was now only a memento of antiquity, without power to impress itself on the mind of youth or only on a small section of youth.

But Soviet education has done more than educate youth out of belief in the *rusalka* and other spirits. A generation of atheist propaganda in word, in symbol, in dramatic performance, has sapped the vitality of religious faith among Cossacks no less vigorously than among peasants. Even the attitude toward icons has changed. Though the Cossack home is as ever resplendent with them, not even older men and women accord them the obeisance that was once universal. Rarely did I see them on entering a home bow before icons and make the sign of the cross over themselves. Likewise on passing churches they seldom displayed their former marks of reverence. External forms so innate in Orthodoxy have lost much of their former hold even on the older generation.

Mothers and grandmothers, fathers and grandfathers who grew to maturity in pre-Soviet days may seek to persuade sons and daughters, grandsons and granddaughters to be married in church and to christen their children. Invariably they call the priest to their deathbeds. With their dying breath they may beg their children to arrange a feast after their burial. Often they may even leave instructions how many chickens to kill for the feast, how much wine and vodka to serve. To be remembered after death is one of their most cherished longings. Yet gone from them is the old belief that if a person is not Orthodox, he is an infidel. Immensely significant is the fact that in Ust Labinskaya a Jewish twelve-year-old boy is one of the great martyrs and heroes of the community. "Think of it," said the mayor, "Cossacks, mourning the death of a Jewish boy."

One of the more decorative features in the landscape of a Cossack village is its ponds and streams. I know no village in the Kuban without the one or the other or both. Now the ponds are overgrown with sturdy reeds, and the surface is often thick with green scum. During the German occupation they remained unattended, and since the liberation, because of a shortage of labor, they have become even more rank with wild growth. Yet on hot days children gather about them, the little ones nude, the older ones in bathing suits. In the old days every one of these children sported a little cross on his neck. Mother or grandmother inculcated in them the belief that without it they would be at the mercy of the *rusalka* or some other spirit. Now, as I watched them running around ponds or splashing in the water, the old symbol of Orthodoxy was rarely in evidence.

Late one afternoon I went swimming in one of these ponds. A crowd of older boys, of high-school age, fresh from the harvest fields, came for a swim. All of them wore bathing suits, and as they swam around, splashing noisily with their feet and shouting hilariously as is the wont of Russians when they are in water, they gave one the impression of being as carefree and happy as boys anywhere. Yet they had been through the German occupation with all the frustrations that it implied for them more than for older people because they were more readily suspected of being in league with guerrillas.

They were full of talk. The Germans, they said, had kept one school in the village open, and some of them had attended it but soon tired of the studies and quit.

"They didn't teach us much," said one of them; "a lot about Hitler being the greatest leader in the world and about religion."

"Didn't you like instruction in religion?" I asked.

"It wasn't interesting."

"Was the church crowded on Sundays?"

"Sometimes."

"Did the young people go?"

"Yes."

"Did they pray?"

"Some of them did, girls mostly."

"Why then did the boys go?"

"There was no other place to go to. The clubhouse was closed. Germans didn't arrest people for gathering in church or in the church courtyard, so we went. We saw the girls there, had dates with them."

Hearing these boys talk as they did made it emphatically clear that, as in other parts of the countryside, Soviet education and propaganda have drained out of Cossack youth, of boys more than of girls, the fealty to Orthodoxy that their fathers and mothers might still be professing. The collapse of Orthodoxy in the Russian village was already manifest in 1923, when I first went to Russia after the Revolution and only six years after the rise of the Soviet Government. For the speed of this collapse neither religion as an idea or a movement or a way of life, least of all Christianity as such, is to blame. It was the historic sins of Russian Orthodoxy that invited the downfall. Throughout the centuries that it had been bound to the Russian state, it had developed none of the inner strength of Protestantism or Roman Catholicism with which to resist the violent intellectual onslaught of the Revolution. So exclusively had it depended for protection on the strong arm of the czars that it did not bother to cultivate inner enlightenment, inner power, inner invincibility.

No one has written more learnedly and more objectively of the history of religion in Russia than the late and scholarly Paul Milyukov, one-time professor of history in Moscow University. Monumental is the evidence he adduces of the disdainful neglect of the Russian church and the Russian clergy to inculcate in the masses the purely spiritual and intellectual appeal of religion. There have been churchmen, philosophers, and literary men who loved Orthodoxy, who spoke of its transcendent values, its transforming powers, but they were a voice in the wilderness. Milyukov speaks of "the immobility of its dogma, the prevalence of administrative activities over the spiritual, the ritualism of the masses and their indifference toward the spiritual contents of religion. "The Russian church," he says, "had been a tool of the state," and again and again he might have added, it was an arm of the Russian secret police.

He cites the reports of various czarist governors made in the 1860s on the state of religion in their respective provinces. Here is what Prince S. P. Gagarin, governor of Astrakhan, wrote:

"Our clergy are uncultured, uncouth and needy, yet because of their origin and mode of life they stand quite apart from the people and exert no influence over them. The performance of priestly duties is marked by a constricted formalism. The priest officiates mechanically at the Mass, the Te Deum, the Requiem, and other church rituals, and there his pastoral duty ends. The Orthodox clergy never deliver sermons, never give instruction on faith and enlightenment on the first principles of true worship, therefore the people remain ignorant of religion."[2]

Under the guidance of Pobedonostsev and Sabler, the last two czarist Procurators of the Synod, the Russian church lapsed into further deterioration. The conservative ideology of the state, says Milyukov, "penetrated the church to its core and paralyzed all manifestation of a free religious life." In the end it tumbled into the degradation of Rasputinism—Rasputin being the name of the Siberian monk who practically ruled the Russian court in the last spasm of its existence.

On my first trip to Russia after the Revolution in 1923 I was astounded at the widespread infidelity that had seized even the older generation of muzhiks. The Cossack was more firm in his adherence to Orthodoxy, because for centuries it had been a dynamic part of his martial spirit and his fighting zest. But he

[2]*Outline of Culture*, edited by Michael Karpovitch. Philadelphia, Univ. of Penna. Press, 1942.

Seventy-three-year-old priest pointing out road to passing guerrillas

Cossack captain instructing twelve-year-old Cossack at the front

Cossack gunfire clearing the road for horsemen

remained as empty of true understanding of religion as the muzhik.

In the early years of the Revolution the Living Church had sought to resuscitate and vitalize it with a new intellectual and spiritual message. But it never gained a following among the masses. It rose with a boom and crashed with a bang until now only a shell of it remains and is certain to be absorbed by the so-called Old or Tikhon Church, which is the only branch of Orthodoxy that is now functioning. Its very powerlessness is one reason for the friendly relationship now between church and state.

Panteleimon Ponamorenko, himself of Kuban Cossack origin but now president of the White Russian Republic, gave me a copy of a letter from a seventy-three-year-old village priest which offers another reason for the changed attitude of the Soviets and the Communist Party toward the Church. The name of the priest is Yakov Fedorov Slabudko, and this is what he writes:

"Since the beginning of the war in 1941 my village of Porechye was blockaded—that is, surrounded on all sides by German garrisons. Though held in a tight ring by the Germans, it was only a short distance from the guerrilla headquarters.

"In September and October 1941 when guerrilla squads were being organized I was among the first to assume the sacred duty of helping guerrillas. I admonished my parishioners to remember that guerrillas were defenders of the fatherland and should be given all possible help. I told them never to refuse guerrillas food, shelter, anything else they might want, and never under any circumstances betray their presence to the enemy. I also called on all our citizens never to collaborate with the Germans, never to work for them, especially as policemen. Russia, I said, was unconquerable, and collaborators would bitterly lament their error.

"I set the example to the people in my village. Guerrilla officers stopped in my house and found there shelter and food.

Rank-and-file guerrillas likewise stopped in my house, day and night. I fed all who were hungry and never refused them anything I had. I gave them cloth for clothes, for grain sacks, for wrappings on their feet. If I ever learned that the men in the forest were without bread, I sent it to them. Between 1942 and 1944 I gave them forty-five poods of rye, contributed 15,000 rubles in cash to the defense fund, and bought a one-thousand-ruble bond.

"All this I did under conditions of military secrecy. But there were spies among the guerrillas, and the last such spy who was in my home is a man named Buketov. He had been in my house twice, and he reported me to the Germans.

"Several times guerrilla colonels Gradov and Grom wanted to present my name for military decorations. But I begged them not to do it, so that nothing would be known about me. But spies did their own work, and I was denounced and the Germans were told of the help I kept giving guerrillas. When the blockade was still in full force, the Germans broke into Porechye, and I was the first man they seized. I was in church at the time. They seized my wife too and, pointing their rifles at us, they drove us to the public square. For three days they kept my wife and me under close guard without permitting us once to leave the place of our incarceration. Revolver in hand, the German commandant kept asking me where the guerrillas were hiding and how many of them there were. I said I didn't know where they were hiding, and because I pitied the people who were in the forest near by, and wanted to scare the Germans, I said that I had heard there were a million of them. My answer made the commandant's eyes bulge.

"I suffered a heart attack and could no longer walk. With the butt of his gun the guard beat me. Then he struck me so powerfully with the fist on the neck that I fell to the ground face down and unconscious. He kicked me in the side, and that brought me back to consciousness, and I started to get up. But the guard shouted 'Halt,' and kicked me again in the side. As I rolled over he saw the sacred cross on my chest. He stopped beating me, went to a doctor and said a pastor had fallen down and lay on the ground. The doctor sent two Germans after me. They lifted me and took me to the doctor's residence. The doctor took my pulse, gave me a double injection, and forbade the Germans to make me walk. Then the Germans received an order to evacuate the village, and thanks to this order I remained at home.

"Later when I recovered and went to my house I was horrified. Everything was gone. Nothing but bare walls remained. Shoes, clothes, kitchenware were stolen or destroyed. . . . Neither my wife nor I had any shoes or any clothes. I served our father and with faith and justice. I am seventy-three years old, my wife is seventy. Having suffered great calamity and great sorrow, I am taking the liberty humbly to request you, our valorous leader and patriot comrade Ponamorenko, to consider my unfortunate position and to find somehow for my wife and myself shoes, top coats, underwear, and bedding."

I quote this letter in full because it is a revealing document. Overwhelmingly priests spurned the blandishments the Germans flaunted before them in an effort to lure them into collaboration. Pyotr Karpovitch Ignatov, leader of the guerrilla squad of scientists in the Kuban, told me that priests in occupied villages were among his best and bravest informants. To the end they remained unshakably Russian and patriotic. "I was once at confession," said an elderly woman, "and as the little father stooped down, a revolver fell from the bosom of his robe. Quickly he picked it up, threw it back into his bosom and said: 'In these wicked times, little sister, when the German antichrist is among us, even a priest must carry a gun.' " Priests not only carried, but used, guns. Not a few of them have been decorated for action with guerrillas.

In the hour of national catastrophe, the Russian clergy overwhelmingly supported the Army, the people, the government. Their patriotism rose above all past grievances, all past recriminations at the hands of the Soviets and the ruling Party. Thereby alone they gained a new position in the country. They lifted themselves to the prestige of being patriots, than which there is no more sacred term in the Russian vocabulary of today.

I do not know what would happen if there were a real and widespread revival of religion in Russia. More people are seeking the consolation of the Church than in prewar days, especially women, among the Cossacks of the Kuban than among the citizenry of Moscow. But until the youth of the country is won by, for, and to religion, it is too premature to speak of a revival. Had there been such a revival, it is doubtful if the state and the Party would countenance it without at least a vigorous intellectual battle. There is nothing in the utterances of leaders and official theoreticians to justify the assurance that they would remain indifferent to a large-scale resurgence of religion. Hints of a contrary attitude frequently appear in official publications. Here, for example, is *Bolshevik*, highly authoritative spokesman of the all-powerful Central Committee of the Communist Party. In the issue of October 1944, a well-known Party theoretician named A. Solodownikov, in a lengthy discussion of art and the revival of folklore, vigorously censures leaders who are "trying to drag into the concert stage the avowedly religio-mystical works of composers and writers of the past under the guise that it is part of our artistic inheritance." There have been other pronouncements of a similar nature only more direct and more blunt. Here for example is a statement on the subject in a recent issue of *Comsomolskaya Pravda*, the daily spokesman of Soviet Youth: "The attitude of the Party toward religion is well known and has not changed." It quotes Mikhail Kalinin, the President of the country, as saying that Bolsheviks regard religion as an error or unreality which must be battled not with persecution but "with enlightenment." Meanwhile there has been no hint of deviation from adherence to the materialist interpretation of history with its negation and scorn of all mysticism. This philosophy underlies all teaching and all thinking in Russian education, inside and outside all schools and colleges.

Yet faith in the Soviet Union is respected as never before since the coming of the Soviets. The most fanatical Bolshevik no longer associates the icon, for example, with the corruption and reaction of the once Czar-sheltered church. In the battle against that church he has triumphed. Orthodoxy has no political power. It has no wealth. It has no relations with a foreign church that may be hostile to Russia, to Sovietism, to collectivism. It is completely independent of foreign control or of foreign allegiance.

Besides, there are no kulaks or merchants any more with whom the clergy might conspire against Sovietism or socialization. Nor are priests themselves any longer property-minded. This is one of the most significant developments in the Russian Orthodox Church. Priests live off the contributions of their parishioners. They neither cultivate nor propagate accumulation of wealth. Quite the contrary. "Christ had nothing," I heard a priest say in a sermon, "why should we covet earthly possessions?"

The Russian clergy speaks a social language which would horrify their pre-Soviet brethren. They do more: in sermons and in private conversations they draw parallels between the social teachings of Christianity and bolshevism. They oppose the infidelity and the rationalism of bolshevism, and there is no official interference with this opposition. But they have effected a philosophical synthesis between Orthodoxy and bolshevism. In the theological schools that are being opened, this synthesis will be the basis of courses in philosophy and sociology. Marxism and Sovietism will be espoused as the social fulfillment of the New Testament.

Thus while there is peace and good will between the Church and the State, the antagonism between Orthodox mysticism and bolshevik rationalism remains unresolved and irreconcilable. This is as true among the Cossacks of the Kuban as in other parts of the country.

CHAPTER XXV

Eating and Drinking among Cossacks

RUSSIANS have always been known for their hospitality. But Cossack hospitality is more than Russian. It is Cossack with a spirit and a technique, a persuasiveness and consummation all its own.

In 1936, on the eve of my departure from Slavenskaya for Novorossiisk, the mayor of the village, as robust and cheerful a Cossack as I have ever known, arranged for one of his assistants to wake me and drive me to the railroad station. The assistant called me an hour before train time. When I protested that I wanted to sleep a little longer, he said:

"But you haven't the time."

"Why not? It's an hour before train time."

"By the time you eat your breakfast the train will be here."

"I don't want any breakfast. I'd rather have more sleep."

"Sorry, but the mayor instructed me to wake you in time for breakfast."

We drove to the railroad station and walked into the little dining room. My guide excused himself and disappeared. Soon he returned, followed by a short plump woman in a white blouse and a white apron. She set the table, went out of the room, and presently came back with a large frying pan sizzling with six eggs and large lumps of bacon.

"I can never eat so many eggs," I said. "I just got up."

"Yes, you can," said the woman. "Anybody can eat *six* fried eggs."

Further argument was futile. She stood by and, motherlike, coaxed and prodded—and won. I ate all the eggs.

In Moscow hotels in prewar times the regulation omelet was four eggs. In the Kuban it was six. It still is wherever eggs are available.

Unlike Americans and Englishmen, Cossacks do not sip their liquor, but toss it down. To the best of my knowledge few Russians do otherwise. The *glotok*—drinking a sip at a time, whether cocktails, cognac, champagne, vodka—like the tiny sandwiches that are the fashion in America and England, leaves Russians puzzled and amused.

At official parties in Moscow and at others not so official—in homes, for example—the potency of the drink determines the size of the tumbler in which it is served. The stronger the drink, the smaller the size of the glass. In Moscow the tea glass is for mineral water or other soft drinks. But not in the Kuban—nor, so far as I know, among Cossacks anywhere. A drink is a drink, whether it is homemade cherry brandy with an alcoholic content of twenty per cent or Moscow vodka with 56 or more per cent of alcohol or pure spirits, medicinal and others. Always the tea glass, often of extraordinary depth, is the measure of a man's or woman's drinking prowess or pleasure.

Taras Bulba's "science of drinking," though worn thin through the centuries, still lingers. On weekdays, when they work in the fields or are busy with chores around their homes, Cossacks drink little or not at all. The temperance propaganda of the Comsomol, the first Cossacks have ever known, has made its impression not only on youth but on fathers and mothers. But the idea of prohibition is anathema. During the dry years of the first World War, the early period of Sovietism, no one so blithely ignored the dry laws as the Cossack. To him a festival is no festival, a wedding no wedding unless accompanied by hilarity and fun and—hearty drinking.

When catastrophe strikes the land and brings scarcity and hunger, as during the collectivization campaign and the German occupation, the people endure the enforced privations as best they can, though not without violent grumbling. But the Kuban is rich. One good crop of wheat, honey, fruits, vegetables, and the coveted grape, all of which are easy to grow, and the proverbial plentifulness, however limited in variety, comes back. Hard as times now are, acute as still is the shortage of meats, dairy foods, sweets, the Kuban already enjoys a superior standard of living than does Moscow.

At the dinner on the collective farm "Red Star," in the village of Plastunovskaya, we were served: borsch, fat and fragrant with chicken; fried eggs, platters full of them; boiled beef garnished with grasslike vegetables; chicken stewed in tomato sauce and fried in butter; beet-potato salad such as Moscow hotels never serve, don't even know how to make; fresh milk, homemade butter, sour cream, wheat bread, hot jam biscuits; cucumbers and tomatoes; apples, plums, pears; two kinds of cake, a tall brownish sponge cake and apple cake much like American pie, only much deeper, with a thicker crust and as tender as any baked at home.

When I complimented my hostess on the excellence of her cooking, she said half apologetically:

"Ah, but this is nothing. You should have been here before the war when we could set before you a real Kuban meal."

Someday an enterprising Russian or foreigner will compile a Cossack cookbook, and it will be a unique even if not overrefined contribution to culinary art.

Salo, raw salt pork, is a favorite food in Russia, but no people are as partial to it as Cossacks, and one has to hear an older Cossack discourse on the subject to appreciate its transcendent virtues. Once I told an older Cossack that Americans never eat it. He was wide-eyed with surprise.

"And I thought," was his comment, "that Americans were a practical people. Why, suppose you go off on a long hunting and fishing trip or on military maneuvers, or suppose you go to war and have a long march ahead of you on horse and saddle?

What raw meats can you take along that'll keep and that won't need cooking? Beef? Lamb? Veal? Fowl? In the first place, you cannot eat such meat raw; in the second place, if the weather is cold it will freeze and if it is hot it will spoil. But consider *salo*. It always keeps fresh, it doesn't freeze in cold or spoil in heat. It is always palatable, always nourishing, and the longer it lies in your sack wrapped in paper or cloth, the more tang it acquires."

I nodded, but the Cossack was not yet finished.

"Do Americans eat any pork at all?"

"Lots of it," I said.

"That's fine, excellent! Then you'll always be a sturdy people. Yes, sir! The pig is man's greatest boon, and don't we Cossacks know it! We've had to live and fight in all kinds of climates, against all types of people. Take the mountaineer Moslem whom we've had no easy time in taming. Had he been a pig-eater like ourselves, we might still have had trouble with him. Off his horse, without gun, dagger, or saber, he never was a match for the Cossack. He shrank from a fight with the bare fists, and for a good reason: he hadn't the strength of a Cossack, because he hates the pig."

He paused, brushed his beard, nodded contemplatively as though speaking to himself, then pursued:

"Think what many uses and luxuries the pig makes possible. Take a suckling calf. Butcher it and you have to eat it all at once or salt it away, and then it's not fresh meat any more. But a suckling pig cooked whole with trimmings inside, the way our Cossack women do, it's so tender, so fragrant, so sweet that even if it were as big as a calf you'd eat it all at once. Your palate would give you no rest until you did. But a suckling pig isn't as large as a calf, so you have no trouble disposing of it in one meal. Or take sausage. Would there be any sausage if it wasn't for the pig? No, sir! Inconceivable, no real sausage, the kind that puts flesh on your bones, pours strength into your muscles, so you feel like going outside, putting your arms around a tree and pulling it up by the roots . . ."

He paused again. I was listening intently, now and then scribbling in my notebook. Encouraged by my attention, he resumed his discourse.

"D'you eat borsch in America?"

"Beginning to," I said.

"My grandmother—there was a cook for you. You didn't want to be sick because you didn't want to miss any of her meals, and if you were sick you forced yourself to get up and go to the table and after lapping up a plate of her borsch you were well again. . . . Come summer she would dump into the huge kettle a bushel or two of tomatoes, half a dozen dressed chickens, as many slabs of pig meat, all necessary seasonings, and there was borsch for you! We ate it morning, noon, and night. We never tired of it. The pig meat and the chicken gave it a smell and a taste the very thought of which made the mouth water, and even though you'd no more than gotten up from the table you looked forward to the next meal as to a holiday. Of course my father was a rich Cossack, very rich. He had forty horses of his own— forty horses!" He paused and with thumb and forefinger twisted his stubby mustaches and sighed for the old days and the old riches. Then he returned to his theme:

"Now consider eggs. Eaten by themselves—boiled, fried, or scrambled—there is nothing to them, no fullness, no complete meal. But fried with lumps of bacon—ah!"

"Bacon and eggs," I said, "and ham and eggs are national American dishes."

"I should have known that," he said. "That's why you're such an energetic people."

"We fry our bacon crisp, sometimes so crisp that you can break it like a rusk."

"You don't say!" His enthusiasm dropped, and he looked puzzled. "Why do you do that?"

"We like it that way."

"But frying it so dry drains all the juice out of it, all taste, all substance!" he said. "You might as well fry your eggs with wood shavings."

"There's no accounting for one's taste," I said.

"Yes, there is. There's reason for taste. There's reason for everything. There should be. If you fry bacon until it just begins to sizzle in its own fat and then eat it with fried eggs, you have something to fill your mouth with, to bite into, to chew on, a mouthful of strength and health, delight and ecstasy."

With Maria Ivanovna Fadeyeva, mayor of the village of Staro-Myshastovskaya, I drove out to a harvest field. We arrived in time to witness the performance of a professional vaudeville company from Krasnodar then touring the harvest fields of the Kuban. The audience sat on the grass, nearly all women with white *kasinkas* drawn low over the forehead to shield their eyes from the glaring sun. The stage was a rug spread on the ground within the shadow of a summer dormitory. The entertainment was long and spirited; there were dancing, music, storytelling, a magician, a woman acrobat, a puppet show, a guitar player, a gypsy dancer and singer. There was also an imitator of bird songs and animal sounds. The grunting of a pig in various states of frenzy and ecstasy evoked the loudest laughter. And there was the inevitable fun-poking master of ceremonies upholding the dignity of his profession by appearing in a black tie.

Said the master of ceremonies in the course of one of his introductions:

"Last year my work was so distinguished that I was awarded a premium. And d'you know what it was? A wrist watch." He paused, then added. "But I still have to receive my premium." There was loud laughter, and when it subsided the speaker continued: "This year I am certain to be awarded another premium, for my work, as you yourselves can bear witness, is excellent. Most likely this year I shall be awarded a gramophone, and most likely I shall see as much of it as my last year's wrist watch."

The audience roared and clapped. Gibes at the failings of the bureaucracy in its services to the people, especially in the war years, are always appreciated by Russian audiences and constitute a constant source of jolly and biting patter of Russian masters of ceremonies. The patter is neither banned nor discouraged; apparently someone in high authority, perhaps Stalin himself, regards it as a salutary tonic. It offers victims the solace of laughter and exposes bureaucrats to public opprobrium.

When the performance was over, the women in the audience went back to work and I stayed for dinner. The president of the farm was a giant of a man in the early thirties with dark hair, heavy-browed dark eyes, and with a strong, handsome, finely chiseled face. I could not help thinking what a superb hero or villain he would make in an American or Russian "Western" movie.

"Why didn't you warn me you were coming with an American guest?" he said to the mayor. "I could've *organized* a real dinner. To be caught unprepared like this——"

"Please don't bother," said the mayor. "We can eat elsewhere, we've come only to see the harvesting."

"Oh no," he said, "you'll have dinner here. Of course you will."

Four sturdy barefoot kitchenmaids bustled about preparing the meal. I saw one of them carry a tray of filled glasses to the dining room. Hot and thirsty, I followed her, and when she set the glasses on the table I reached out for one and started drinking. My lips tingled and I stopped immediately. What I had mistaken for water was high-powered vodka. The extraordinary depth of the glasses, larger than the usual tea glass, had dispelled all suspicion as to the nature of the contents.

"Go ahead, please," urged the young woman. "We've got lots more."

"I thought it was water," I said.

"It'll quench thirst."

"Not the kind I have," I said. She laughed and brought me a drink of water.

We sat down at the table, I beside the host. He set a tall glass of vodka beside me.

"I don't think I can drink that much," I said.

"Of course you can. It's mild enough, the *moskva* brand, only 56 per cent spirits."

"I'm sorry, I can't."

"No excuses, please," rose a woman's voice. It was the mayor with her hand on the glass beside her plate.

"Will you drink yours?" I said.

"Of course," she answered.

"All of it—at once?"

"Naturally."

"Then I will, too."

"Wonderful!" exclaimed the host and at once stood up and proposed a toast, which is a part of the ritual of Russian hospitality, especially when a foreigner is the guest.

"This is an unusual occasion for us and for me in particular, because this is the first time in my life that I have seen an American in the flesh," he said.

"In this war we here in the Kuban have learned a lot about the American and British peoples, and we want more and more of their citizens to come here and get acquainted with us. We all know what American *dobrota* [kindness] is. Many of our homes are more cheerful than they would have been, now that the bestial Germans have been kicked out, because of the shoes and dresses, the sweaters and coats which the American Relief Committee [Russian War Relief] has sent us. So I propose a toast to the friendship of the gallant American people and the valorous Russian people."

We clinked glasses, nodded to one another and started drinking. I drank and drank, and there seemed no end to the flow from my glass. I could drink no more and set it down. It was still half full. But the mayor, a diminutive woman with stooping shoulders and shiny blue eyes, like the others, had drunk hers to the last drop and appeared none the worse for it, with no sign of discomfort in her expression or manner. The sight of my half-filled glass stirred a murmur of surprise and consternation. Why couldn't I, out of sheer Russian-American friendship, perform the traditional Kuban rite of sociability?

"Don't Americans drink?" asked the host with surprise. "I mean drink *pochelovecheski* like human beings?"

"Some do," I said. "I'm afraid in this respect I'm a poor example."

We started eating tomato soup, then proceeded with chicken. Hardly had we started with the chicken when the mayor was on her feet. Immediately all glasses were refilled. Lifting her glass, the mayor said:

"Our Cossack women are doing heroic work in the field. On them lies the sacred duty of growing food for our civilian population and for our fighting brothers and sisters at the front. And we know that our American sisters are doing their share in this war against fascism. Millions of them are working in defense industries. Others are helping their valiant army and their valiant navy. So I propose a toast to the patriotism of the Russian women and of their American sisters." I applauded heartily. But I only lifted the glass to my lips. I held it there until the others had drained theirs; then I set mine down back of the plate so it would not be too visible. But my host caught sight of it instantly.

"Now really," he chided, "you're offending me, you're making it appear that you are not enjoying our hospitality. Of course it is modest. I didn't know you were coming—and besides, we aren't as well off as we were before the war—you've seen what the Germans have done to us—how they've plundered and looted us. . . . But we're giving you the best we have."

"I appreciate your hospitality deeply," I said. "See how heartily I am eating this wonderful food." I helped myself to another leg of chicken.

"But food isn't enough."

I lifted my glass, took a few sips, and set it down again.

"That's better," he said, "but not good enough."

We finished the chicken and started on boiled river crab.

"Won't you say a toast?" said the host.

"Of course I will."

Glasses were refilled, and I rose to my feet.

"Let's drink to your valiant armies fighting in the east and to the American and British armies fighting in the west." There was a loud and hearty cheer. Again we clinked glasses and again

I only lifted mine to the lips. My host frowned, shook his head, smiled and said:

"*Nu!*"

I shook my head, and the young president of the collective motioned with his hand, as though in disgust.

For dessert we had the Kuban regulation omelet.

Now came another toast from a visiting Party worker.

"To victory and to friendship between the Soviet Union, England, and America." This time the president wouldn't drink until I did. I drained half of my glass, but he hadn't yet touched his.

"This is the last toast," he said, "and if you don't want to make me think I've failed in my duty as a host you will empty your glass." I did.

The dinner over, we walked outdoors. The sun was hot, but a cool breeze was blowing and I felt refreshed. My head reeled, and I climbed into the jeep and sat down. The mayor and the president stood near by talking about the wheat crop, the deliveries to the state, the probable date of the completion of deliveries. Neither showed the least trace of tipsiness. Finally the mayor climbed into the jeep, sat down beside me, and we drove off. She was as alert and clear-minded as though she had only been drinking water.

"How are you feeling?" she asked.

"Fine," I said lamely.

"That's good. The president was so pleased you came. He thanked me for bringing you and made me promise that next time I bring an American to the harvest field I'll let him know in advance so he can *organize* a real meal."

"You look so fresh and composed," I said.

"Why shouldn't I? It was fun to be out here and have a bit of relaxation."

"I envy you," I said.

She laughed and replied:

"You must come again, when we are richer than we are now, so we can treat you like a real guest."

I stayed several days in the village of Dinskaya, an old and formerly prosperous community of fifteen thousand, now reduced to half its prewar population. Vasily Demyanovitch Ognenoy, the agricultural expert, or county agent, was my official host. A stocky man in the thirties, of medium height, with powerful shoulders, powerful hands, his face was pockmarked and his small eyes round and blue. He spoke in a low voice with a melodious intonation. He piloted me around streets, homes, fields, showed me the battered and burned ruins of what in the prewar days were new public institutions. On the outskirts of the village on a large plot of land was the shell of a lone building. The grounds were overgrown with weeds and littered with broken playground equipment, with here and there the head of a bright flower peeping orphanlike out of a mass of debris.

"This was our children's nursery," said Ognenoy, "a model nursery, and Dinskaya was so proud of it. From all over the Kuban people came to see it, admire it, and ask us how to build one like it. We had been working on plans to dot the great Kuban with nurseries like it or better ones. Now look at it—a tottering shell." We walked inside. Nothing was left, not a table, a chair, or picture, not a pane in any of the windows, not a scrap of plumbing—a tottering structure, a ghost-haunted box!

On my last evening in the village Ognenoy "organized" a farewell dinner. He invited the mayor and the Party secretary, both of whom had been away in the harvest fields, and because they arrived late the dinner didn't start until midnight. All the time I was in the village I had been having meals in the home in which I was staying or on some nearby collective. There were no celebrations, no toasts, little drinking, and the meals were modest. But a farewell dinner was something else. It was a celebration and a commemoration. "You have seen much of Dinskaya," said Ognenoy, "you may never come again." So it had to be a "nice little" dinner. It was.

The first toast was to Roosevelt, Churchill, and Stalin. The second toast was to the peoples of England, America, and Russia.

I only lifted the glass to my lips. When Ognenoy saw me set my glass down as full as it had been when I had lifted it, his mouth opened wide.

"How could you——" he began without finishing the sentence.

I said that I'd listen to toasts, I'd make toasts, I'd applaud toasts, but I could not possibly do them bibulous justice. I ended by declaring I was already feeling "stabbings" inside of me.

"That's fine," said Ognenoy, whose surname, translated, literally means "the fiery one."

"Why is it fine?" I asked.

"We have a saying that to drive out a wedge you drive one in, so if you drink more you'll drive out the 'stabbings,' they'll be washed out."

I shook my head. Ognenoy looked hurt.

"Please!" he said.

Again I shook my head.

"You're our guest," he pleaded, "and you must understand——"

"Doesn't a guest have rights?"

"No, sir, not in the Kuban. A guest does as his host wills."

I remained unconvinced, so Ognenoy went into a long speech.

"Maybe you don't understand. So listen. We don't drink by ourselves. We haven't the time. Look at our secretary and our mayor. They've been up night after night in the harvest fields. They have hardly had a wink of sleep. They have been running from one thrashing crew to another to see that the work goes well, that the people have all the gas, all the oil, all the spare parts they need. When this dinner is over, they'll drive out again to the harvest fields. The gathering of our bread is our most important job. Not an ear of wheat must remain ungathered and unthrashed. We don't even bother with regular meals during the harvest season. Yet the secretary and the mayor took time off, and so did I, to show you that, busy as we are, we don't neglect our duties as hosts. Therefore, you mustn't neglect yours as guest."

The secretary laughed. The mayor laughed. The other guests laughed. There was gay talk and lively banter. But Ognenoy was a picture of agony.

"You'll make me weep," he said.

"Why?"

"Because you're so stubborn. I feel tears already coming to my eyes."

"Nonsense, you're a powerful man, and your name is Ognenoy, the fiery one."

Meekly and with supplication he pursued a new line.

"It doesn't have to be vodka," he said. "We've got lots of homemade cherry brandy. It's weak enough so a child can drink it—only 20 per cent spirits."

"Very well," I said, "you drink vodka and I'll drink cherry brandy."

"Oh no. We cannot do that. We drink what you drink. If vodka isn't good enough for you, it isn't good enough for us. So it shall be cherry brandy."

The dinner livened up. Toast followed toast, long toasts, brief toasts, gay and solemn toasts, poetic, impassioned, fighting toasts, to the armies of the Allies, to the death of fascism and fascists, to the glory of democracy, to American women, British women, Cossack women, Chinese women, to the women of all the world except the fascist countries. Songs followed, ancient and modern, songs of mirth and songs of sorrow, love songs and marching songs, fighting songs and victory songs. . . . Ognenoy was so happy his face beamed; sweat glistened on his forehead, under his eyes; he embraced and kissed me Russian fashion and complimented me on my belated but hearty appreciation of Kuban hospitality.

Dawn was breaking into the house when the party broke up. The secretary and the mayor left for "a few winks of sleep" before returning to the harvest fields. All the guests were gone. Somehow I made my way to the window, opened it and looked outside. Roosters were crowing. That was all I heard. The world was spinning round and round to some fatal eclipse. . . . Then nature came to my aid and claimed for the good Kuban earth all the toasts my body was only too willing to shake out of itself. I staggered to my bed and fell soundly asleep.

CHAPTER XXVI

The Cossacks Discover America

IT WAS NOT the letters and money orders of relatives in America, or the American-invented tractor and combine, American movies and American jazz, not even Jack London and Mark Twain, that first made Cossacks in the Kuban aware of America. It was the American leghorn hen! To her belongs the credit of making the Kuban for the first time in its history look to America as to a land of glamor and miracle.

Though Cossacks were richer and better farmers than muzhiks in the old days, they followed a traditionally Russian and backward pattern of tillage. Their land was famous for its wheat, its fruit, its horses. Because they were Cossack, the horse was their favorite animal, the one they strove most to improve. On the horse they lavished their choicest eloquence and their sturdiest efforts. Other branches of livestock were of secondary or little significance. There was no poultry science. The setting hen perpetuated her species and, because of the wheat and the corn she was fed, could be depended upon adequately to fulfill her mission of supplying the Cossack with eggs and chicken. The incubator was as unknown as the tractor.

But in 1928, the first year of the first Five-year Plan, leghorns were imported to the Kuban and they created a sensation. Here was a bird whose virtues were unmatched by any of the native breeds. It was smaller in size, but it was alert and spunky and could fend for itself as no other hen that had ever squawked in a Cossack courtyard. It was a magnificent layer, better than any hen the Cossack had ever known. The eggs were white and shiny. They were pretty to look at and they were a "mouthful" to bite into. The white leghorn proved a *chudo* (miracle), and all over the Kuban collectives and individual Cossacks started raising it. In time it crowded out most of the native breeds.

Soon afterward collectivization swept the land. It signalized the greatest revolution in Russian agriculture. It marked an end to the old mode of individual ownership and individual tillage with its dependence on hand and horse, on ox and cart, on tradition and habit. The American tractor superseded the horse and ox. The American combine supplanted the scythe and the cradle. The American incubator made the setting hen an antiquity and a nuisance. Science and technique supplemented tradition and habit. A new age and a new dispensation shook the Russian countryside.

The Russian language was deficient in technological terms. There were no available Russian equivalents for the names of American machines that were pouring over the Russian land. They could have been easily enough rendered into Russian. But that was not done. The original American names were retained, and now such words as "tractor," "combine," "motor," "incubator," "cultivator," "leghorn," "disk," "gillette" (safety razor), "silos" (silo) "separator," "excavator," are as much and as familiar a part of the Cossack vocabulary as "borsch" and "vodka."

Because collectivization rolled into the Kuban on the wheels of the American-made or American-invented machine, it invested the very word "America" with fresh meaning and fresh appeal. Ideology or no ideology, without the American machine there would have been no collectives in Russia, just as without the engine there would have been no automobile and no airplane.

The Soviet idea ever has been that entertainment must go hand in hand with toil and sacrifice. However low the standard of living at any given time, however arduous the task at hand, there must be recreation, especially for the youth. Therefore, under collectivization as never before the clubhouse or town hall became the community center in the Kuban villages. Nowhere else in rural Russia were clubhouses built so rapidly; nowhere else were they so large, so up to date with such spacious auditoriums and such adequate stage equipment. These Soviet "Yimcas," as one may speak of them, fostered amateur theatricals, choral singing, amateur bands and orchestras, dances, lectures, motion pictures. Soon enough and despite original Soviet disapproval, the clubhouses of the Kuban resounded with the strains of American jazz, with the beat of the American fox trot, with the sway of the "Boston"—the American waltz. Thus a fresh trickle of Americanism flowed into the Kuban and became a part of the everyday life of its youth.

More and more American films were shown in these clubhouses. Audiences roared with mirth over the antics of Harold Lloyd and Charlie Chaplin, the broad farce of Harold Lloyd was no less appealing than the subtle comedy of Chaplin. They clamored for more and more of such films, and since new ones were infrequent, old ones were welcomed back, over and over. To this day not only in the Kuban but elsewhere in Russia the silent films of Harold Lloyd and Charlie Chaplin pack the largest auditoriums.

As collectivization gathered momentum and the Kuban boomed with new plans and new schemes of farming, with new crops and new breeds of livestock, still more American "culture," as Russians say, seeped in and was assimilated. Rich in fruit and vegetables, the Kuban became Russia's most affluent canning country. The canning factories were built according to American blueprints, were equipped with American machinery or machinery patterned after American models. Thus the new civilization that was sweeping the Kuban, "collectivist in form, socialist in content," as Russians speak of it, was lavishly interwoven with American invention and American adventure. How richly this was the case and how romantically Russians often speak of it I did not fully realize until I visited the village of Dinskaya.

In the preceding chapters I have already spoken of Vasily

Demyanovitch Ognenoy, the county agent of Dinskaya. Late one afternoon we went walking outside the village. Pausing in front of a rim of low hills, Ognenoy said:

"D'you know what we had on these hills? American windmills. They pumped water into our cow stables. What a marvelous invention! You did not need an engine or gasoline. Nature did the work for you, did it superbly with its own energy without cost or trouble to the collective. If anything went wrong, you climbed up the wheel with hammer and monkey wrench and in a few minutes you had the wheel turning again, turning and turning, easily, beautifully, and you could go on with your work in the field or in the barn without needing to worry about water for the cows. Such a glorious invention!"

He paused, looked contemplatively at the hills, now bare of windmills, bare of anything but grass, and added emotionally:

"The Germans smashed them all. Not one windmill have they left, the foul, two-legged beasts!"

Let no one underestimate the meaning that the word "America" holds for men like Ognenoy. There are literally tens of thousands of them all over Russia. Such men are concerned, not with American politics or America's social system, but with American scientific progress, American inventiveness, America's enormous contribution to the modernization of the Russian village and Russian agriculture. To them America is a land of glamor, the glamor of steel and engines and all manner of mechanical contraptions with which to unlock nature's riches and place them at the disposal of man. Whatever the future relations between the United States and Russia, this glamor will continue to excite the imagination and the admiration of the Ognenoys and of all others who have staked all their hopes and all their faith on the capacity of the machine under Soviet control to bring them the bountiful life for which they yearn and which the Soviets have so eloquently promised them.

The more I traveled in the Kuban the greater was my awareness of the immense popularity that America has achieved there. Here, for example, was the village of Novo Titerovskaya. I was having breakfast in a Soviet restaurant. A woman named Yefrosia Ivanovna Kolchenko was waiting on me. No sooner was my glass of milk empty than she was beside me, pitcher in hand, refilling it and saying, *"Kushaite, kushaite* [Eat, eat]." The meal was nearly over when she came up again, this time with nothing in her hands, and said:

"I want to give you a message to the kind American people. When the war broke out my husband went to war, my son went to war, my daughter Yelena, who was born in 1924, went to war, and I too enlisted. We are a one hundred per cent fighting family. My husband and son are still fighting. But when the enemy was driven out of here my daughter and I came home. We were needed here. Our home was looted of everything, especially the clothes we had left behind, though we had carefully hidden them. We wore our army clothes because we had none other. Then we got two parcels from the American Relief Committee. The one I received contained a dress, the one my daughter received contained an overcoat, a skirt, and a blouse. I cannot tell you how rejoiced we were. Our village was ruined, our home was looted, and of a sudden in faraway America people thought of us and sent us those pretty clothes. . . . My daughter is so proud of them she puts them on only on Sundays or when she goes to a dance. I wrote my husband and son about it, and so did my daughter, and my husband wrote back that the American gift will encourage him to kill more Fritzes."

Barely had Yefrosia Kolchenko finished her words when another woman came out of the kitchen and said:

"I too got a parcel from the American Relief Committee, a dress for my thirteen-year-old girl, and she and I are very proud of it. I wrote my husband at the front about it, and he was so pleased. He said, 'Americans are real allies.'"

I asked Rozhnov, mayor of the village, whether many families had received American gifts.

"Quite a few," he said. "We have already had three shipments. The last has just arrived—280 parcels—and we shall distribute them according to the needs of our people, always looking first after war widows and after families whose sons and fathers are at the front."

The people of the village, he said, were so proud of the gifts, they always wrote about them to the men in the Army, and the men wrote back glowing tributes to America.

In the evening a group of young people came to see me. Most of them were high-school graduates or already in college. They asked endless questions about American colleges, American youth, American life, and those who said they would specialize in surgery hoped that someday they might go to America for a postgraduate course. Before we parted they said:

"Take our addresses and give them to college students in America. Tell them to write to us, and we shall be glad to correspond with them."

Said one girl: "I wish I were in America now—there are more men than here."

From Novo Titerovskaya I drove to Goryachi Klutsh—Hot Springs—one of the most scenic villages in the Kuban, in the foothills of the Caucasian Mountains. Because of the scenery, the climate, the mineral waters, the abundance of fishing and big game in the mountains, the village was in prewar days rapidly becoming a popular resort. Now it was desolate. The Germans had laid waste most of its buildings, trees, parks, rest homes. Only the birds and the mountains and the wild flowers remind one of its prewar glories.

Arkady Perventsev, the novelist, was vacationing there with his family. I called on him, and he insisted on arranging dinner. Among the guests was a young woman, a physician from the Board of Health. Since the expulsion of the Germans from the Kuban she had been organizing children's homes and special feeding stations for children. There were toasts during the meal, one by the physician.

"When I first came here," she said, "the Kuban was devastated and poverty-stricken. The Germans looted the people of mirrors and gramophones, sewing machines and bicycles, livestock and cereals. My problem was to feed the children, and I want to tell you I don't know what we should have done had it not been for the lend-lease food which your country has sent us. It was a life-saver. I propose a toast to your country and your people for the great gift of food they sent us for our children."

Katerina Ushchuzhnaya is principal of the high school in Dinskaya. Vasily Ognenoy introduced me to her. A native of the village and a graduate of Moscow University, she is one of the most beautiful women in the Kuban, with golden hair and blue eyes, and in her manner is the acme of courtesy and refinement. She showed me around the shattered school building which pupils and teachers with the help of local citizens had only partially restored. She invited me to attend a county teachers' conference which she was supervising, and as she did so she picked up a book and showed it to me. It was a textbook on psychology and pedagogy. "It is the only copy we have in the whole county because the Germans burned nearly all of our books."

Then she asked if I should like her to arrange a *vecher*—entertainment by her students. I said I should.

The entertainment was held in the town hall, which likewise had been only partially restored by the young people of the village. All stage equipment was gone, seized by the Germans; all chairs and decorations were likewise looted. Instead of chairs there were long benches which squeaked and rattled whenever anyone sat down or moved about. Yet the auditorium was crowded. People were sitting on window sills and standing in the aisles. Children, many of them barefoot, jammed into the space on the floor between the stage and the first row of benches.

The audience was a revelation. It was almost exclusively feminine, and the women and girls no longer wore the sweat-soaked work clothes and slip-overs and misshapen shoes and sandals in which I had seen them walking about and working in the daytime. They dressed as for an exalted occasion. When I spoke of the striking contrast in the appearance of the audience now and during the day, the school principal said:

"Ah, but you should have seen our women before the war. We had real Sunday dresses. Cossack women love to dress. But the Germans and Rumanians looted our wardrobes, and we'll have to wait until the war is over before we can hope to get new clothes."

A high-school student, a boy of sixteen, was chairman of the evening. Tall, well groomed, his hair neatly trimmed and parted on the side, only his freshly polished, tight-fitting boots, reminiscent of ancient Cossack fashion, distinguished him from an American high-school boy of his age. Completely at ease before the overcrowded auditorium, he proved not only an excellent extemporaneous speaker but surprisingly American in his platform technique. After introducing the first number, he said:

"Now, folks, let's give him a hand. Come on, everybody," and himself led the applause.

So unexpected was this demonstration of what I had always regarded as American Chautauqua technique that I said to the principal:

"Where did he learn it?"

"We always do it here," was her reply.

"That's distinctively American," I said.

"Really? I'll tell my pupils. They'll be so pleased."

To her, as to so many Russians, the term "American," when applied to an immediate concrete task or object, implied superior quality. It was completely divorced from politics and ideology. It was associated with competent execution, with superior fulfillment, with liveliness of manner.

The program was long and varied, with much singing and dancing, reciting of peasant dialogue and poetry, and an unusually skilled tap dancer.

Especially memorable was the declamation by a girl named Rumyantseva of a war poem with the fighting refrain of: "Kill him—every time you see him, kill him; whenever you catch sight of him, kill him." Festiveness fled, gaiety vanished, vengeance was rife, passion was hot, the war was real, hate was overpowering, and the auditorium shook with applause. When the recitation ended and the next number was introduced, a ten-year-old boy in the rendition of a popular sailor song, the audience snapped out of its fighting passions and was itself again, relaxed, good-humored, festive.

It was one of the most singularly original audiences I have ever known. If it enjoyed a number it was breathless with attention. If it was bored it started talking until the conversation drowned out the voice of the performer. One number was a duet by two girls. So melodious was the singing that the audience would not stop the applause until the girls came out for an encore. This time one of the girls pitched her voice so high that instead of melody and harmony there was only a cacophony of sounds. For a while the audience listened patiently, then it started applauding and laughing, louder and louder, until, covered with embarrassment, the girls left the stage.

It was midnight when I returned to the home in which I was staying. No sooner did I enter the house than my hostess, a little woman with brilliant dark eyes and a lively manner, whose husband was at the front, a colonel in the Army, came to me and said:

"Wasn't it a splendid audience? To think that so many of them would come when harvest is at its height and they work so hard in the field. . . . And do you know why they came? They heard that an American would be present, and they like your country so much in this village, and they wanted to see you and talk to you."

We talked about the audience and the program, and then she said:

"Some of the women said they envied me because you are staying in my house. They'd have felt so honored to entertain you."

Statesmen and diplomats may wrangle violently over the meaning of the language of international agreements. They may clash fiercely over territorial issues and political problems in Europe and in Asia. The American press may be sizzling with denunciations of Russia for her failure to fulfill this or that provision of this or that agreement. Moscow's *War and the Working Class* and *Pravda* may be answering the attacks or launching their own in language no less violent and vituperative.

Yet over and above the diplomatic wrangling there is in the common folk not only of the Kuban but all over Russia deepseated and warm admiration for America, far more than for any other country in the world. If in the Kuban this admiration is more vocal and more eloquent, it is because Cossacks are naturally more loquacious and more rhetorical in speech.

Quite untrue are the stories I have heard and read since my return home that the Russian people know little or nothing of the immense amount of aid Russia has been receiving from America through the Red Cross, lend-lease, and the Russian War Relief. I have yet to meet a Russian in or out of the Army who does not realize it, who has not benefited from it, directly or indirectly, and who is not profoundly grateful. The Russian press and radio have not dramatized this aid, but not an American statement on the subject, whether by the late President Roosevelt or anyone else, but has been duly and fully recorded in word and in figure by the press of the country. Nothing pleases a Russian more in these harsh and cruel times than to know that he has friends in other Allied countries. The receipt of an American gift makes a holiday; it is talked about by everyone in the village, and what is especially worthy of emphasis, the men at the front learn of it from the letters they receive from wives, mothers, daughters, or sisters. As one Cossack woman has expressed herself: "It is not so much the gift as the feeling that people in your country think of us and remember us."

Some American foods Russians like better than others. They think our sausage is without tang, but they love our lard. I know housewives who prefer their fat rations in lard, when they can get it, to any other food. They "butter" their bread with it and find it a tasteful delicacy. It must be remembered that because of the stern climate Russians are partial to fats. Seldom will a Russian butcher hear a housewife say that she would prefer a lean to a fat cut of meat.

What particularly entrances the Russians is the way we do things, the manner in which we pack our parcels. Our wrappings and labels evoke rhapsodic eulogy and admiration, and so do the simple and eminently workable little gadgets with which to open cans and other metal containers. Again and again I have heard Russians speak with ecstasy of the packing of our cigarettes, our chocolate bars, the boxing of our cereals and other foods. "How much we have to learn from you!" is an expression I have heard over and over from hardheaded Party executives as well as poor common folk.

They are learning. Greedily they devour whatever new idea of service presents itself to them in the course of their contacts with things American. Anyone on a train or in any public place with an American catalogue, whether of automobiles, planes, washing machines, typewriters, fountain pens, any machinery, or anything else from silk stockings to cosmetics, will easily gather around himself a crowd of eager-faced questioning Russians seeking a peep at the decorative pictures and engravings. Among other things, American aid during this war has flooded Russia with new conceptions of service which will not be lost on them, for service is the weakest link in Soviet economy, and Russians are certain to put to use much of what they have learned. . . .

Stupendous as has been Russia's advance in the elevation of the machine age since 1928, the first year of the first Five-year Plan, the achievements up to date are a bare beginning of what she hopes to attain in the future. In 1939 Molotov could already proclaim that 90 per cent of Russia's mechanized farm equipment came out of Russian factories, and Russian pioneering in their famous *katushas*—rocket guns—the high quality of their tanks and artillery, amounted to extraordinary industrial achievement.

"To catch up with and surpass" capitalism in production and distribution, which is the slogan and the goal of Soviet economy, means primarily to attain and to outclass the American level of production and distribution in the manufacture of heavy industry as well as of everyday household and personal necessities. Anyone who has been in Russia, anyone who has read sober Russian appraisals of their successes and their shortcomings, knows only too well the enormity of the distance Russia has to traverse before she begins to approach the American level of production in quantity no less than in quality, or the American gospel and science of service.

Foreigners who have had occasion to eat Russian canned fruit or vegetables speak with admiration of the skill with which Anastas Mikoyan, Russia's Commissar of Foreign Trade, has organized the new canning industry. But anyone, Russian or foreigner, who has had occasion to use a Russian can opener has only words of execration for the manufacturers of this lowly household implement. Some time ago *Crocodile*, Russia's humorous weekly, defined a "gillette," which is the Russian word for safety razor, as an instrument which in foreign lands removes the hair from a man's face, but which in Russia removes also a part of the flesh on a man's face. The inferior quality of so many of Russia's consumers' goods is a constant object of scathing denunciation in the official press as well as of the biting patter of Russia's masters of ceremonies at entertainments in clubs and on the stage. The heavy and defense industries have absorbed so much of Russia's engineering and business energies that the so-called light industries manufacturing consumers' goods have had to plod along as best they could.

With the knowledge and experience she has already acquired in industrial development, with the engineering skill and talent she has already cultivated, Russia can, if necessary, continue her onward march into the machine age without foreign aid. Yet were she cut off from American contact, were American help denied her, for whatever reason, the speed and the tempo which are the soul of Russian planning, the fire of Russian hoping, would be thwarted and halted. There would be none of what Russians call "the dynamism" which has featured and fostered the Five-year Plans and which have been the driving force in all of Russia's pioneering and in all her dreams of the new society.

Machine-minded as Russians are, with a passion for the machine as the deliverer of man from all want and distress, they think of America as the land which has elevated it to the highest level ever achieved. Men like Ognenoy in the Cossack Kuban speak with ecstasy of American windmills, American tower silos, American milking machines, because without these and without the American-invented tractors and combines, trucks and incubators, there would have been no collectives in the villages and no flowering of the new culture in the immense and far-flung Russian countryside, in the Kuban more than elsewhere.

Unless diplomatic clashes between this country and Russia lead to a rupture of relations, thousands of Russians of both sexes will be coming here to explore, study, and perfect themselves in American methods of doing things, big things and little things, from the building of harbors and ships, apartment houses and public schools, automobiles and electric refrigerators, typewriters and fountain pens, the management of air passenger travel and motion-picture production, to plumbing and the wrapping of cigarette packages. Insatiable is the hunger of Russian youth for new knowledge and new experience in the one problem that haunts every Russian from Stalin to the most faraway sheep-herder in the Caucasian Mountains, namely, skill and efficiency in production.

Shortly after my return from Russia I happened to be visiting the State Agricultural College of Clemson, South Carolina. At milking time I went to the dairy barn, and I could not help thinking how fascinated a Russian dairy expert, indeed any Russian, would be with the up-to-date mechanized and labor-saving contrivances that were so lavishly installed there—the shower bath of the cow before milking, the specially built cage of steel bars into which she automatically walked after the shower bath, the pumping of the milk from the milking machine into an elevated glass container that was fixed into an automatic scale for the weighing of each milking. . . . To a Russian such a dairy barn is quest and fulfillment, prose and poetry, adventure and reward, one of the highest rewards known to man in his search of ever increasing bountifulness from nature's vast storehouse of riches.

Were there to be a rupture of relations between this country and Russia, it would be a severe blow not only to the growth of Russia's new economy, but to the really warm pro-American sentiments of the people. To the best of my knowledge neither the Kremlin nor anyone else has thus far manifested the least inclination to check or counteract such sentiments in the masses of the people.

PART FOUR

The Cossack of Tomorrow

CHAPTER XXVII

Work and Freedom

———◆———

"Roosters crow again in our village," said Tatyana Zaharova, president of the collective farm in the village of Mayevsky, "and cows bellow and goats too bleat once more." Before the war this kolhoz of three thousand acres boasted a mechanized dairy barn, four hundred horses, one of the choicest orchards and one of the most productive truck farms in the Kuban; hardly a family but was the proud possessor of three bicycles, a sewing machine, a gramophone. The acquisition of these city-manufactured articles was the measure of the prewar prosperity of the people. Nowhere else in rural Russia were they as universal as in this village and all over the Kuban. In terms of manufactured goods, the welfare they signalize is nowhere nearly as high as in the average rural community in America. But then Russia is Russia, with her own history, her own geography, her own social order, her own economic system, and this writer has never applied American standards of living or liberty or achievement to Russia.

Now the mechanized dairy barn in Mayevsky was gone, few of the cows and horses were left, the truck farm was a forest of weeds, the orchard was thinned, scrubby, and neglected; there were no bicycles, no gramophones, only a few sewing machines. The Germans had looted the village and left it bleak and desolate.

But roosters crowed again, and cows bellowed and goats bleated; "and," added Zaharova, "this is only a beginning." In simple words this energetic woman summed up the condition of

her village, the task and the struggle ahead not only in Mayevsky but in all the Kuban, in all liberated Russia. While in the outside world discussion of Russia rages round power politics, Russia's international claims and ambitions, her agreement or disagreement with this or that ally, inside Russia people are preoccupied with the rehabilitation of their shattered economy and
shattered lives. The war and the occupation have forced the
standard of living almost as low as I knew it in 1932, the year of
the completion of the first Plan. Nothing Russia needs more than
consumers' goods—shoes, clothing, hardware, chinaware, bicycles, sewing machines, soap, paper, pencils, pens, in fact everything. Nothing the people crave more, clamor for more, hope
for more. Nothing would dismay them more than the threat of
another war and the continuance of privation and frustration.

So everywhere work is the slogan and the goal, and how the
people work! From dawn until dark, from dark until dawn,
often enough even in the rich Kuban with implements which
in prewar days were deemed fit only for museums.

Emphasis on work and production have ever been the key to
Soviet internal policy and internal aspiration, and this is as good
a place as any to examine them in their larger aspects, particularly
in their relation to the freedom that Anglo-Saxon peoples know
and cherish. Production in the Soviet view is the source of
national security and of a rising standard of living. It is the sole
such source, the soil out of which grow the good things in life.
Therefore it must and does take precedence over everything
else in the nation. Civil liberties can wait, individual freedom in
the Anglo-Saxon meaning of the term can bide its time. But the
manufacture of pig iron and steel, of electric energy and machinery, of wheat and cotton, cannot be held in abeyance, not
for one day, not for a single hour. With backward and stunted
production, especially in pig iron and steel, which to the Russians is the basis of all production in the modern world, there
is neither national security nor individual welfare, neither life
nor elevation. There are only stagnation and paralysis, and in

time of war defeat and subjugation or, worse still, annihilation. In the Soviet view liberation from economic want and scarcity, the presence of an abundance of material satisfactions for the mass of the people, is the basic condition of ultimate and unhampered individual liberty. We may argue that they put the cart before the horse, but their emphasis on economic achievement as a prerequisite to political emancipation, though in these days their spokesmen never quite express themselves in such frank language, is what makes their economic collectivism such a sharp and irreconcilable contrast to America's or England's economic individualism or, as we more commonly express ourselves, "free enterprise." Hence Soviet or Bolshevik preoccupation with production, especially of pig iron and steel.

As early as 1913 in an article bearing the title, "How to Increase the Per-Capita Consumption of Russia," Lenin wrote:

"Russia is still an incredibly backward country, backward to an unheard-of degree, poor and semibarbarian, which, in equipment of modern instruments of production, is four times worse off than England, five times worse off than Germany, and ten times worse off than America."

Again and again Lenin returned with vigor and bitterness to the subject of Russia's industrial backwardness as exemplified by her inferior production of iron ore and her scanty use of steel. In 1913 he made comparison between feudal Hungary and Russia. In Hungary, he said, out of 2,800,000 peasant households, 2,500,000 used wood-framed plows and wood-framed harrows, but "the poverty, primitiveness, and neglect of the overwhelming majority of our peasant farms is incomparably worse than in Hungary."

"In 1900," he wrote again, "the per-capita production of pig iron in czarist Russia was one eighth of that of the United States, while in 1913 it dropped to one eleventh of that of the United States." During the thirteen-year interval annual production, by comparison with America, had actually receded by one eighth! To Lenin nothing could so abundantly fulfill the promise of the

revolution of which he had dreamt and which he had been plotting since his high-school years as adequate manufacture of pig
iron and steel, as the lifting of all Russian production to a higher
level than any capitalist land had attained. He made it obvious
that the triumph of socialism in Russia was not a matter solely of·
propaganda, doctrine, Party line, ideology, political police. All
these would blow away like the smoke that rises out of the
peasant's thatched cottage if production were not boosted to a
height unachieved by any nation in the world, including the
United States. "Either perish," he proclaimed, "or overtake and
outstrip the advanced nations economically"—first and foremost,
he might have added, in the manufacture of pig iron and steel.

Literally and rigorously Stalin, Molotov, Zhdanov, the others
who have been shaping Kremlin policy, have adhered to the
principle Lenin laid down. Production has been the great god
at whose feet they laid their own most earnest thoughts and
efforts and the nation's and the people's greatest offerings. Whatever the charges that Stalin's enemies may be leveling at him for
his failure to observe this or that postulate in Marxism or to
fulfill this or that tenet in Leninism, in his ceaseless and impassioned emphasis of the supreme, indeed transcendent, value
of production as the basis of Russia's new civilization he has
remained an unimpeachable disciple of Lenin. His speeches teem
with emphasis and overemphasis on this one overwhelming task,
and to him perhaps even more than to Lenin the outputs of pig
iron and steel are the unfailing stars by which to chart internal
policy, to move internal social forces, and on which, to a larger
measure than appears on the surface, to build foreign diplomacy.

Speaking at the Sixteenth Party Congress in 1930, Stalin said:
"We are outrageously behind the foremost capitalist countries
in the level of industrial production." Like Lenin before him,
like every Marxist revolutionary in Russia, Stalin saw in Russia's
backwardness her greatest calamity and her greatest danger. It
haunted him as no other problem Russia was facing. Privately
even more than publicly he has never ceased to hammer at it.
Hence the conception of the Five-year Plans and the feverish,

ruthless, breathless drives for their fulfillment as the sole condition of survival and advancement.

Speaking at a conference of managers of Soviet industry on February 4, 1931, a year of grim political repression and acute material want, of continued liquidation of kulaks and of mass exile of people who disbelieved in or opposed, however indirectly, the fulfillment of the first Plan, Stalin delivered one of the frankest, most prophetic, and most memorable speeches of his career. Though I have quoted it in an earlier volume I am reprinting part of it again, for Russians never tire of citing it to foreign observers who voice disappointment with this or that lack in Russian politics and in Russian life. Stalin speaks of himself as a Marxist, but save for a phrase here and there any Russian historian might have uttered his harsh and unrelenting words. Stalin said:

"The history of old Russia is the history of defeats due to backwardness.

"*She was beaten by the Mongol Khans.*

"*She was beaten by the Turkish beys.*

"*She was beaten by Swedish feudal barons.*

"*She was beaten by the Polish-Lithuanian squires.*

"*She was beaten by the Anglo-French capitalists.*

"*She was beaten by the Japanese barons.*

"*All* beat her for her backwardness—for military backwardness, for cultural backwardness, for agricultural backwardness. She was beaten because to beat her was profitable and could be done with impunity.

"Do you remember the words of the pre-revolutionary poet,[1] 'You are both poor and abundant, you are both powerful and helpless, mother Russia'? These words of the old poet were well known to those gentlemen. They beat her, saying, 'You are abundant, so we can enrich ourselves at your expense.' They beat her, saying, 'You are poor and helpless, so can be beaten and plundered with impunity.' Such is the law of capitalism—to beat the backward and the weak; the jungle law of capitalism. You

[1] Nikolai Nekrasov.

are backward, you are weak, so you are wrong, hence you can be beaten and enslaved. You are mighty, so you are right, hence we must be wary of you. *That is why we must no longer be backward.* . . . Do you want our socialist fatherland to be beaten and to lose its independence? If you do not want this you must put an end to this backwardness as speedily as possible and develop genuine Bolshevik speed in building up the socialist system of economy. *There are no other ways.* That is what Lenin said during the October revolution: 'Either perish or overtake and outstrip the advanced capitalist countries.' *We are fifty to a hundred years behind the advanced countries. We must cover this distance in ten years. Either we do this or they will crush us."*

These are brutal words, and only a man who lived not in the present but in the future, who was callous to the sacrifices of today because he was supremely aware of the threats of tomorrow, and sought either to avert or effectively to meet them, could speak with such unconcern of the immediate needs of the people for better food, better clothes, more freedom. . . . Yet ten years, three and a half months later, Nazi Germany, boasting the most powerful and most mechanized war machine the Western world had known, and buttressed by the agricultural and industrial resources not only of Germany but France, Austria, Czechoslovakia, Poland, Holland, Belgium, Norway, Denmark, Italy, Yugoslavia, with free access to the high-quality iron ores and no small amount of the manufactures in neutral Sweden, with millions of cheap laborers recruited from all conquered lands, this steel-clad, war-fevered Germany flung herself on Russia with the avowed aim not only of conquering her but of exterminating millions and millions of her people, driving her beyond the Urals into Asia and keeping her there, poor, primitive, and subjugated. It is no accident that all over the Kuban, as everywhere else they penetrated, the Germans centered their destructive fury on the obliteration of the achievements of the Five-year Plans and on the degradation of the country and its people to a state of pre-Machine Age ignorance and primitiveness.

The human cost of the Plans was enormous. Let moralists and philosophers decide whether or not, in the light of the war and the victories of the Red Army, the sacrifices were ethically justified. The indisputable fact is that the achievements of the Plans in industrial development, in large-scale mechanized agriculture, in technical and general education of the people, saved Russia from defeat and from the worst fate any conqueror had ever sought to impose on her.

Stalin again returned to the subject of production in March 1939, this time with a new approach. "We are still lagging economically," he said, "as regards the volume of our industrial output per head of population." He cited figures showing that in 1938 Russia was producing twice as much pig iron as England and almost twice as much steel. "It might seem," he continued, "that we are better off than England." But materially Russia was not and could not be better off than England because, as Stalin pointed out, her per-capita production of pig iron for 1938 was 87 kilograms, of steel 107, whereas in England it was 145 kilograms for the one and 226 for the other.

The comparison with America was still more unfavorable to Russia. In the boom year of 1929 America produced 43 million tons of pig iron, and for 1942, the final year of the third Plan, Russian output of the metal was to rise only to about one half that amount. For Russia to attain America's level of per-capita output in iron and steel on the basis of the figures of 1929, Russia would need to lift her production of both to fifty or sixty million tons annually. Stalin was hopeful that within ten or fifteen years, or on the conclusion of two or three more intensive Plans, Russia would achieve the coveted goal.

But the war upset schedules of peacetime production in Russia as well as America, in Russia in the occupied regions destructively, in America everywhere creatively. There have been no recent official pronouncements on when Russia would "catch up with and outstrip" the most advanced capitalist nations in production, at least in the output of pig iron and steel. If Russia were to keep up with America in the manufacture of steel and pig iron on the basis, not of the boom year of 1929 but on the present war years, Stalin would need to revise completely his estimate of the time it would take Russia to equal or to exceed American achievement. By Russian admission American industry performed a prodigious miracle by lifting the output of pig iron to over 62 million tons and of steel to almost 90 million tons in 1944. To the average Stalin-minded Russian, perhaps to Stalin himself, this figure is not only a miracle but a dream which Russians at this stage of their industrial development can only admire and envy.

I have dwelt at some length on the place of production in the Soviet scheme of things, especially on the output of pig iron and steel, because, as already suggested, with it, as with no other circumstance on the Soviet scene, are bound up internal policy, including the whole sphere of civil liberties, not in the present Russian but in the traditional Anglo-Saxon meaning of the phrase. The right to criticize official policy, leaders of the Soviet state and of the Party, Russians are denied. Only a Party leader in high position would dare lodge a complaint against the political police, which does its arresting, its questioning, its trying, its sentencing, whether to exile, hard labor, or death, in secret. The public trials of political outstanding offenders are an exception to the rule. Within the framework of official policy the Soviet citizen, unless his record is stained with political opposition, enjoys a number of basic rights such as the right to work, to education, to the choice of a career, and to an array of other social benefits, also the right to criticize the faulty execution of a policy, provided it is not concerned with anything the political police may do. He is guaranteed equality of race or nationality, sex equality which implies not only the right of women to receive equal pay for equal work but to hold office on an equal footing with men. But the right to disapprove or question official policy, whether in internal life or international relations, is as vigorously denied as the right to open a business of one's own.

In his speech on March 10, 1939, in speaking of the immediate tasks confronting the Communist Party, Stalin listed in fourth place the need "steadfastly to carry into effect our socialist constitution; *to complete the democratization of the political life of the country.*" The italics are mine, because Stalin's pronouncement on the subject cannot be too vigorously underscored. Were there as much political democracy in Russia as the Soviet press so often assures its readers, there would have been no need for Stalin saying that its enactment needed to be completed.

The question arises when will civil liberties in the Anglo-Saxon meaning of the phrase become living facts instead of, as they now are, literary provisions in the Constitution of 1936?

In the absence of official pronouncements on the subject, one can only speculate on the answer. In my judgment it must be sought, not in political doctrine, however eloquently phrased, but in figures on Russian production, particularly of pig iron and steel. Barring a war or a tense international situation, the real test will come when the annual outputs of the one and the other approximate fifty or sixty million tons. With such an output of these metals the Soviets will have the secure and stable foundation for the two conditions which have been in the forefront of their thinking and planning, their acting and dictating, namely, national defense and an adequate standard of living. Until then there will be modifications and abatements. There already have been, as testified—for example, in the study of literature and history in schools and colleges. In all the years that I have been going to Russia I have never known pedagogues and students to apply to both subjects as much objective understanding as now. It was more than a surprise to me when I heard students in the senior class of a girls' high school in Moscow speak of Chekhov's heroes and heroines not as "contemptible exploiters" but as "charming and lovable noblemen," as "tender and kindly noblewomen." There is far more freedom in the study of literature than there is in its writing. There is far more flexibility of thought in the study and appreciation of the literary and artistic creations of the past than there is in the demands made on the writers and artists of today. Significantly enough, in the October issue of *Bolshevik*, the highly authoritative organ of the Central Committee of the Communist Party, A. Solodownikov, in discussing this subject, writes: "The Party and the Soviet Government have always striven to put art to the service of the high aim of creating the new socialist society and the education of the new man."

Yet it must be remembered that feudal societies, such as Russia was essentially in pre-Soviet days, always have repressed civil liberties and still do. There is not a single feudal land in the world, whether in South America, Asia, or Africa, but stanchly and often enough brutally suppresses the freedom which Anglo-Saxon countries have for centuries striven to maintain. Old Russia was no exception. To the intellectuals and to the rising middle class, civil liberties had meaning and appeal. Feudalism shackled their hands and their minds, and during the years of the fateful Dumas they strove to rid themselves of these shackles. But to the mass of the people in rural Russia especially, without the education of the intelligentsia and the middle classes, with their own burden of want and woe, civil liberties in their political sense were only words. In the peasant revolutions in Russian history the word "freedom" was a fighting slogan. Stenka Razin and Pugatchev were highly skilled propagandists, and both flaunted the promise of *volnitsa*, the Cossack word for "liberty," in every appeal and every document they put forth. But neither Cossack leader had the least conception of liberty in the Anglo-Saxon sense. To them and to their followers the word carried the promise of free land and freedom from the tyranny of landlords which were the essence of Cossack ideology and which evoked a ready and violent response in the serf-ridden peasantry. The emphasis is not on political but on material gains. . . . It is well to remember, as I have already pointed out, that Stenka Razin was a contemporary of John Milton, and that his revolt occurred shortly after the Cromwellian revolution in England. Yet nowhere is there the least indication in anything Razin said or did which could even remotely be interpreted as an approximation of the political language or the political ideology of the two spokesmen of the great Puritan revolution in England. Nor did the illiterate Pugatchev have any inkling as to the meaning or importance of political liberty, though in the year he was executed, to quote a previous passage, "the farmers of New England fought the battle of Concord and Lexington. The following year came the Declaration of Independence and within four years the great French Revolution."

To the very end of its days czarism had meant feudalism, and despite the rise of vigorous liberal and revolutionary movements, had withheld from the common man, particularly the peasants and the Cossacks, the opportunity to become grounded in the very concept of civil liberties. The Soviet Constitution of 1936, whatever else it may or may not achieve, is at least a means of inculcating this concept in the minds of the people. Its study is a "must" subject for everyone in the country. Its fulfillment, in the sphere of civil liberties in the American or British sense, is something else again.

The war has tested Russian production as no other event in Soviet history. It has met the test well. Yet the question of security in the future rather than the present must still weigh heavily on men like Stalin and his immediate associates, if only because, with the ruin of the industry of the Ukraine during the war and the German occupation, the output of pig iron and steel is perhaps no further advanced than it was on the eve of the German attack. Besides, Russia's primary and crying need now is for consumers' goods. The war has pushed the standard of living to as low a level as I have ever known it. The people of the Kuban remember with longing the days before the war when food was no longer a problem, when manufactured goods were arriving in increasing quantities, when surplus wheat, corn, sunflower seed, meat could be exchanged for shoes, textiles, bicycles, gramophones, other commodities. Immense will be the attention that the Kremlin will now devote to the output of consumers' goods. Yet this task is as inextricably linked with the manufacture of pig iron and steel as is national security. Whatever, therefore, the energies that will be devoted to consumers' goods, in the immediate future as during the first three Plans, steel and pig iron will continue to be the number one problem and the number one concern of the Kremlin. Only when the manufacture of these is lifted to fifty or sixty million tons annually and security and consumers' goods have attained the desired status, will the question of freedom in *all* its ramifications and *all* its implications face its real and overpowering test in the Soviet Union. Until then, barring an internal or external calamity, as figures on production keep mounting, the ensuing relaxations may prove more startling than anyone now anticipates.

I use the word startling advisedly, though in relation, not to Anglo-Saxon, but to Russian history and experience. Only those who interpret history and social relations in the narrowest meaning of the Marxian class struggle would deny that civil liberties in Anglo-Saxon countries have been a way of life, a mode of self-expression, a weapon of advancing social progress and individual welfare. Any effort to deprive the citizenry in these countries of such liberties by whatever methods and for whatever purpose would provoke the cruelest civil war. It is inconceivable that any state could "shut the mouth" of the thinking or the unthinking Englishman or American—for long, anyway. No institution, no organization is so severely disciplined as an army, especially in time of war. Yet anyone who has lived with American or British troops during World War II knows only too well how freely they have been "griping," how gloatingly they have been "cussing" anybody and anything they have disliked. All this is a result of history, of tradition, of habit, of the psychological unfolding of peoples who have been nourished on the civil liberties which their ancestors long ago wrested from unreasonable rulers. Abuses here and there, however flagrant, may have thwarted but have not stifled the urge to take advantage of the freedom they guarantee.

Had the Russian people been heir to a similar history, tradition, habit, to a more or less identical psychological unfolding in the course of the past centuries or even since the emancipation of the serfs in 1861, there is no reason to assume that they would have been markedly different from the peoples in Anglo-Saxon countries. For one thing under a condition of civil liberties they would not have been faced with the formidable burden of industrial backwardness and the formidable task of production which has ever haunted the Soviets. The three Plans exacted from the people an inordinate amount of sacrifice in freedom and good living, but, to repeat, it is the achievements of the Plans that fortified Russia with the education, general and even more technical, and the industrial and agricultural resources with which to battle Germany as she did.

Yet there is a dynamic flexibility in the Russian Revolution which it would be easy for the subjective-minded student of Russia to disregard and underestimate. The years of the first Plan were a time of severest dictatorship and harshest repression. Yet the Russia of today is not the Russia of those times. Sweeping have been the relaxations of former restrictions, the reinterpretation of doctrine, principle, policy. The study of the class struggle had then supplanted the study of history. Now history ranks as a leading subject in schools and colleges. So does literature. The classics, both Russian and foreign, are accorded a hallowed place in the curriculum. Belinsky, Dobrolubov, Pisarev, Russia's great literary critics of the nineteenth century, who are also among her foremost preachers and prophets of humanitarianism, have been embraced with a passion that is in marked contrast to the frigid, often contemptuous indifference with which "class-conscious" writers and pedagogues once regarded them.

I remember vividly the words of the late Felix Kon, directing head of the arts, who in reply to a question I put to him said that the Russian proletariat did not need Rachmaninov and Tchaikovsky, but only such music as would further the fulfillment of the Plan. Now the most class-conscious Bolshevik would laugh or fume at anyone who cast the least aspersion on these world-famous composers. None other than Glebov, secretary of the Party in the Commissariat of Education, once proclaimed that Leo Tolstoy could not possibly have done any distinguished or significant writing because he was only a *pomyeshchik*—landlord! Now Tolstoy is by far the most widely read author in Russia, and the most beloved.

In those days Russia's past was all evil and horror. Now the past is linked with the present and the future and is cherished and revered. The reversal of attitude toward sex and the family could not have been more complete. Not a shred is left of the one-time harshness toward the Church, toward Cossacks, toward sons and daughters of the bourgeoisie and kulaks. One may think what one chooses of Russian elections, based as they are on a one-party system, but the fact that the voting is no longer by a show of hands but by secret ballot carries its own implications for the future far more than for the present. Nor must we ignore the ever increasing emphasis on the *individual* possession of usable goods. The mayor of Novorossiisk told me that in the rebuilding of the city emphasis will be laid on one- and two-family cottages with lawns and back yards rather than on many-storied apartment houses. The abolition of the inheritance tax in 1942 is only a means of enabling the individual citizen to acquire increasing amounts of such goods.

It would take a bulky volume to trace out the shift of policy and practice since the days of the first Plan. The undeniable fact is that in the prewar days the rise in the output of heavy industry and the increase in the amount of consumers' goods in shops and market places were accompanied by a growing sense of external and internal security and resulted in increasing abatements of the severity of the dictatorship. Yet I must reiterate that the political offender is still "*the* enemy of the people" and is at the mercy of the political or security police. Only when production of pig iron and steel attains an annual output of fifty or sixty million tons respectively will civil liberties in the Anglo-Saxon meaning of the phrase be subjected to the most crucial test.

It may be argued that as long as the Communist Party monopolizes power in Russia, as it now does, there is no hope of real freedom ever being allowed. An Allied statesman with whom I discussed this subject, quoting Lord Acton, said, " 'Power corrupts, absolute power corrupts absolutely.' " Having enjoyed the adventure, the privilege, the ecstasy, the benefits of power, he insisted, the Communist Party will not of its own accord relinquish it. All one can say in reply is that highest Communist authority is against such a supposition. Not only Marx, Engels, Lenin, but Stalin speaks of the dictatorship as *transitional.* They see the state under socialist rule undergoing endless changes. "The forms of our state," said Stalin on March 10, 1939, "are changing and will continue to change in line with the development of our country and with the changes in the international situation." Manifestly the changes that have already taken place testify not to a rigidity but to a flexibility of the dictatorship.

Besides, if it is the intention of the Kremlin and the others who fashion policy in Russia to cling to power for its own sake regardless of the condition of the country, and even when it has attained an economy of abundance, why proclaim a document such as the Constitution of 1936 and make it compulsory study all over the country? Why inculcate the concept of all conceivable freedoms in old and young? Why place such stress on the study of the classics, especially the Russian? Why not only encourage but oblige the young generation to "soak itself," as one Soviet school superintendent once expressed himself, with Pushkin, Gogol, Turgenev, Dostoevsky, Gorky, Chekhov, and above all Tolstoy, whose humanitarianism and love of freedom shine out of every story he wrote? Why open up to the youth of the land the vast spiritual riches of Belinsky, Dobrolubov, Pisarev, the more fervent Herzen, and the more coldly intellectual Chernyshevsky, who was no less ardent an apostle of freedom and democracy?

In my judgment the dictatorship that now prevails in Russia will in time have to yield to the mentality that the writings of Russia's foremost men of letters are fashioning. When Stalin's promise of saturating the country "with consumers' goods" and "with an abundance of products" comes true, the pressure from everywhere for increasing freedom in all avenues of human thought and human pursuit will be all the more insistent, too insistent for any dictatorship to ignore or to resist.

Of course I am only speculating. But the severest critic of Soviet Russia must reckon with these considerations. Not to take cognizance of them or to underestimate their significance, or to interpret Russia solely in terms of the event and the condition of today is to miss some of the most dynamic forces on the Soviet scene.

Yet never before on any of my journeys in the Cossack country have I observed as close a relationship between government, Party, and people as now. This was one of the most revealing features of my journey in the Kuban, a feature which the over-cluttered bureaucracy of the capital, the incivility and obtuseness of many of the uniformed bureaucrats, the vigilance of the political police in the relationship between Russians and foreigners, obscure, often hopelessly, from the view of the foreign observer.

In the Kuban, as all over rural Russia, life and politics are not beset by these man-made obstructions. The two most important functionaries in the village are the mayor and the Party secretary. Not once did I see the office of the one or the other guarded by an armed sentry. Both are approachable. Both listen to complaints and demands, however loudly voiced. Both live simply and not always in the best houses of a village. Both are constantly in the midst of community affairs and public enterprises, whether selling bonds, fulfilling the Plan in plowing, seeding, harvesting, thrashing, delivery of produce to the state, or finding textbooks for a school. Neither wears a uniform. In appearance both are indistinguishable from other villagers. Their wives and children work on a basis of equality with others. Nowhere do they and their families constitute any kind of an exclusive social set, and no task is too small for them. I have known mayors and Party secretaries to spend hours in an effort to find a new carburetor or some other spare part for engines and other machinery. Nor do their salaries begin to compare with the income of the efficient presidents of collective farms, if only because they receive their salaries in money and not in produce. Grigory Kupayev, the fifty-one-year-old president of the collective farm "Red Star" in the village of Plastunovksaya, told me that his pay for 1944 would be six tons of wheat and barley, half a ton of sunflower seeds, a ton of corn, four and a half tons of hay, 450 pounds of grapes, 112 pounds of honey, some sugar, the amount depending on the crop of sugar beets, and 4,500 rubles in cash! Not even Mikhail Bessonov, the governor of the Kuban, enjoys as high an income, which in the case of Kupayev is further supplemented by produce from the garden and from what little livestock the kolhoz has already managed to secure for the individual use of its members since the expulsion of the Germans. . . .

These leaders as I observed them in the Cossack country are a new type of Soviet executive. They are young, in the twenties or early thirties, and there is about them, their speech, their appearance, their manners, a businesslike air which was nowhere nearly as manifest in men in their position on my previous visits to the country. They are smooth-shaven, their offices are uncluttered with books and papers, their desks are clean. They are as statistical-minded as Stalin and know by heart the figures on almost any subject within the sphere of their jurisdiction. They live in a world of figures even more than in a world of ideas, for the fulfillment of the Plan, whether in the wheat crop or in the increase of livestock, in the restoration of schoolhouses, in the purchase of textbooks, in the operation of nurseries, in any and every task that is before them, is their most sacred duty, the faulty execution of which may result in dismissal or demotion and the ending of any hope of advancement in a chosen career.

What I liked best about them was their candor and their informality. I could call on them any time I wished—in their offices, their homes, or in the harvest fields. Like Bessonov, the governor of the province, and the experts I met in Krasnodar, they are proud of the Cossackhood of the Kuban, but see its future destiny in the dedication of the people to ever increasing production of grains and fruits, of meats and milk, of eggs and other consumers' goods and the constant elevation of its cultural level. They act and talk and look like the business executives that they are, and their chief burden of work is in the promotion of the business of living and learning and laboring, on a collectivist basis, of course, in the villages in which they function.

"We are poor now," said the schoolmaster of Plastunovskaya, "but we'll work harder than ever to catch up with and surpass the good life we had before the war in our Kuban. We shall have not only gramophones and bicycles but motorcycles and automobiles. Give us time, give us time!" In one form or another I heard these words repeated everywhere I traveled.

I carried away the conviction that these men are absorbed in the destiny of Russia as in nothing else in life, and that if ever the Soviets were to embark on a war for the forcible sovietization of the world they would need to be as forcibly re-educated and reconditioned as were the surviving internationalists to whom "socialism in one country" meant betrayal of the Revolution.

CHAPTER XXVIII

The New Cossack

As I DROVE AROUND the Kuban I could not help thinking of an incident which the agricultural editor of the Krasnodar newspaper had related to me in 1926. As a means of popularizing the cultivation of cotton he had induced groups of school children and individual Cossacks in various villages to plant the crop on small patches of land. In one village a Cossack was especially successful with the crop. But there was a drought in the village, and the people were alarmed, especially the *stariks,* older folk, all the more so because the village had rarely been struck by drought. The priest held a special Mass in the fields and prayed for rain. But no rain came, and wheat, corn, sunflower crops were wilting.

The panicky stariks called a secret meeting and decided that someone in the village had invoked on it divine wrath. But who could be the sinner? The man who was growing cotton! If the Lord had sanctioned its growth in the village, it would have long ago been cultivated. To appease the wrath of Providence, the stariks swooped on the cotton patch in the dark of night and plucked up every plant. In the light of all I was now seeing and hearing in the Kuban, the incident sounded unbelievably medieval.

Cotton is now one of the industrial crops of the country. An array of other new crops has been acclimated—peanuts, rice, the soya bean, the castor bean, citrus fruits, Italian hemp, tea, new brands of tobacco, and still others were in process of experimentation. No starik would now attribute drought or any natural calamity to man's infringement on divine dispensation. The lowliest and most backward of them has heard too much of the new science of agriculture, has observed too closely its beneficent results to question the suitability of a new crop on grounds of theological rectitude. Superstition, if it still lurks in the minds of the stariks, has been pushed into the background of their consciousness.

In 1926 the *borodatch*—the bearded one—still colored the social scene of the Cossack village. He more than anyone else was the embodiment of the old tradition, the old wisdom, the old authority, the old faith, the old way of life, and he more than anyone else resisted the Soviet onslaught on the old Cossackhood. During the civil war and collectivization he suffered the direct penalties. The Cossackhood he knew and loved, with its unbridled warrior spirit, its special liberties and privileges, the gift of free land on the birth of a son, the economic individualism it fostered, the wild pastimes it emulated, were to him the acme of human attainment, the glory of Cossack civilization. For him there was neither life nor hope, neither present nor future, outside of the old Cossackhood.

Now the *borodatch* is so rare a sight that he is invested with a romantic halo. He is almost as much a part of history as the superstitions he espoused and the social order he upheld. Gone is the centuries-old animal abandon he symbolized. Taras Bulba's "science of drinking" has been refined into a social usage embroidered with much of the old·decorative and rhetorical amenities, but without the old-time animal explosiveness. Mass fist fights are now a memory. Were anyone to suggest them, he would not only be mocked, he would be brought before the law. Mass animosities between one part of the village and another, between Cossacks and peasants, are a legend. Mass disbelief in "learning," especially for women, mass contempt for books and bookishness, mass exaltation of physical prowess and mass veneration of soldierly achievement as the height of manly self-realization, are no longer even voiced save as an echo of the past. What could be more revealing of the psychological shake-up and intellectual upsurge in the Cossack than the presence in the medical school of Krasnodar of more than seven hundred Cossack girls, all from villages, most of whom wanted to be surgeons? Between 1926 and 1944, the years of my first and my last visit to the country, the Kuban, as already stated in the Preface, acquired more "learning," that is, education, received and read more books, mastered more science, put on the land more up-to-date mechanized equipment than in *all* preceding years of its history as a Cossack territory. Never before had there been so many elementary and high schools in the country as in the pre-war days, so many libraries, so many tractor stations, so many reading rooms and clubhouses, so many experiment stations. There is hardly a collective farm but maintains its own laboratory which carries on experiments under the direction of an agricultural expert or a college experiment station. Talking to men in charge of these laboratories gives one a feeling that in their inconspicuous little offices and in the outlying patches of land they cultivate, the Cossack country is acquiring new knowledge and evolving a new force that will lift it to new heights of achievement in agriculture.

I asked General Kirichenko why so many Cossack girls wanted to be surgeons, and his reply was as pithy as it was enlightening. "Why," he said, "should a Cossack girl want to bother with pills and powders, drops and iodine swabs? Any girl can administer these. But to amputate an arm, a leg, to cut open a body and slash out malignant tissue—that's a *delo* [real job], and we Cossacks believe in doing real jobs."

I know of no more modernized and cultivated Cossack than the general. He reads the classics, Russian and foreign. He goes to the theater, the ballet, the opera, concerts. He speaks with loathing of war per se. He and the college of which he is now president sponsor an orphan asylum and engage in other social work and in a host of intellectual activities, including the study of Marxism, which were alien and abhorrent to the Cossack of old. Yet his speech vibrates with an energy and an expressiveness that are unmistakably and triumphantly Cossack. Real jobs, worthy or unworthy, depending on one's social approach and historical appraisal, have ever been the Cossack's specialty and joy. Whenever he made a stand on an issue it was always with a violent decisiveness. He made alliances with and against Turkish sultans and Tatar khans. He fought with and against Polish kings. He crossed swords with and in behalf of Russian czars. Whatever the motive, the partnership itself during the period it lasted was no halfway measure. Unless he deemed it fun or it suited his fortunes to scrap an agreement or treaty, the Cossack fulfilled his share of it with spirited militancy. If he suffered defeat he expected no mercy and was accorded none, whoever his conqueror, whether Tatar, Pole, Turk, Muscovite, or Bolshevik.

The Cossack never was a dawdler and a doubter. His has ever been an attitude of affirmation. Whatever the cause he championed, baneful or beneficent, whether it was support of autocracy or Orthodoxy, the championship or the suppression of revolution, the acceptance or the rejection of sovietism and collectivization, his conviction was as firm as his sword was mighty. Lost or won, the battle usually lasted until strength waned, weapons were spent—defeat was imminent. Proud of person, stubborn in aim, fierce in execution, his direct approach and his will to be always saved him from doom and obliteration, always conjured forth, as if by magic, a circumstance that brought forgiveness of past sins and recognition of innate virtues.

This was so in the reign of Catherine the Great, for example. Fearful of his rebelliousness, the mighty Czarina broke up the Dnieper Republic. But no one else in Russia could combat the fighting Tatar like the Cossack. In the conquest of the Crimea and the Kuban he was indispensable and irreplaceable. Therefore shortly after the dissolution of the *setch*, Potemkin and other men high in the state and military councils of the Czarina made overtures to him with words of flattery and with sumptuous gifts, and the Cossack became once more the warrior with the saber, battling for a new cause and upholding a new authority.

Fearful of fresh uprisings, the Soviets, while Lenin was still alive, had disbanded and outlawed Cossackhood. They stripped the Cossack of his uniform, his horse, his weapons, and degraded him to the level of an ordinary muzhik, whom he had always despised. They invested the very word "Cossack" with obloquy and contumely. But when war clouds were beginning to thicken over the Russian horizon, when Hitler's campaign of hate against Russia and all Slavs was assuming threatening magnitude, the Bolsheviks, no longer disturbed by the Cossack's opposition, and trusting in his loyalty to the new regime, exhumed him from the oblivion and disgrace into which they had flung him, and lifted him and his Cossackhood into national eminence.

During World War II there were disloyal and treacherous Cossacks. How many? No figures are available. As in all other parts of Russia which they had occupied, the Germans recruited their police force from the local population.

The burgomaster of Krasnodar was a Russian lawyer. So was

his assistant. The *starostas*—elders—of the various city districts were largely schoolteachers, some bona fide collaborators, others disguised spies for the guerrillas in the mountains. All over the Kuban young girls fraternized only too intimately with enemy soldiers and officers. Hundreds of them retreated with the Germans. Those who have remained home are receiving medical treatment, if they need it, and unless they have been active collaborators—denounced Party men, Jews, Soviet officials to the Germans—they have not been molested. Nor have been those women who have had children by Germans or Rumanians. The children are treated no worse than other Soviet children.

Yet all German efforts to revive the old type of Cossack, with the old type of military and social trappings, collapsed. Even the clergy overwhelmingly refused to be baited and bribed into collaboration. Andrey Vlasov, the Russian general who in the early months of the war deserted with an army to the Germans, had recruited among captive Cossacks no small number of followers. But loyal Cossacks never took the Vlasovites as prisoners. In the battle of Korsun in the Ukraine, the Red Army encircled ten German divisions. Among them were two thousand of Vlasov's Cossacks. The Kuban Cossack division which formed one of the links in the Russian encirclement shot and sabered to death every one of them.

The new Cossackhood does not spell a resurrection of the Cossack caste. There is no such caste any more. It does not carry with it a restoration of the old Cossack privileges. There are no such privileges any more. Under a system of collectivization there is no discrimination of the sexes and no grant of free land for a newborn son. The Cossack mother enjoys no more and no less state aid than any other mother.

The Soviets have diluted the old Cossack population, which was derived pre-eminently from the peasantry, with fresh racial and national strains.

The newly broadened social base embraces all residents in Cossack territory, regardless of their pre-Soviet antecedents. Gypsies, Tatars, Armenians, Greeks, members of other non-

Cossack groups or of non-Russian nationality are privileged at their choice to wear Cossack uniforms and are encouraged to take up horsemanship and participate in Cossack races and Cossack war games.

The Soviets have resurrected the martial-mindedness of the Cossack and the science of Cossack warfare. They have dramatized the Cossack's military attainments and his military virtues—his fearlessness of death, his audacity in battle, his horsemanship, his skill with the gun and the saber, his patriotism, his love of adventure which the purely soldierly qualities make possible. But they have not stopped there. They have initiated and familiarized the Cossack with the most up-to-date weapons and methods of warfare. They have mechanized and modernized him, though not to a point, as General Kirichenko explained, to hamper his chief virtue in war, which is his mobility.

The Soviets have done more, they have extolled the individual and social virtues for which the Cossack of old, in spite of all his wildness, was noted—his respect for elders, for parents, his family loyalty, his love of horses, his pride in ancestry, his personal integrity, his decisiveness of mind, his love of action. Nowhere else in Russia is the horse so favorite an animal. Nowhere else do boys and girls, especially boys, "adopt" newborn colts so eagerly, care for them, play with them, grow up with them, ride on them for pleasure as well as for training in Cossack war games.

The Cossack is not the professional soldier that he once was. He serves no longer a term in the Army than does any other citizen. In time of peace he is exclusively a farmer. He toils more strenuously than he ever did under the czars, for his livelihood depends not on special subsidies but on the "labor days" he earns in the kolhoz, on the produce he grows in his own garden, and on the foods he obtains from his own livestock. He does not even own the horse on which he rides and practices war games. All horses are the property of the kolhoz.

The old Cossackhood is dead. The new Cossackhood presupposes a new individual and a new civilization. In time of war the new Cossack is still a formidable force, as, despite the non-Russian prophecies to the contrary, World War II has so dramatically demonstrated—all the more so because his ancient and historically unfailing mode of warfare is now integrated with modern strategy and tactics and modern weapons. As the years roll by, the Cossack will become more and more modernized, almost streamlined, as a soldier and a fighter. But in time of peace his immense energies will be devoted to peacetime pursuits, to creative purposes.

Such he is destined to remain until such time, if it ever comes, when armies and wars are only a memory of the barbarism of the past.